A complete history of the Isle of Man : containing the situation and geographical description thereof; the ecclesiastical and civil histories; the whole order of the governments from the earliest account; the nature of the soil; the produce of the country

John Seacome

Nabu Public Domain Reprints:

You are holding a reproduction of an original work published before 1923 that is in the public domain in the United States of America, and possibly other countries. You may freely copy and distribute this work as no entity (individual or corporate) has a copyright on the body of the work. This book may contain prior copyright references, and library stamps (as most of these works were scanned from library copies). These have been scanned and retained as part of the historical artifact.

This book may have occasional imperfections such as missing or blurred pages, poor pictures, errant marks, etc. that were either part of the original artifact, or were introduced by the scanning process. We believe this work is culturally important, and despite the imperfections, have elected to bring it back into print as part of our continuing commitment to the preservation of printed works worldwide. We appreciate your understanding of the imperfections in the preservation process, and hope you enjoy this valuable book.

CONTENTS
OF
THE ISLE OF MAN.

	PAGE.
The introduction	3
Description of the Isle of Man	8
The act of surrender made by Reginald, to the see of Rome	18
The continuation from the Scotch conquest to the settlement under the House of Stanley	28
The king's proclamation for continuing officers in the Isle of Man	38
A topographical description of the Isle of Man	42
The succession of the bishops of Man	61
A catalogue of the governors of the Isle of Man since Sir John Stanley's time, till the year 1741, with the north and south divisions	93
Review of the state of the island under the dominion of the House of Stanley—Excessive alarm excited by the revestment in Great Britain—The revival of prosperity and general amelioration of character and manners resulting from a better order of things—Prejudice against the Duke of Athol, whence it originates, and how maintained	97
Tour round the island, commencing at Douglas—Description of that town and neighbourhood	105
Tour continued—Castletown—Derby haven—The Calf—Peel town and castle—Ramsay—Lazey, and the road returning to Douglas again	113
Agriculture—Its great advance of late years in the Isle of Man—Scale of population at different periods—State of buildings—Advantages possessed by the Manx farmer over those of neighbouring countries—Roads—Manure—Notice of some particular improvements effected by individuals	129

CONTENTS.

	PAGE.
Herring fishery, and trade in general	147
The revenue—Exports and imports	153
The laws—House of keys—Civil officers—Juries, &c.	161
Comments on the state of the laws, with some cases adduced in proof of the assertion that they require amelioration	170
Comments on the actual state of society in the island—Characteristics of the natives—The clergy—Methodists	177
Further observations on the society—An example presented to the ladies for their imitation, deduced wholly from *native* excellence—The peasantry—Review of the state of society at different periods—Contrast between the natives and strangers—Anecdote of the latter	185
Some characteristic superstitions of the Manx	199
Prices of provisions—Rent—Servants' wages, &c.	206

CONTENTS TO THE APPENDIX.

No. 1. Rev. Mr. Wilson's letter to the Earl of Derby	211
2. Bishop Wilson's character of his wife	213
3. Bishop Wilson's address to his children	215
4. Bishop Wilson's letter to the keys	216
The answer of the keys	217
No. 5. The petition of Thomas Wilson, D. D., in behalf of his father the Bishop of Man and the inhabitants of the island	219
No. 6. Letter to the king	220
Letter to his son	221
No. 7. Heads of a bill, proposed in Tynwald, for amendment of the criminal law	222
Manx coin	236
Traditions and superstitions	238
The scenery of the island—longevity of the islanders, &c.	240
Extract from the journal of a modern traveller; or, a trip with the Manx herring fleet in 1821	243

A HISTORY OF THE ISLE OF MAN.

THE INTRODUCTION.

THIS island appears but little, or but darkly known to the ancients; and amongst all our modern historians and geographers there is not one has given any tolerable account of it before Mr. James Challoner, Governor for the Lord Fairfax, and the great and learned Mr. Blundell, of Crosby, who prudently retired thither during the time of the usurpation, whereby he preserved his person in peace and security, and his estate from all manner of depredation. This gentleman being a person of polite learning, employed his leisure hours in collecting the History and Antiquities of the Isle of Man; and by his manuscripts, which I have seen, gave posterity the clearest and most correct account thereof.

But as to the rest of our English historians, few of them, especially the ancients, so much as mention it. Mr. Cambden indeed is the first that gives us any light or insight into it; after him the great Lord Cook and Doctor Heylin; but they all abound with so many errors and mistakes, that it is very unsafe and uncertain adhering to any of them.

Having said this, give me leave to observe what natural

misfortunes this country is said to labour under, which I am informed, and apprehend from some of its natives, is frequent penury, and want of many necessaries of life, occasioned by a thin unfertile soil, requiring more experience, labour, and manure, than the inhabitants in general are qualified to bestow upon it; for though there are few here that can be properly said to be rich, so neither are there many can be esteemed miserably poor. But were they so happy as to have the encouragement of some manufactures, and a more extensive trade of their own product, the country would not only be improved, but grow rich, and able to supply themselves by their own labour and product.

It is true they want many necessaries for the common service of life, as timber, salt, wrought iron, and coals, &c. But with all these they might be easily supplied by the countries round them, had they equal products to give in exchange, or indeed were there a herring fishery as certain and plentiful as formerly, it would supply all those wants, and to spare. But as blessings of this nature very much depend upon proper seasons and the bounty of heaven, they must pray for the one, and patiently wait for the other; and with thankful hearts and virtuous lives endeavour to merit those favours.

As I have given you the common, or rather accidental wants and misfortunes of this little part of the globe, I cannot but in justice show the blessings and advantages it enjoys beyond all the nations round about it.

The first whereof is a perfect unanimity in matters of religion, strictly conformable to the doctrine and discipline of the church of England by law established.

The next after this is the rectitude and goodness of their laws, so wisely formed, and so admirably adapted to their constitution, that the great Lord Cooke saith, "that the Isle of Man hath such laws as are not to be found in any other place."

Every man there pleads his own cause, without council or attorney, or any person who gains by encouraging strife. All chancery business is ended in twelve or fourteen weeks, to wit. Four court days, matters of common law are something more dilatory by reason court days come but twice a year; but the ease of the government, and every man's interest, draws all suits and controversies to as speedy a conclusion as can possibly be contrived.

There is in this little world, besides this happiness, an universal plenty and cheapness in all seasonable times, which makes it the resort of many people in distress and low life. Their own ale has been long esteemed of equal goodness to any of its neighbours; their importations by themselves or strangers, of wine, brandy, rum, sugar, fruit, lemons, silks, velvets, coffee, tea, and china ware, are very large. And could they be once favoured with the exportation of them to their neighbouring nations, upon a just duty, and proper and well regulated conditions, England and its neighbouring friends would, in the opinions of experienced persons, be better supplied, and with less hazard to our manufactures, and more advantage of his majesty's revenue.

But be that as it will, as God has been pleased to give them plenty, he hath also given them hearts to enjoy it. The people are naturally of a cheerful, sociable, and debonair temper, much inclined to music and freedom among themselves, very loving, but a little choleric. They were formerly reputed courageous, and eminent for many excellent military commanders, as will appear more fully from the history, as likewise the respect their kings had among foreign princes, of which Macon (not to mention more) was a most remarkable instance.

But above all, they have been famous for their hospitality to strangers, as great numbers of English in the late civil wars, and many thousand of Irish Protestants, in these late devastations of that kingdom, in 1689, can witness.

Nor were they less famous in former ages for sheltering distressed princes, of which I will venture to give my reader one instance.

Eugenius, when prince of Scotland, took sanctuary in the island for nine years, and was afterwards recalled by the nobility and people, and crowned King of Scotland: to omit Ederias, and Corbred, sirnamed Gald, from his travelling and learning, who were educated in this island, even before Christianity; for it is not improbable these princes might choose the Isle of Man for their retreat, because it was then and many ages after accounted the only seat of learning under the Druids, nor was it less remarkable under their first pious bishops.

Hector Boetius says, Man was the fountain of all honest learning and erudition; others of the Scotch nation tell it was the mansion of the muses, and the royal academy for educating the heirs apparent to the crown of Scotland, as Eugenius the Third himself, who likewise sent three of his sons, to wit, Ferguard, Fiacre, and Donald, into the Isle of Man, to be educated under Couranus, whom they write Bishop of Sodor; two of which sons, Ferguard and Donald, were successively Kings of Scotland, as both Hector Boetius and Hollinshead can witness; who likewise inform us, that even before this Couranus, (by Doctor Heylin writ Goran,) ordered that the three sons of his brother Congel, to wit, Eugenius the Second, Cougatus the Third, and Kinatellus the First, should be brought up in the Isle of Man, says Boetius, under the government of certain instructors and schoolmasters, to be trained up in learning and virtuous discipline, according to an ancient ordinance thereof made and enacted. So celebrated was the discipline of those ages, that it seems to have passed into a law, that the princes of Scotland should be educated in this island.

Having thus far shown wherein the ancient honour of this island consisted, I think it proper my reader should know that it had formerly an order of nobility, for I find both earls and viscounts mentioned, but especially barons, who I conceive were the governors of the out Isles. In those days the Comes were the first magistrate in the country, and the Vice Comes his substitute; but of latter ages they have been appropriated as marks of honour to particular families.

There were likewise formerly several ecclesiastical barons in this isle, as the Abbot of Rushen, and the Abbot of Furness, and the Bishop of Man, who still retains that honourable title, and in regard thereof is to hold the lord's stirrup, when he mounts his steed, at the Tinwald.

But because those pious foundations lie buried in their own ruins, I shall crown my work with what is esteemed the greatest glory this world affords, viz. That it was a kingdom, if you will take the words of my Lord Cook: The ancient and absolute kingdom of Man, in Calvin's Case, Lib. 7, Chap. 21. Though since it fell under the homage of the crown of England, it was never granted but by the title of the Island and Lordship of Man, except to Sir John Stanley, who is styled King and Lord of Man, in their records as before-mentioned; so that it pretended to no such absolute dominion, for allegiance to the crown of England was reserved in all public oaths.

Not but that it still retains most of the essential marks and insignia of regal power, as making laws for its own government, of pardoning criminals, of holding courts in the lord's name, the patronage of the bishopric, the admiral of those seas, the coinage of money, and many other inferior articles of regality; which as they were derived from the favour of the crown to the house of Derby, so the constant and uninterrupted loyalty of that noble house may be justly esteemed to have deserved it, especially since they have managed that great trust and power with so much tenderness and care of the people under them, by which they have stood as lasting examples to all in power, and transmitted to the remembrance of all posterity, that by their care, vigilance, and justice, there is one little spot of earth in the world where law, justice and equity, true religion and primitive integrity, have long done, and still do flourish, in contempt of faction, sedition, contention, want or division, or whatever else the world calls miseries and misfortunes.

DESCRIPTION
OF
THE ISLE OF MAN.

THE Isle of Man hath been called or known by divers names amongst ancient writers. By Cæsar it was called Mona, and is still so styled in their own records from all antiquity; by Ptolomy, and by Pliny, Monada; by Secunda Ninius, Eubonia; by the Britons, Menaw; by the natives, Manning; and by the English, the Isle of Man.

The length of the isle from north to south is more than thirty miles, and the breadth between eight and ten. It lies between 55 and 56 degrees of northern latitude, and 15 degrees of longitude. Castletown seems to be in the same parallel with York. A certain author says, it is placed in the navel of the sea; and in truth it seems to be the centre of the king of Great Britain's dominions, as it is almost equally distant in the north from Galloway, in Scotland; in the west, from Ulster, in Ireland; in the east from Cumberland; and in the south from Anglesea.

The Isle of Man lying nearer to the counties of Lancaster and Cumberland, than to any other of England, the inhabitants very much follow and partake of the customs and usage of those counties, especially Lancaster, with whom they have a constant trade for their cattle and other produce of the island, and in return supply themselves with salt, and all other necessaries wanting there. They have a natural respect for the people of Lancashire; whether it arise from their lord's usual residence in that county, or their being mostly supplied with their principal officers from thence, as governors, bishops, archdeacons, and many others of less note, I know not; but they have such an esteem for the people of that county, that it is a common maxim with them, that a good Lancashire Justice of the Peace generally makes the best Governor of the Isle of Man.

This island was many ages governed by its own kings, natives of the place; but through a long descent, and great variety of changes in the government, it is rendered too difficult to be pursued in a lineal and regular manner without many and long digressions; and as I conceive, it would appear more like a needless curiosity than of any service or useful information to the reader, therefore I shall neither give him nor myself more trouble than is needful on that head, to introduce the description and history of that island more clear and intelligible.

Beginning first with King Olave, the third son of Goddard Crownan, whose family had long reigned in the island, which was styled the kingdom of the isles, as will appear more fully in the sequel hereof. This young gentleman being greatly oppressed and harrassed by the more powerful kings of Norway, Denmark, Scotland, and Ireland, applied himself to Henry I. King of England, and offered him the kingdom of the isles. He was then a prince in the flower of his youth, peaceable, just, and liberal, but especially to the church, and therefore pious.

He assumed the government anno 1102, and by his princely address and prudent negociations procured the King of England for his patron, and by that king's intercession the Kings of Scotland and Ireland for his confederates; so that having nothing to fear from abroad, he applied himself to public works of mercy and piety at home.

First, by reforming the laws and the manners of his subjects. And wisely weighing that religion and good education greatly soften the temper and actions of a brutish and vicious people, for that purpose, in the year 1134, he gave the abbey of Rushen to Evan, Abbess of Furness, to serve as a nursery to the church; and hence it is that the Abbots of Furness had the approbation of the Abbot of Rushen, and some believe the right of electing the bishop himself, and a sort of chapter to his diocess.

Olave having thus laid the ground-work of his establishment, greatly endowed the whole church of the isles with large franchises, liberty, and immunities; the revenue of which was set out from the most ancient and apostolic manner, to wit, one third of all the tythes to the bishop for his maintenance; the second to the abbey, for the education of youth, and relief of the poor, (for those good monks were then the public almoners, and by their own labours rather increased than diminished the public charity;) the third portion of the tythes was given to the parochial priests for their subsistence.

Olave having spent near four years in all the calm enjoyments of peace and plenty, at last resolved to visit the King of Norway, and in the year 1142 did homage to Hengo, King of Norway, by whom he was honourably received, and before his departure crowned King of the Isles. He left his son Goddard to be educated in the Norwegian court, and then returned to Man, where he found the long peaceable course of his affairs quite altered; for the three sons of his brother Harold, who had been educated in Dublin, raised great forces, and demanded one moiety of the kingdom of the isles. Olave desired time to consider of it, and on the day appointed to receive his answer, the principal persons on both sides met at Ramsey, where both sides being drawn up in lines opposite to each other, Reginald, one of the brothers, standing in the middle, as talking to some principal persons, being called by the king, turned himself of a sudden, as if he designed to salute him, but at the same time lifted up his battle-axe, and at one blow cut off his head. The nobility depending upon Olave, being all dispersed or slain, Reginald divided the country among his own followers.

Olave left by his wife Affrica, daughter of Fergus, Lord of Galloway, one son, who succeeded him.

The sons of Harrold, flushed with this success, had thoughts of conquering all before them. Immediately therefore they transported their forces into Galloway; but the people there behaved with such bravery and resolution, that they quickly forced them to return with shame and confusion, into Man, where they exercised all the cruelties upon the men of Galloway that shame, disappointment, and revenge could invent. But the justice of heaven suffered not so many villanies to go long unpunished; for, in the year 1143, Goddard, the son of good King Olave, returned from Norway, to whom the whole island immediately submitted. Upon which he ordered two of the sons of Harrold to lose their eyes, and the third, who had murdered his father, he caused to be executed. And having by these acts of justice cleared his way to the crown, by the unanimous and hearty consent of all the people he assumed the government.

Goddard was then in the flower of his youth, brave, active, and generous, with the mein and stature of a hero, and polished by education in a foreign court; all which, joined to the merit of an excellent father, attracted the hearts not only of his own people but of strangers also; and all the neighbouring provinces admired and envied the happiness of the Manx nation, and every one wished for a king like theirs.

But as all human affairs are subject to frequent changes and unforeseen accidents in life, and the most moderate and prudent government in the world is not secure from faction and sedition at home, as well as enemies abroad, so it fell out with this good king; for one Thorfinus, the son of Otter, at that time the principal of all the natives, having been dispossessed of some lands he had a pretence to, and denied some favours he expected, grew a mal-content, and setting up for a patriot gained to his party several factious and seditious subjects; and by their aid, and such others as he could bring into his way of thinking, designed to work his own private revenge.

He therefore goes into Argyle to Summerled, who had married a daughter of good King Olave's, and persuaded him to make his son Dulgall king of the isles, in right of his mother. Summerled, being a prince of a hot, enterprising, and ambitious temper, embraced the proposal; and Thorfinus, by his own influence and persuasion, brought several of the western islands under his obedience. However the majority of the people as yet adhered to their lawful king; among these was one Paul, a person of great loyalty, interest, and virtue, who gave Goddard notice of all Thorfinus's projects, and Summerled's preparations.

Upon which the king equips eighty ships, and in the year 1156 a bloody battle was fought at sea, where both sides wearied with the slaughter made, and the victory still doubtful, the two generals agreed to divide the kingdom of the isles, by which all the northern fell to the son of Summerled. But he, not contented with a moiety, in the year 1158 came into Man with fifty-eight ships, and the people, either weary of the war, or the misconduct and unkind usage of their prince, all submitted to him; so that Goddard, by letting a discontented people slip from him, now found himself no more a king, but forsaken and slighted by all, especially by those who had been the instruments of his severity and misconduct, and found no safer way to make their court to their new master, than by exposing the old, agreeable to that stated maxim, that he that will do ill to please his prince, will certainly do the same against him, when it appears his interest and advantage in so doing. Whilst these things were transacting, the dethroned King Goddard found means to escape into Norway, there to reserve himself to his better fortune. A lively instance of indolence and neglect, which presently degenerate into violence and unwarrantable measures, by which the gaining of a crown may sometimes forfeit the virtue which renders a man worthy of it.

Summerled, flushed with these petty victories, set no bounds to his ambition, but in the year 1164 raised a fleet of a hundred and sixty sail, with a resolution to master all Scotland; but, attempting to land his men at Rheinfern, was conquered by a few, himself and his son slain, with most of his people. The people were glad to be thus delivered; for they found, by dear bought experience, a sensible difference betwixt a passionate and misguided prince, and a real tyrant.

Every one now began to think of Goddard, their exiled king, whose six years' absence, and his own generous qualities, had blotted out the errors and mistakes of his youth and former government; so that all the hearts of the people inclined to his restoration.

At which time Reginald, his bastard brother, had gathered and armed a multitude of loose fellows of different nations, resolving with them to carry the kingdom of the isles.

The Manxmen stoutly defended their king's cause. The battle was fought at Ramsey, and the people lost the day by the treachery of a certain count, who probably dreaded Goddard's revenge upon him; but Goddard being truly informed of the island's good intention towards him, landed the fourth day after the battle with a powerful assistance from the king of Norway. The people received him with joy, all former errors were mutually forgot, and Reginald was seized, and his eyes put out; and all those who might render the succession disputable were stripped of all power. From this time Goddard began to settle his affairs with prudence, gentleness, and moderation; and Macloten, son of Maccartack, King of Ireland, gave him his daughter Fingala to wife, by whom he had a son named Olave.

The year following the king took a progress through the isles, to settle the confused state of affairs there. During his absence, Emoreal, one of the blood-royal, attempting some novelty, brought a great multitude to the Isle of Man, who at first dispersed some few that guarded the coasts; but, the same day, the Manxmen rallied their whole force, and slew him and all his followers; and thus the king continued composing and settling the affairs of his government till the year 1187, in which he died, on the ninth of September, in a good old age.

This prince had tried both extremes of government, first ruined by success, and the ill conduct of his youth; but being made wiser by afflictions and experience, became a fortunate and happy prince.

This prince left three sons, Reginald, Olave, and Ivar, and appointed Olave his successor, because born in lawful wedlock; but Olave being then but a minor, the Manxmen sent for the eldest son Reginald out of the isles, and made him king, anno 1188.

Reginald was then of a ripe age, endowed with great qualities, as wit, courage, and resolution, mixed with craft, dissimulation, and revenge, which added to the natural injustice to his brother Olave, rendered his reign, though long, unhappy. Reginald, in the sixth year of King John of England, had done his homage for the Isle of Man, for which the king granted him a knight's fee in Ireland, and his protection, *pro feod* and *servitio suo*, says the record.

Reginald being at this time absent in Ireland, with all his forces, and all his principal officers, by which the people of the island had been great sufferers, began to think of their injustice to Olave their lawful prince, then in the vigour of his age, and master of all those refined qualities that render princes agreeable to their people, or men to one another; mild, just, sedate, pious, and liberal; to which was added, an admirable symmetry of body, which rendered him the darling of the ladies, who by their interest at home sometimes make the strongest abroad.

Reginald, returning into Man, and viewing the desolation of his country during his absence, and at the same time perceiving the lost affections of his people, resolved to remove his brother Olave, the idol of their hearts, out of his way; but not finding it safe to do it by open violence, he caused him to be seized and sent to William, King of Scotland, where he was kept in chains seven years, at the end of which, King William dying, was succeeded by his son Alexander, who at his coronation ordered all the prisoners to be released, among whom was Olave, who speedily returned to the Isle of Man, well attended by the nobility, and good wishes of the people, and presented himself to his brother Reginald, who received him with all apparent affection, and married him to the Lord of Cantyre's daughter, named Lavon, and sister to his own queen, but gave them nothing but the islands called the Lewis's, which necessity compelled Olave to accept of, since he could get no better. But coming into the Lewis's he found them barren, and altogether insufficient to support him and his retinue; therefore, urged on by despair, necessity, and justice, but more than all by the Viscount Skey, he resolved to push his good fortune to the utmost, and taking hostages of all the great men of the isles, set sail in the year 1215, with thirty ships, and landed in the Isle of Man; but the nobility and people interposing, the brothers came to an agreement, and divided the kingdom of the isles betwixt them, of which Reginald, besides his moiety, had the Isle of Man allotted him.

Olave having refreshed his men, returned to his part of the isles. But Reginald, greatly regretting to be dispossessed of above a hundred isles, that he had been so long master of, sent to Allen, Lord of Galloway, for assistance, and the year following sailed into the out isles, with a design to dispossess his brother Olave; but the people absolutely refusing to fight against their natural prince, obliged him to return home without effecting any thing.

Reginald, restless and impatient with this second disappointment, pretends a necessity of a journey to England. The people cheerfully supplied him with a hundred marks towards his journey; but instead of going to England, he carried his daughter into Galloway, and married her to the son of that lord. But as nothing discontents a people more than the misapplication of public generosity, especially when they see themselves imposed upon, and betrayed to a foreign power, considering with indignation the ingratitude of Reginald, and their own injustice to their lawful prince, they by universal suffrage sent for Olave, and declared him king, in the year 1218. Reginald, seeing his error, though too late, resolves in good earnest on a voyage to the court of King John.

It is certain, as we have observed, that King John, in the sixth year of his reign, took Reginald, King of Man, into his protection, and granted him one knight's fee in Ireland; and also granted him one hundred quarters of corn, to be delivered at Drogheda, on the 26th of May, Anno Reg. sui 14. Anno Dom. 1212.

And King Henry III. Anno Reg. sui 2do. Anno Dom. 1219, granted to Reginald, King of Man, letters of safe conduct to come to England, and do him homage, &c.

And in the fifth year of his reign, 1221, the same king writes to his justice in Ireland, the fourth of November, to deliver to Reginald, King of Man, his knight's fee, two tons of wine, and one hundred and twenty quarters of corn, granted him every year, by the charter of King John his father.

Now if it be allowable to compare so small a prince with an English monarch, there never was a nearer resemblance than in the fortunes of these two; both had obtained their government by injustice to the lawful heirs, both lost it by their ill treatment of the people, both of mischievous designing tempers, and both lived to feel the effects thereof on their own heads: only in this they differ,—John had offended the clergy, and Reginald his people. John had, some years before, made the most infamous submission to the pope that was ever heard of in story; Reginald, to complete the similitude, must do the like, either because it was the fashion, or that he could hope for no assistance without it.

HISTORY OF THE

THE
ACT OF SURRENDER
MADE BY
REGINALD, TO THE SEE OF ROME.

Reginaldus, Rex Insulæ Man, constituit se vasallum sedis Romanæ, et ex insula sua facit feudum oblatum, Londini 10. Cal. October, 1219.

SANCTISSIMO Patri et Domino Honorio Dei gratia summo Pontifici, Reginaldus, Rex Insularum, commendationem cum osculo pedum. Noverit sancta Paternitas vestra, quod nos, ut participes simus honorem quæ fiunt in Ecclesia Rom. juxta admonitionem, et exortationem dilecti patris Domini P. Norwicen electi, Camerarij et Legati vestri, dedimus et obtulimus nomine Ecclesia Romana, et vestro, et Catholicorum vestrorum successorum, Insulam nostrum de Man, quæ ad nos jure hereditario pertinet, et de quæ nulli tonemur aliquod servitium facere, et deinceps nos, et hæredes nostri in perpetuum tenebimus, in feudum dictam insulam ab Ecclesia Romana, et faciemus ei per hoc homagium et fidelitatem, et in recognitionem dominij, nemine census nos et hæredes nostri in perpetuum annuatim solvemus Ecclesia Romana duodecim marcas sterlingerum in Anglia apud Abbatiam de Furnes Cistertiensis Ordinis in festo purificationis B. V. Mariæ. Et si non esset ibi aliquis ex parte vestra vel successorum vestrorum, deponentur dictæ duodecim marchæ per nos et hæredes nostros penes Abbatem et Conventum, Ecclesia Romana nomine. Hanc donationem, et oblationem dictus Dominus Legatus recipit ad voluntatem et bene placitum vestrum, et post receptionem factum ab eo sic ipse Dominus Legatus dictam insulam dedit mihi, et hæredibus meis in feudum perpetua possidendam et tenendam nomine Ecclesia Rom. et me inde per annulum aureum investivit, &c. Actum Lond. in domo militiæ templi 10 Kal. Octob. An. Dom. Millesimo, ducentesimo, decimo nono. Et ne super his aliquando possit dubitari, has literas fieri fecimus et sigillo nostro muniri.

Codex juris Gentium Diplomaticus per Godefridum Gulielmum Liebnitzium, impressus Hanoveræ 1693, folprodromus, page 5.

Reginald, King of the Isle of Man, constitutes himself a Vassal of the See of Rome, and of his island makes the offered Grant, at London, 22nd of September, 1219.

TO the most Holy Father and Lord Honorius, by the grace of God supreme Pontiff, Reginald, King of the Isles, kisseth his feet, and sendeth greeting. Be it known to your Holy Paternity, that we, as being partakers of the benefits derived from those things that are done in the Roman church, according to the admonition and exhortation of the beloved Father in God, Peter, Lord Bishop of Norwich, Elect Chamberlain and Apostolic Legate, have given and offered in the name of the church of Rome, and your's, and of your Catholic successors, our Island of Man, which belongs to us by right of inheritance, and for which we are not bound to do service to any; and henceforwards we and our heirs for ever will hold the said island as a grant from the church of Rome, and will do homage and fealty to it. And as a recognition of dominion, in the name of a tribute, we and our heirs for ever will pay annually to the church of Rome twelve marks sterling in England, at the Abbey of Furness, of the Cistertian Order, upon the feast of the Purification of the B. V. Mary. And if there should not be any person there on the behalf of you or your successors, the said twelve marks shall be deposited by us and our heirs with the Abbot and Convent, in the name of the church of Rome. This grant and oblation the said Lord Legate accepts, according to your will and pleasure; and after acceptance so made by him, he the said Lord Legate gave to me and my heirs the said island, to be possessed and held in fee for ever, in the name of the church of Rome; and thereupon invested me therewith by a ring of gold, &c. Done at London, in the house of the Knights Templars, the 22nd of September, Anno 1219; and that no doubt may remain concerning the premises, we have caused this instrument to be made and sealed with our seal.

Vid. Codice juris Gentium Diplomaticus per Godefridum Gulielmum Liebnitzium, impressus Hanoveriæ 1693, fol. Prodromus, page 5.

Whilst Reginald by this infamous surrender was endeavouring to recover his lost estate, his brother Olave, for above two years, enjoyed an undisturbed possession in the government of the Isles, till at last compelled by the disorder of affairs to visit the remote parts of his scattered kingdom, and being well affected by the nobility and soldiery, he left the Isle of Man exposed to the fury of his brother Reginald, who upon this occasion embraced the opportunity, by returning from London; and, by the assistance of Allen, Lord of Galloway, and Thomas Earl of Athol, landed a great army in the Isle of Man, with which he laid the whole south side waste, murdering all the men they met, burning even the very churches, and committing all the inhumanities a tyrant, heated by resentment and revenge, could invent. Till at last, glutted with so much barbarity, or perhaps apprehending his brother Olave's return, he drew off his forces, and Allen, Lord of Galloway, left his bailiffs to collect the revenue; but Olave speedily returning, drove away those collectors, and used all possible means to recal such as had escaped the fury of Reginald, so that the country began to be repeopled, and the natives to settle themselves in peace and security.

But the ambitious spirit of Reginald rested not here; for the same year, in the midst of winter, and in the dead of the night, Reginald, accompanied by the Lord of Galloway, landed a second time, and by his plausible insinuations debauched the whole southern division to his service. Of so mutable a nature are the vulgar, that those very people that had been just before so harrassed by burning their houses, murdering their kindred and relations, now publicly take arms in his defence.

King Olave flies for protection to the men of the northern division, who unanimously resolve to defend him and his cause; whereupon the two brothers engage in battle, at the place called the Tinwald, the public field of council and of arms. Reginald lost the day, and was slain in the heat of the action; and thus fell that restless and ambitious soul, who for above thirty years had disquieted himself and his people. His body was carried by the monks of Rushen to the Abbey of Furness, and buried in a place formerly chosen by himself.

Olave now hoping to enjoy all the fruits of his labours, and the rights justly due to him, resolves on a voyage to Norway, anno 1220; where, during the contest between the two brothers, the accustomed respect had not been paid, which occasioned the king of Norway to appoint a nobleman, one Heusback, to be king of the Isles, and gave him his own name, Haco, who on his arrival there was slain in storming a certain castle in the Isle of Bute, and never reached the Isle of Man.

Upon this Olave returning into the Isle of Man, brought with him Goddard, the son of his late brother Reginald, and by the consent of the people the isles were divided betwixt them, as a means to preserve a future tranquillity in both. Olave had Man allotted to him. Goddard, going to his share, was slain in the Lewis's, by which the whole kingdom of the isles devolved upon Olave, who for the better security thereof resolved to apply to the court of England; and in the year 1236 obtained from King Henry III. letters of safe conduct for Olave, King of Man, to come to him, to treat with him on business of moment; and being come to King Henry, he the same year gave him his commission, with forty marks, one hundred quarters of corn, and five tons of wine, for his homage and defence of the sea coasts, as long as he shall faithfully perform that service, which he enjoyed to the year 1237, the time of his death, which happened on the 18th of June that year, in Peel-Castle, in a good old age, greatly lamented by his people, as a prince worthy of better times, a better kingdom, and better subjects. He lies interred in the Abbey of Rushen, and was succeeded by his son Harold.

Harold was then about fourteen years of age, a youth of great hopes, and rare endowments both of body and mind; but before he was well settled in his new government, (led either by the necessity of his affairs, or a youthful curiosity) resolved on a progress through his whole kingdom, which consisted of near three hundred islands, but dispersed, and many degrees remote; and for the security and good of the island, he appointed one Logland, his cousin, to be his lieutenant, who probably did not execute that trust with the care and fidelity expected from him; of which the king being informed, sent the autumn following three sons of Noil, viz. Dufgall, Thorgall, and Malemore, with his trusty friend one Joseph, to examine and consult about his affairs in the island, and report the conduct of Logland to him.

Upon this a general meeting was appointed the twenty-fifth day following, at the Tinwald, their usual place of assembling for public affairs; but one side accusing, and the other defending, instead of counsel and composing the differences then subsisting, they fell to arms, the shortest way of ending controversies in those days. Dufgall, Malemore, and Joseph, fell in the quarrel. Upon information whereof, the king, greatly incensed, returned into Man the spring following, and Logland justly apprehending his displeasure, attempted to fly into Wales with Goddard, a younger son of Olave, but suffered shipwreck in his passage, with the young prince and all his retinue.

The power of the kings of Norway to this time had been the terror of the northern parts of Europe; but Harold had not paid that personal attendance at that court as was expected, therefore that king, in the year 1238, sent Jospatrick, and Giles Christ, the son of M'Kerthanck, to seize the revenue of the island to his own use. But Harold the year following took a voyage into Norway, where he conducted himself with that prudence and discretion, that after two years stay he was restored to all the isles enjoyed by his ancestors, to him and his heirs and successors, under the broad seal of Norway.

Harold, now secure of the inheritance of his predecessors, in the year 1242 returned into Man, where he was received with the universal applause and good wishes of the people, which he endeavoured to improve by all those public diversions which render youthful princes agreeable to their subjects. But considering nothing secures a lasting happiness like peace abroad, he entered into a strict alliance with the neighbouring princes of Scotland and Ireland; and to secure himself of the good affection of the monarchy of England, he procured letters patent from Henry III. dated the thirty-first of his reign, by which he was permitted to come into England, where on his arrival he was welcomed with all the public compliments due to his character.

The king honoured him with the Order of Knighthood, which in those days was never conferred, but upon persons of high birth and merit. In all places he was entertained with a generosity natural to the English nation; and at last was nobly presented by the king. In the same year he returned to his own country, where good fortune was at once showering down all the blessings of this life upon his head.

He received an invitation into Norway, whither he went, attended by Lawrence, late Archdeacon, now Bishop elect of Man, with a numerous train of nobility and ladies, and there was married to the king's daughter; and after a long and noble entertainment, with all the festivity usual on such occasions, he returned to Man, but was unhappily driven upon the coast of Radland, in Wales, where he suffered shipwreck, and perished with his beautiful young queen, his bishop, and almost all his nobility, and the ladies her companions; a sad conviction, that the highest felicities this world affords are too often but a more solemn introduction to our ruin, which was unhappily verified as in himself, so in his brother and successor.

Reginald, his brother, assumed the government, Anno 1249, on the sixth of May; and the thirtieth of the same month was slain in the meadows near the Church of the Holy Trinity, commonly called Kirk Christ Rushen, with all his party, by a knight called Ivar. Whether the cause of their quarrel was love or revenge is not mentioned, or whether he had assumed the government without the consent of the people we are not informed of by record, further than that Reginald left one daughter very young, named Mary, who in the year 1292 claimed the kingdom of the Isles, and did homage to our King Edward I. in Perth, or St. John's town. And though we do not find in all the Norwegian line any pretence to a female succession, yet this gave ground for a plea, near four hundred years after, in which sentence was pronounced in favour of the heirs general of Ferdinand, Earl of Derby, against his brother, Earl William, in the following case, wherein question was moved concerning the title to the Isle of Man, which by Queen Elizabeth was referred to the Lord Keeper Egerton, and divers Lords of the Council, and to three of the Judges of England, who in Trinity term, fortieth of Elizabeth, 1598, upon hearing of the counsel on both sides, and mature deliberation thereon, resolved on five points, viz,

First, That the Isle of Man was an ancient kingdom of itself, and no part of the kingdom of England. Secondly, They affirmed a case reported by Kelwin, the fourteenth of Henry VIII. to be law, to wit, Michl. fourteenth of Henry VIII. an office was found, that Thomas, Earl of Derby, at his death was seized of the Isle of Man in fee; whereupon the countess his wife, by her counsel, moved to have her dowry in the chancery: but it was resolved by Brudnel, Brook, and Fitzherbert, justices, and all the king's counsel, that the office was merely void, because the Isle of Man was no part of England, nor was governed by the laws of this land, but was like to Tourney in Normandy, or Gascoine in France, when they were in the King of England's hands, which were merely out of the power of the chancery, which was the place to endow the widows of the king's subjects, &c.

Thirdly, It was resolved by them that the statute of William II. de jovis conditionalibus, nor the twenty-seventh of Henry VIII. of uses, nor the statutes of the thirty-second and thirty-fourth of Henry VIII. of William, nor any other general act of Parliament, did extend to the Isle of Man, for the causes aforesaid; but by special name an act of Parliament may extend to it.

Fourthly, It was resolved, that seeing no office could be found, to entitle the king to the forfeiture of treason, that the king might grant by commission under the great seal to seize the same into the king's hands, &c. which being done and returned of record, is sufficient to bring it into the king's seizure and possession, and into charge, &c.

Fifthly, that the king might grant the same under the great seal, because he cannot grant it in any other manner; and herewith agreeth divers grants under the great seal of this isle.

Sixthly, it was resolved that a fee simple in this isle, passing by the letters patent to Sir John Stanley and his heirs, is descendible to his heirs according to the common law; for the grant itself by letters patent is warranted by the common law in this case; and therefore, if there be no other impediment, the isle in this case shall descend to the heirs general, and not to the heirs male, upon which this affair was afterwards settled by act of parliament, as aforesaid.

During the race of Goddard Crowman, three qualifications seemed requisite for the descent of the government, to wit, a male succession, the consent of the people, and the approbation of the King of Norway, who was then acknowledged for the sovereign; and where any of these were wanting, it generally proved fatal to the prince and people.

Olave had left a third son, named Magnus, who probably was not in the island at his brother's death; so that Harold, the son of Goddard Don, grandson of Reginald, for a time usurped the name of king, and dispossessed all the nobility, depending on the successors of Olave, of their employments and commands. But the King of Norway sent for him, and made him prisoner for his unjust intrusion; and in the year 1252 sent Magnus, the lawful heir, to the Isle of Man, who was chosen king by the universal consent of the people: but finding it unsafe to trust to that title only, he the next year went into Norway, where after two years attendance he was declared King of the Isles, and the title confirmed to him, his heirs, and successors, Anno 1254.

These little princes had a nice game to play, as they lay surrounded with so many potent states. The Kings of Norway began to decline, and the Scottish Kings, from whom these islands had been taken, to recover strength; so that during the last vacancy they designed to have recovered them, had not their king died in the midst of the preparation. The monarchy of England was now almost their only refuge; so in the year 1256, Magnus resolved on a voyage to that court, where he was honourably received by King Henry III. as his brother Harold had been some years before, and was knighted by that king, as the greatest compliment that could be paid to strangers by our monarchs in those days of chivalry.

In the year 1263, Aquinus, King of Norway, resolved to revenge the affront the Scottish nation had designed against him, and accordingly made a descent upon that kingdom, but was so warmly received by their new King Alexander, (a generous and active prince,) that he was forced to take shelter in the Orcades, where he died, at Kirkwall.

This was the last feeble effort of that nation, which had spread its arms over all Europe for five hundred years past. It hath given kings to England and Sicily, dukes to Normandy, and held the sovereignty of those isles for near two hundred years past; but the continual throwing off of such vast numbers of the natives had so weakened itself, that some time after it became subject to the more potent and growing kingdom of Denmark.

Thus nations have their periods as well as persons and families; and the most enterprising generally destroy themselves soonest by their own ambition. The little kingdom of Man, deprived of the protection of Norway, could not support itself much longer; for Magnus dying anno 1265, in his castle of Rushen, was buried in the Abbey church of St. Mary, which he finished and caused to be dedicated, and left no child behind him.

He was the ninth and last of the race of Goddard Crowman, who for two hundred years had enjoyed the name of king, though in effect little better than lieutenants to the crown of Norway, and their inheritance became an insensible addition to the kingdom of Scotland, which rather took away an evil than conferred a good; for though the addition of a neighbouring country may increase a territory, yet different laws, interest, and religion, rarely cement themselves into a well compacted or united state.

THE CONTINUATION FROM THE SCOTCH CONQUEST

To the Settlement under the

HOUSE OF STANLEY.

ALEXANDER, King of Scotland, being informed of the death of Magnus, began to seize such of the out isles as lay most convenient for him, while the affairs of the little kingdom of Man were wholly distracted; but Magnus, King of Norway, son of Aquinus, thinking to apply some remedy to them, sent his chancellor into Scotland, with offers to surrender the Isle of Man and Bute, on condition he should peaceably enjoy the remainder. But Alexander bravely rejected the offer, with a protestation he would win or lose them all; and in pursuance thereof began to reduce them singly with success. But during his engagement therein, a new commotion arose in the Isle of Man, which gave him some concern and uneasiness, as intending to unite the whole kingdom of the isles to that of Scotland, and apprehending little opposition from that of Man.

But the Manx History informs us, that the widow of the late King Magnus, a woman of a haughty and intriguing spirit, who by the death of Reginald had cleared her own way to the kingdom, and secretly in love with a certain knight who had slain Reginald, her late husband's brother, named Ivar, now thought him the fittest person to supply the vacancy, there being no lawful successor, except the daughter of Reginald, and she but a child. The danger from Scotland seemed pressing; but what will not love and the temptations of a crown persuade men to?

Ivar, then in the vigour of his age, gay, generous, and popular; the boldest, the bravest, and the best of all the natives; one that had virtues enough to save, and vices enough to ruin a nation; readily embraced the offer of his kind friend the widow, his mistress, who had entirely forgot all affection, as well as duty and allegiance, to her late husband's niece and legal successor the Princess Mary. Her pride, ambition and aspiring lewd temper could think of nothing less than a crown.

But the child Mary was so happy as to be left under the care and guard of just, sincere, and affectionate friends, who, whilst the widow and her bully, Ivar, were making their way to the government, took care to have Mary secretly conveyed into England, with all the public deeds and charters, equally fearing the danger she was in at home as well as from abroad; but, being got into safety, we will leave her for a while to attend and wait her good fortune.

In the interim, Ivar vigorously prepares for the defence

of his new kingdom, and at least resolves to deserve, if not enjoy the crown. But the Isle of Man could do little singly with the more potent kingdom of Scotland; for Alexander having now reduced all the out isles, sends a numerous army under Alexander Peasley and John Commin, who landed at Rannesway, now Derby Haven, in the year 1270. Ivar, though much inferior in number, (as being deprived of all assistance from abroad,) received them with a resolution natural to the Manx nation, and fought them stoutly, and as bravely fell with the expiring liberty of his country, and with him five hundred and thirty-seven of the flower of the people.

Thus the kingdom of the isles was wholly reduced, in which the King of Scotland had spent four years, to wit, from 1266 to 1270. The King of Norway, now seeing the kingdom of the isles lost, sent his chancellor a second time either to redeem it or compound for a tribute. The first was absolutely rejected; but to end farther disputes, a peace was concluded under several articles; of which the payment of four thousand marks ready money, and one hundred pounds by way of tribute, were the principal. No notice was taken of Mary, the child, nor her right, though last of the family of Goddard Crowman, which had held the government two hundred years, and were now succeeded by Alexander, King of Scotland, who enjoyed it by a mixt title of arms and purchase, and governed by his thanes or lieutenants: the first of whom was Goddard M'Manus, too honest a man to make a good governor in his prince's sense, who, for refusing to be concerned in the murder of three brethren descended from the former race, was removed after he had held this station four years.

To him succeeded Allen, a man that understood his king's pleasure better than how to govern his people well. He was imperious, cruel, hard-hearted, inexorable, too much of the bully for the governor, and too little for the soldier. The people till this time had followed their hereditary kings with a cheerful, active obedience, by which they were enabled not only to secure themselves, but often to make conquests abroad; but instead of the generous firmness of their ancestors, they were now degenerated into a sullen and supine negligence, and their only study was how they might legally disobey. This increased the thane's severity; for the more a people suffer, the more men of brutish and cruel souls insult.

At last, grown desperate by their miseries, the natives universally rose against the Scots nation, with a resolution either to extirpate them, or fall to a man themselves; but by the interposition of their good bishop, they agreed to end the dispute by a combat of thirty on a side. The thane, who had been the occasion of the quarrel, as he stood spectator of the fight, was pressed to death by the multitude.

The Manxmen lost the day, and all their thirty combatants fell; the Scots lost twenty-five. This last struggle of the Manx nation made the Scottish king sensible of his false policy.

He therefore sent over Maurice Okerfair, a wise and worthy magistrate, one whose prudence made him reverenced in peace, as his honour did in arms, which rendered him terrible in war, dreadful to the stubborn, tender to the poor, and merciful to the afflicted. In him the exactness of the soldier gave an air and vigour to the laws, and the fineness of the gentleman softened their vigour in execution, by an excellent mixture of moderation and severity. He made it his business to allay the animosities of the two factions, and so far succeeded that he caused thirty cross marriages to be celebrated in one day. He held the government three years, and died in 1282, equally lamented by both nations.

Okerfair was succeeded by one Brenus, who pursued the gentle and moderate principles of his predecessor; and taught the people the art of fishing. He was unhappily slain in some rencounter with the Highlanders, in the year 1287.

Brenus was succeeded by Donald, a person of great birth and reputation; but how long he had the government is uncertain, for in the year 1289 King Edward I. gave the Isle of Man, &c. to Walter de Huntercomb; for upon the surrender of the island by Richard de Burgo, who probably had been intrusted with it by one of the competitors of the crown of Scotland, King Edward, in the eighteenth year of his reign, committed the custody of this island to the aforesaid Walter de Huntercomb, a very brave and honest man, who the year following, by his master's order, surrendered it to John Baliol, King of Scotland, with a salvo, notwithstanding, to King Edward's right, and that of all other pretenders.

Whether he was ever possessed of it doth not appear, for the Scottish nation was at that time greatly embroiled by the factions of Bruce and Baliol, competitors for the crown. King Edward was chosen as arbitrator of their differences, and being at Perth, or St. John's Town, Mary, the last of the old family, and wife of John de Waldeboef, made her claim, and offered to do her homage for the Isle of Man, but was answered, she must claim it of the King of Scotland, who then held it.

It also appears by petition to King Edward I. in Parliament, in the thirty-third year of his reign, that while this isle was in the hands of John Baliol, King of Scots, Mary, the wife of John de Waldeboef, presenting her right to the Isle of Man, was answered, she must prosecute it before the King of Scotland, who then held it as above. But she dying in the prosecution, the right descended to William, her son and heir, and from him to John his son, and from him to Mary his daughter, who survived her brother, and then claimed the Isle of Man, as true and lawful heir, and was answered, Let it be heard in the King's Bench, and justice done.

In the thirty-fifth of the aforesaid prince's reign there is a memorable record extant, in Mr. Prinn, of our king's right, and seizure of the Isle of Man, for his own use, upon the dispossessing of Henry Bello Monte; the custody whereof was granted to Gilbert de Makaskall, during pleasure, who had expended one thousand two hundred and fifteen pounds three shillings and fourpence, in defence of it against the Scots, and likewise laid out three hundred and eighty pounds seventeen shillings and sixpence in victuals, which delivering to the governor of the castle of Carlisle, to victual it against the Scots, both the sums were allowed him upon his petition, and ordered to be paid.

King Edward I. soon after dying, was succeeded by his son, the second of that name. This fickle prince made no less than three grants in one year, to so many of his favourites, to wit, Percy de Gaveston, Gilbert de M'Gascall, and Henricus de Bello Monte. The grant to the last is to be seen at large in Mr. Challoner. These uncommon proceedings put the island in great disorder and confusion, which gave King Robert Bruce an opportunity of ending all controversies, by asserting the right of the crown of Scotland; and in the year 1313, sat down before the castle of Rushen, which for six months was obstinately defended by one Dingay Dowill, though in whose name we do not find. But not long after, it was granted to Robert Randolph, Earl of Murray, during whose government, in the year 1316, Richard Le'Mandeville, with a numerous train of Irish, landed at Rannesway, (now Derby Haven,) demanding victuals and money, which being denied them, they divided themselves into two troops, and under the hill Warefield, now Barrowl, found the natives drawn up, but their spirits so dejected by their loss of liberty, invasions, depredations, and frequent change of masters, that they made little or no resistance.

The conquerors grievously spoiled the whole island and abbey of Rushen, and after a month's stay returned into

Ireland. After this the Scotch writers tell us of a grant to the Duke of Albany, the year uncertain; and lastly, to Martholine, the King's Almoner, who was sent over to take care of religion, and the reformation of manners, then wholly degenerated there.

He wrote against witchcraft, a practice too frequent in that place in those days. And for the better circulation of business, he is said to have minted a certain copper coin, with the king's effigies on the one side, and a cross on the other side, with this inscription, *Crux est Christianorum gloria:* the cross of Christ is the glory of Christians. To say truth, we have so little certainty of those times, that we rather expose their ignorance than inform ourselves; only this is certain on all hands, that in the year 1340, and in the seventh of Edward II. this island was retaken by the Scots, and John de Egarda, at that time a potent and eminent man in this isle, and his family, were driven from thence, after great losses sustained, into Ireland. Whereupon the king, upon his application, wrote to his Justice Chancellor and Treasurer of Ireland, to allow him a competent maintenance for his brave endeavours to serve him; who, after having refreshed himself, and collected his friends together, with what forces he could possibly raise, returned to the island, expelled the Scots, and restored the king's authority. Upon which the king again wrote to his officers in Ireland, to allow him a competent maintenance for himself, his family, and soldiers, *anno octavo regni sui.* Brave actions merit agreeable rewards, instanced in the loyalty, duty, and integrity of the above gentleman, and the justice and generosity of the prince in return thereof.

We come next to Mary, the last of the family of Goddard Crowman, whom we left attending her fortune at London, where she married John de Waldebeof, a gentleman of eminent note and figure, by whom she left a son named William, who entered his claim in Parliament, in the thirty-third of Edward I. but died before any thing was determined therein, and left a daughter Mary. This lady coming to England with her grandmother's deeds and charters, cast herself at the feet of King Edward III. imploring his majesty's assistance. That generous prince not only gave her his protection, but married her to Sir William Montacute, whom Mr. Speed styles the chief star in the firmament of England; for he was magnanimous, affable, active, and generous even to a fault. His merits had acquired him the esteem of the greatest of our English monarchs.

The king gave him both soldiers and shipping to prosecute his lady's right, which he did so successfully, that in a short time he recovered the island from the Scottish government; and the Manx History says, that excellent prince caused him to be crowned, and styled King of Man, anno 1344, according to Daniel and Stow.

But as the gaining a man's right often costs him more than it is worth, he had contracted so great a debt, that he was obliged to mortgage the island to Anthony Beck, Bishop of Durham, for seven years. This bishop was styled Patriarch of Jerusalem, a proud, busy, crafty, covetous prelate of little good nature, but abundance of grace; and as usurpers generally gripe hard when they have got possession, so he obtained a second grant thereof from Richard II. for his life, after whose decease the island devolved upon William Montacute, Earl of Salisbury, the descendant of the above William, who, in the year 1393, sold it to Sir William Scroop, Chamberlain to the king, as appears by record, viz. *Wilhelmus le Scroop emit de Domino. Wilhelmo Montauto insulam eubonix est Mannix, est nempe jus ipsus insulæ ut quisquis illus sit Dominus Rex vocetur ni etiam fas, est corona aurea coronari.*

This Sir William Scroop, afterwards Earl of Wiltshire, is said to have had all the vices of a great statesman, subtle, fawning, false, designing, timorous and unjust, covetous and ambitious; and to support his own authority, misled a weak prince into a separate interest from his people, which in the end proved the ruin of them both; for the nobility, not able to bear his insolence and ill usage, rose against the king, though unsuccessfully, among whom the great Earl of Warwick, a true maintainer of English liberty, was banished to the Isle of Man, but soon after recalled.

For the Duke of Lancaster (afterwards King Henry IV.) landing in England, was universally received by the nobility and people, and Sir William Scroop, Earl of Wiltshire, had his head struck off without any formal process, for misgoverning the king and kingdom; and the Isle of Man was granted by King Henry IV. to Henry Piercy, Earl of Northumberland, upon condition he should carry the Lancaster sword (with which the king was girt when he entered England,) on his left shoulder at his own coronation, and his successors the Kings of England for ever.

This earl was a hot, enterprising, haughty, and ambitious man, a zealous assertor of the power of the nobility, for which he fell under an attainder; but was, not long after, restored to all his lands and honours, the Isle of Man only excepted, which he was deprived of by act of Parliament. The Isle of Man at first was ordered to be seized by Sir John Stanley and Sir William Stanley for the king's use only.

But in the sixth of Henry IV. the king made a grant thereof to Sir John Stanley for life, in the month of October; and on the sixth of the ensuing April, Sir John Stanley delivered up the said grant to be cancelled in chancery; and the king, in consideration of the said surrender, and other valuable causes and concessions by Sir John Stanley, regranted the said island to him, his heirs and successors, with the castle and peel of Man, and all royalties, regalities, franchises, &c. with the patronage of the bishopric, in as full and ample a manner as it had been granted to any former lord, to be held of the crown of England, *per homagium legium*, paying unto the king a cast of falcons at their coronation, after such homage made, in lieu of all demands, customs, &c. whatsoever. Anno 1406.

In the reign of his late majesty, George I. the Parliament taking into consideration the injury that was done to the revenue, by the peculiar situation of the Isle of Man, for running foreign goods into this kingdom, (which could no way be avoided, as it was a private property, and governed by particular laws of its own,) proposed to the Duke of Athol, the proprietor thereof by right of marriage into the Stanley family, to deliver it into the hands of the government, for a stipulated sum, supposed to be equivalent to its value. But the duke, unwilling to alienate so large a property of his family, and which had been enjoyed with so much dignity by his ancestors, used all his endeavours to stop such a proposal, and exerted all his interest to suppress the prosecution thereof. Accordingly for some time the affair was suspended; but the abuses appearing more and more flagrant, and the injury every day increasing, in spite of the power of acts of Parliament to suppress it, the Parliament passed an act, empowering certain persons to treat with the duke for the purchase thereof, which, after several delays, was determined, upon condition of the government's paying at a stipulated time the sum of £70,000, for the use of the then present Duke and Dutchess of Athol, or their heirs, or the heirs of either of them. In the year 1765, the time fixed, the money being lodged in the bank of England, pursuant to the agreement, as above, the following proclamation appeared in the gazette, which finally determined this great and important affair.

BY THE KING.

A PROCLAMATION,

For continuing Officers in the ISLE of MAN.

GEORGE R.

WHEREAS by an act made in the last session of Parliament, entituled, "An Act for carrying into execution a contract made, pursuant to the Act of Parliament of the twelfth of his late majesty King George I. between the Commissioners of his Majesty's Treasury, and the Duke and Dutchess of Athol, the Proprietors of the Isle of Man, and their Trustees, for the purchase of the said Island and its dependencies, under certain exceptions therein particularly mentioned,"—It is enacted, That from and immediately after the payment into the bank of England, by us, our heirs, or successors, in the names of John Duke of Athol, and Charlotte Dutchess of Athol his wife, Baroness Strange, Sir Charles Frederick, Knight of the most honourable order of the Bath, and Edmund Hoskins, Esq. or the survivors or survivor of them, of the sum of seventy thousand pounds, on or before the first day of June, in the year of our Lord one thousand seven hundred and sixty-five, the island, castle, peel, and lordship of the Isle of Man, and all the islands and lordships to the said Island of Man appertaining, together with the royalties, regalities, franchises, liberties, and sea ports to the same belonging, and all other the hereditaments, and premises, therein particularly described and mentioned, (except as therein is excepted,) should be, and they were thereby unalienably vested in us, our heirs, and successors, freed and discharged, and absolutely acquitted, exempted, and indemnified, of, from, and against, all estates, uses, trusts, entails, reversions, remainders, limitations, charges, encumbrances, titles, claims, and demands whatsoever. And whereas we have caused to be paid into the said bank of England, in the names of the said Duke and Dutchess of Athol, Sir Charles Frederick, and Edmund Hoskins, the said sum of seventy thousand pounds, on the seventeenth day of May last past, whereby, and by virtue of the said act of Parliament, the immediate care of our said island, and of our loving subjects therein, is now devolved upon us. And whereas by our commission, bearing even date with these present, we have constituted and appointed our trusty and well-beloved John Wood, Esq. to be our governor in chief, and captain general, in and over our said island, peel, and lordship of Man, and all the islands, forts, castles, and lordships, thereunto appertaining. We, being desirous to provide for the due and regular administration of justice within our said Island of Man, and the territories and dependencies to the same appertaining, and to secure the peace and good order thereof, and to promote, to the utmost of our power, the happiness and prosperity of all our loving subjects residing within the same, have thought fit, with the advice of our privy council, to issue this our royal proclamation, hereby strictly commanding and requiring all manner of persons whatsoever, to pay due regard and obedience to the said act of Parliament, and our said royal commission, and cheerfully and dutifully to submit themselves to our said governor so appointed by us as aforesaid, and to be aiding and assisting to him, and all other our magistrates and officers, in the lawful discharge of their authorities, to them committed and intrusted, as they will answer the contrary at their perils. And our will and pleasure is, that all officers and ministers who now are, or at the time of the publication of this our royal proclamation within our Island of Man shall be, concerned in the administration of justice within our island aforesaid, and particularly our clerk of the rolls, attorney general, and two deemsters, and all other persons whatsoever, who at the times aforesaid are or shall be duly and lawfully possessed of, or invested in, any civil employment, (except only the officers appointed and employed by the late proprietors of our Island of Man, in collecting and receiving the revenues arising within our said island, and the territories and dependencies of the same,) shall from henceforth hold their respective offices, places, and employments of, from, and under us, our heirs, and successors, and shall continue in the exercise thereof, and shall enjoy the same, with such salaries, fees, profits, and emoluments, as have hitherto belonged to the same respectively, until our royal pleasure in this behalf shall be further known. And we do strictly command and enjoin all and every the said persons, of whatsoever rank, condition, or degree, to proceed in the execution of the said respective offices, and to perform all the duties thereunto belonging, upon pain of our highest displeasure. And we do further charge and command all and every our said magistrates, officers, and ministers, and all persons whatsoever, who shall hold any office, place, or employment, ecclesiastical, civil, or military, within our said Island of Man, and the territories and dependencies of the same, that within the space of one calender month from and after the publication of this our proclamation within our said island, they do take the oaths appointed to be taken by an act of Parliament passed in the first year of the reign of his late Majesty King George I. entituled, "An Act for the further security of his Majesty's person and government, and the succession of the crown in the heirs of the late Princess Sophia, being Protestants; and for extinguishing the hopes of the pretended Prince of Wales, and his open Abettors;" and also make and subscribe the declaration mentioned in an act of Parliament made in the twenty-fifth year of the reign of King Charles II. entituled, "An Act for preventing dangers which may happen from Popish Recusants," in the presence of our said governor, his lieutenant, or deputy, or in the superior court or courts of record in our said island, upon pain of our highest displeasure, and as they will answer the contrary, at their utmost perils. And our will and pleasure further is, that all jurisdictions and authorities whatsoever, which were heretofore carried on and exercised in the name of the Lord of our said Island of Man for the time being, or of any other person or persons whatsoever, and which are now vested in us, our heirs, and successors, by virtue of the said act of Parliament, shall be henceforth carried on and exercised in the name of us, our heirs and successors only; and that all writs, precepts, processes, orders, injunctions, and all other forms of law and justice, and all acts of state and policy, for the due ordering and government of our said island, and the territories and dependencies thereunto belonging, shall be issued and executed in the name and by the authority of us, our heirs, or successors, or our governor or lieutenant, or deputy governor, for the time being, appointed, or to be appointed by us, our heirs, and successors, and in no other name, and by no other authority whatsoever. And we do hereby strictly command and enjoin our said governor, and all other our magistrates and officers, within our said island, and the territories and dependencies to the same belonging, to see this our royal proclamation duly carried into execution; and to cause the same to be publicly read in all the principal towns of the said island, between the hours of eleven in the morning, and two in the afternoon; and printed copies thereof to be affixed in the most public places of the same, and to be distributed to all the ministers of churches, chapels, and other places of religious worship, within our said island, and the territories and dependences thereunto belonging. And we do hereby lastly charge and command all ministers of churches, chapels, and other places of religious worship aforesaid, publicly to read this our royal proclamation therein, on the next Lord's day after they shall receive the same, during the time of divine service, immediately before the homily or service, upon pain of our highest displeasure.

Given at our court at St. James's, the twenty-first day of June, 1765, in the fifth year of our reign.

GOD SAVE THE KING.

A TOPOGRAPHICAL DESCRIPTION

OF THE

ISLE OF MAN.

THE most general division of this isle is into north and south, each of which has its castle, deemster or judge, and vicar general; and both are subdivided into seventeen parts or parishes, distinguished by the name of kirks. The saints to whom they were in old time dedicated, viz.

Kirk Christ, of Rushen.

Kirk Harbery, dedicated to St. Columbus.

Kirk Melue, dedicated to St. Lapus.

Kirk Santon.

Kirk Bradon, which signifies a Salmon in the Manx language.

Kirk Marcom.

Kirk Concan, dedicated to St. Conca, mother to St. Patrick.

Kirk Cannon.

Kirk Maughald.

Kirk Christ, of Ayre.

Kirk Bride or Bridget, a Parsonage.

Kirk Andrew, the Archdeaconry.

Jorby, or St. Patrick, of Jorby.

Ballough, a Parsonage.

Kirk Michæl.

Kirk German.

Kirk Patrick, of Peel.

Their parishes are again divided into sheadings, as the people call them, viz. the sheading of Kirk Christ, Rushen, the middle sheading, the sheadings of Garf and Glanfaba, Michæl sheading, and Ayre sheading, each of which has its coroner, as the parishes have every one a captain and minister, and every fort its constable, having three parishes in every sheading, but that of Glanfaba, which has but two parishes in it. The island was formerly more populous than now it is. At present there are but four principal towns, viz.

I. Rushen, the chief town, situate on the north side of the isle, and from a castle and garrison in it commonly called, by the English, Castletown. It is the usual residence of the governor, and hath a market and fort, but is under no special officers, as a mayor, aldermen, &c. as corporations are, but offenders are apprehended and brought to justice by the officers of the fort, or constable, as in all other towns and parishes. The castle is a noble piece of antiquity, said to be built by Gutred, the second of their Orrys's, grandson of the King of Denmark. At the foot of the castle is a creek, where ships sometimes venture in, not without danger; but a mile distant is a good harbour, called Derby Haven, secured by a fort, built by the late

Earl of Derby. Pope Gregory IV. or rather St. Patrick, who came into the isle, erected an episcopal See here by the name episcopal Sedorensis, and his jurisdiction was extended to all the Hebrides; but now it is limited to this island. The bishop was formerly reckoned a baron, but never sat in the house of Peers, because he held of a subject, the Earl of Derby, and not of the king, yet hath the highest seat in the lower house of convocation.

II. Douglas, situate on the east side of the isle, the most populous town, and the most spacious and best haven in the isle, the mouth of which is secured so well by a fort, that there is not any attempting either the town or harbour from the seaward. In times of peace it is much frequented by French and other foreigners, who come hither with bay-salt, wine and brandy, and buy up coarse wool, leather, and salt beef, to carry home; by which means this town is become the richest in the isle, and has a good market.

III. Ramsey hath also a good haven, defended by a block-house, built by the late earl.

IV. Peel or Pile, anciently called Holmtown, hath a fort, erected in a small isle, and defended with a strong garrison which secures the harbour. The castle has a platform round it, well secured with cannon. In it stands the ancient cathedral, dedicated to St. German, the first bishop, and repaired by the Earls of Derby, as also a ruined church dedicated to St. Patrick, their apostle. Within this circuit is the lord's house, some ruinous lodgings of the bishop's, and other noble remains of antiquity.

There are some other towns of lesser note, but are remarkable for some particulars, as,

Balaeuri, on the south side of the isle, where the bishop generally resides.

Laxy, which has the largest haven of any town in the isle.

This isle is compassed with huge rocks round about.

The air is sharp and cold in winter, and on the south-west side it lies open to the chops of the channel, and so is liable to a salt vapour, which sometimes has bad effects, but generally is very wholesome to live in, having no damps or venomous vapours arising out of the earth. They have some frost, but short and seldom.

The soil in the north parts is very healthy, sandy, and gravelly; and the north-east has a large tract of meadow called Curragh, which was formerly under water, but is now drained and well improved; but in the south there are good meadows and pastures.

All parts of the isle produce store of wheat, barley, rye, and oats, of late, since they have learned the art of liming their lands, and manuring them with sea-weeds; and some places have plenty of honey, flax, and hemp, and export yearly some fish-oil.

Towards the middle it is mountainous; and the highest hill, called Sccafell, yields a prospect into England, Scotland, and Ireland, in a clear day.

They have cattle of all sorts; but their meat and horses are small and poor, yet will endure a great deal of labour.

Their sheep thrive well, are fat, and well tasted; and their wool is very good, especially that which they call Laughton wool, which when carefully dressed makes a cloth near a hare-colour, which is one of the greatest natural rarities of the country.

They have plenty of goats and hogs of the ordinary size, besides a small kind which live wild in the mountains, called purs, which are admirable meat; and some red deer in the mountains: but they belonged, before the late cession to the government, to the lord of the isle, the Earl of Derby, who had lately stocked the Calf, a pleasant isle adjoining, with fallow deer, and made it a beautiful park.

Their hares are fatter here than in any other country, and they want not otters, badgers, and foxes.

Fowls also of several kinds are found here, as hawks,

which in King Henry IV's time were in such esteem, that Sir John Stanley, the first King of Man, in his patent, was obliged, in lieu of all other services, to present that king and his successors, upon the day of their coronation, with a cast of hawks, geese, hens, ducks, falcons, and wild fowl in plenty.

On the south side of the isle is another island, called the Calf of Man, which is stored with a sort of sea-fowl, called puffins, whose flesh is unpleasant; but being pickled, may vie with anchovies or cavear. They breed in holes like rabbits, and are never to be seen but in the months of June and July, which are their times of sitting.

There is also another kind, called barnacles, which are a kind of ducks and drakes, said to be bred out of rotten wood, but found, upon search, to be produced of eggs as other fowl.

Partridges and farkers will not live here, nor any venomous creature propagate their kind.

Here are many small rills of fresh water, and springs of a pure pleasant taste.

Here is also a pool in the mountainous parts near Kirk Christ, Rushen, of so vitriolic a quality, that no ducks or geese can live near it, which probably proceeds from the frequent spewings of copper that are discovered on all sides of those mountains.

They have sea-fish in abundance, as salmon, ling, cod, haddock, mackarel, ray, thornback, plaice, especially herrings, crabs, lobsters, and cockles, but few or no oysters; but what they have are very large.

They have no wood in the isle, nor is there a tree to be seen, though in former times there was great plenty, as appears from Goddard Crowman's hiding 300 men in a wood, and from the church called Kirk Arbory, which seems to be so called from *arbor*, a tree, as also from the timber found in their bogs, and especially in the meadows called Curragh; nor have they as yet discovered any sea coal for firing in their soil, only they have plenty imported. The poorer sort make use of gorze, heath, ling, and broom, and a coarse sort of turf or peat in digging, when they often find oaks laying under ground.

They have some good stone quarries, especially limestone, on the sea shore, and the rocks called Minehaugh give very probable signs of other minerals. They have also lately found iron, lead, and copper, and there is great probability of finding coals.

This island seems to have been peopled from the Hebrides, or Western Isles of Scotland, and their language is a kind of Scotch-Irish, mingled with Latin, Greek, and English.

We have a specimen of the Manx language given us in the Lord's prayer, printed in Bishop Wilson's Enchiridion, and a collection of the Lord's prayer in above a hundred languages, printed in the year 1703.

The peasants are tall in stature, of a dull surly temper, and live in poor huts made up of stones and clay, and thatched with broom.

Their gentry are courteous and affable, and imitate the English in their carriage, apparel, and housekeeping.

The families of gentlemen named Christian and Caunel are of great antiquity, and out of them their deemsters or judges are usually chosen.

It is almost certain, that this island was never in the possession of the Romans, and so retained their original simplicity longer than the rest of Britain.

The original government of this island was a sort of aristocracy, I had almost said theocracy, under the Druids, admirably adapted to the good of mankind, and so mixed with the prince and priest, that religion and the state had but one united interest.

All controversies were ended by an amicable composition, and the integrity of their rulers was such, that their awards were instead of laws.

This was the true patriarchal government, to which virtue, not birth, was the best title, and is supposed to have continued here till the end of the fourth century, when, according to Mr. Cambden, out of Nenaius, this island was conquered by one Bailey, a Scot, who overturned the ancient form of government, and ruled all by his own will, which force, not reason, swayed, till necessity obliged his successors to agree in some rules and laws, which were the foundation of their present constitution.

The laws and statutes of this island are such, as the Lord C. J. Coke saith, that the like are not to be found any where else.

They were governed of old by a *jus scriptum*, which was committed to the fidelity of their deemsters, a certain sort of judges chosen every year to decide all controversies, a custom received probably from the Druids.

All possible care is taken for the speedy execution of justice.

The government of this isle hath, ever since its conquest by Bailey, been reputed monarchial, and was governed by kings of their own, who claimed the whole revenues of the isle; and all the inhabitants were tenants at will to him; but growing weak in power, they were made tributaries to the Kings of England, Scotland, or Norway. Their names are,

Monnan-Mac-Lear, son of the King of Ulster, and brother of Fergus, King of Scotland. Him the Manx believe their founder and legislator, and have him in great admiration for his wisdom.

Towards the end of his reign, St. Patrick, in his second voyage to Ireland, landed here.

The names of his immediate successors are lost, till

Brenus reigned, A. D. 594, who was succeeded by

Ferquard, Fiacres, Donald, Gutred, Reginald, Olave, Olain, Allen, Frigall, Goddard, Macon, or Macutus, Syrric.

Goddard, the son of Syrric, who reigned   A. D. 1065
Fingal, son of Goddard,   1066
Goddard, son of Harold,   1066
Lagman, son of Goddard,   1082
Dopnal, son of Tade,   1089
Magnus, King of Norway,   1098
Olave, third son of Goddard,   1102
Goddard, son of Olave,   1144
Reginald, natural son of Goddard,   1187
Olave, the lawful son of Goddard,   1226
Harold, son of Olave,   1237
Reginald II. his brother,   1249
Magnus II. his brother,   1252
Alexander, King of Scots,   1260
William Montacute,   1305
Anthony Beck, Bishop of Durham,   1306
Pierce Gaveston,   1308
Henry Beaumont,
Thomas Randolph,
Alexander, Duke of Albany,
William Montacute, Earl of Salisbury,   1340
Who sold it to William Lord Scroop,   1395

Who forfeiting it by treason, it fell into King Henry IVth's hands, who gave it to Henry Earl of Northumberland.

But he was banished four years after, and being deprived of this isle, it was given to Sir John Stanley, in whose family it has continued through many descents ever since, by the style and title of Lords of Man.

The Duke of Athol, as Lord of Man, was Admiral of the Isle, and had an absolute jurisdiction over the people and soil; so that he was immediate landlord of every man's estate, some few barons only excepted: and reserving his homage to the crown of England, no prince had a more full and ample authority.

He was sole patron of the bishopric, and all parsonages

and vicarages except three, which are in the patronage of the bishop.

He had power to make and repeal laws by the advice of his deemsters and twenty-four keys, who must have had his approbation, or he would reject them from the assembly.

He had power of holding courts in his own name; might hang and draw, or pardon malefactors, in his own jurisdiction.

All wrecks, royal fishing, &c. were his by regality, with many other prerogatives.

The civil policy of their government was managed by the lieutenant, who was the duke's immediate representative, and had often been of his family; with other inferior officers.

The lieutenant or governor has a power to call a Tynwald or Parliament, or any other Court, which cannot sit without his warrant. He swears inquests, is sole chancellor, and hath the sole military power to place or displace officers in garrisons, or otherwise; and whoever opposes him in any place or thing wherein he represents the king, robs him of his horse or arms, beats his servants, or breaks his house, is a traitor. Sometimes there has been a captain general, but it was only in some extraordinary cases. The other officers for the duke's service are,

A Receiver General or Treasurer of the Island. He has the charge of the revenue, and pays all the salaries of the civil list, but is accountable to

The Comptroller, who always sits with him both on receipts and payments, and is the auditor of the general accompts. He sits sole judge in all trials for life in the garrison, keeps the records, and enters the pleas of the several courts, where he is allowed fees.

The Water Bailiff, who is in the nature of the Admiral of the Island, and sits judge in all maritime affairs. He has the care of the customs, fishing, wrecks, &c.

The Attorney General, who sits in all courts to plead for the king's profit, as suing for felons, goods, forfeitures, deodands, &c. and is to plead the causes of all widows and orphans, they giving him twopence for his fee.

All the aforesaid officers act by commission from the king during pleasure, and upon his decease their power of acting all expires with him; in the absence whereof the sword takes place, and the chief Commanding Military Officer, who is generally styled Major, takes upon him the preservation of the peace of the island, by seizing the castle and forts, preventing all tumults and disorders, and all persons from going off the island to the prejudice of the inhabitants, until the civil power is restored and re-established by new commissions from the succeeding king.

All the said officers were esteemed of the household or court, and formerly had their diet in the family, where a constant table was kept for them and their attendants. These officers are all by their places justices of the peace, and are in all things to act for the king's profit. The king may call them as a counsel to his assistance, when he thinks proper, or occasion requires, either for the service of himself, or the country.

The deemsters, or judges, are the first public magistrates of the state, but were never part of the household or family. They sit as judges in all courts, either for life or property; they have always been two, one for each division of the isle. They are styled in the ancient court-rolls *Justiciary Domini Regis*. Whether they have their names from the old word to deem, judge, or determine, or to doom, sentence, or condemn, I am not informed, nor can take upon me to ascertain; but by the advice of the twenty-four keys they may, in all new and uncommon cases, declare what the law is, in such cases wherein the law is not fully expressed.

By the ancient law of the isle it is provided, that if any person accuse the deemsters of injustice or mal-administration, he forfeits life and limb. The summons or process used by them is the same with the governor, to wit, a slate stone with one or two letters of their name made upon it; and to counterfeit or misapply this process is as highly penal in their law as the counterfeiting the lord chief justice's warrant is with us.

After the deemsters the twenty-four keys are the representatives of the country, and in some cases serve as the grand inquest of the isle. They are the last traverse in all cases of common law, are present at all trials for life, and in conjunction with the governor and officers of the household aforesaid make the legislative power of that little nation.

The next officers are the coroners of each sheading or division, who act in the nature of sheriffs, and are subordinate to the twenty-four keys.

Every parish hath likewise an officer called a moar, which is the lord's bailiff, and each of them have a subordinate officer not worth our notice.

The courts of judicature are usually twice in the year, to wit, about May and Michaelmas. The first are called sheading courts, and in the nature of our hundred courts, or courts leet and baron; these are held for the king's profit, and relate to all breaches of the peace, and all presentments are here made upon any violation of their laws or public orders.

Immediately after these are held the common law courts, where all actions relating to men's properties are tried. These courts were formerly held in every sheading distinctly, but now have proper places appointed for the holding of them, with all due regard to the ease and benefit of the people.

Next after these follows the grand court or general gaol delivery, in which are managed all trials for life; and perhaps there is no place in the universe where men have a fairer trial, nor where the taking away life is more tenderly regarded.

In this court the governor presides, assisted by the king's officers, with the bishop and his clergy.

The deemsters sit as judges, with the twenty-four keys, to advise with in case any new matter arises. The criminal must be first found guilty of the crime he stands charged with by the grand inquest, and if the case be treason or murder, the witnesses have a very particular and solemn oath administered to them, to wit. The clerk who administers the oath opens the book of the gospel, and the witness or evidence lays his right hand open upon it, then the clerk says to him;

By this book of truth, by all the holy and sacred body of the church, by all the wonderful works and mighty miracles God Almighty wrought in six days and seven nights, in heaven above, and earth beneath, you shall speak the truth, and say nothing that is false for love or fear, favour or affection, consanguinity or affinity, or any other consideration whatsoever; so may you be helped by the Son of God, and by the contents of this book whereon your hand now lies. Then the witness kisses the book.

After this, a peculiar jury of four out of every parish in the island is empannelled, and the prisoner may make his exception against fifty-six and no more. And if his case be felony only, and he suspects it will go hard with him, he may put himself to the king's mercy, and so evade the trial and sentence by the court; and the king, by their law, as well as his prerogative, grants him his grace in such manner as he thinks proper.

But if he stands his trial for life, when the jury come into court, and before they deliver their verdict, the deemsters ask them whether the bald pates (to wit, the clergy,) may sit; and if the foreman answer no, then the bishop and clergy withdraw, as not proper for them to sit or pass sentence in cases of blood; and then the verdict is delivered, and the criminal found guilty, and executed as the court directs; or, if acquitted, discharged.

There is likewise another court, called the Debet Court, in which all fines are set; and there is an Exchequer Court, which is held as often as the governor pleases, or occasion requires. There is also a Court of Chancery, which anciently was held weekly, but at present is kept monthly, wherein the governor sits sole chancellor, and may call the king's council and the deemsters to advise with, as he sees proper.

All actions brought in chancery are entered in the comptroller's office, of which the plaintiff presents the governor a copy, who grants his token upon it to summons the defendant, who may refuse appearance for three court days, but on the fourth he is brought in by a soldier, and the matter heard and determined. So speedy is the justice of this little government that it may challenge the world.

The religion professed in this isle is exactly the same with the church of England; but they have not the Bible in their own language. The ministers turn the English translation into the Manx language in reading the lessons.

The Manxmen are very respectful to their clergy, and pay their tithes without the least grudging.

The clergy are generally natives, who have had their education in the isle. They are sober and learned, and are allowed a competent maintenance of fifty or sixty pounds a year.

The people are so strictly conformable, that in uniformity they outdo any other branch of the reformed church.

There were anciently in this isle three monasteries, viz.

1. The monastery of St. Mary, of Rushen, in Castletown, which was the chief, and the burying-place of the Kings of Man.

It was a goodly fabric, as appears by the ruins. It consisted of an abbot and twelve monks, who had good revenues. The chapel was the largest place of God's worship in the island, except the cathedral.

It was a daughter of Furness Abbey, as were some other

monasteries in this isle. The abbots of it were barons, held courts for their temporalities, and tried their own tenants.

2. Douglas, a priory for nuns. This house is said to be built by St. Bridget, and the prioress was a baroness of the island. It is the most pleasantly situated in the isle.

3. At Brinnaken, a house of the friars minors, a small plantation of the Cistertian order.

The abbots also of St. Bees, of Whittern, in Galloway, and Banchor, in Ireland, were Barons of Man, because they held lands in this island, upon condition of attending upon the kings and lords of it when required.

Having now with some pains and perplexity of thought attended and brought my reader through the obscure and intricate history, constitution, civil government, and antiquities of the little kingdom of Mona, and corrected and amended what I have judged error or mistake in former writers on that subject, what remains before I conclude, but that I give the world the ecclesiastic history of this little kingdom, from its first conversion to Christianity, with the growth, state, and government of the church, its bishops, pastors, and overseers, from the earliest date, and the most approved authorities I have been able to collect from the various writers and histories of those ages?

The first mention I meet with of Christianity's appearance in the Isle of Man, is in Capgrave's Life of Joseph of Arimathea, wherein he tells us of one Mordaius, a king of that isle, being converted to Christianity, about the year of salvation 63, who had his residence in a city called Sodora. If this story be true, (which I much doubt on, as hereafter,) Christianity had an early plantation in this island. But it is matter of wonder to me, that this conversion of the king should not have had a more general influence over the people; for in all the authors I have met with, I find no mention of Christianity in this part of the world of near 400 years after this story, except in another such like story, by Hector Boetius, who relates that one Amphibalus was bishop here about the time aforesaid. But as this story is rejected by most men of learning, except Archbishop Spotswood, I shall with deference consider him so far as to give you his relation thereof from his own words, Book 1st, fol. 3rd, and then make my remarks thereon.

He acquaints us, that one Cratilinth coming to the crown, in the year 277, made it one of his first works to purge the kingdom of heathenish superstition, and expel the Druids, a sort of priests held in those days in great reputation. Their manner was, to celebrate their sacrifice and other rites in groves, with leaves and branches of oak. And from thence, saith Pliny, they were called Druids, which doth signify an oak.

Cæsar, in his Commentaries, gives us this further account of them, that besides the managing of sacrifices, which were committed to them, they were intrusted with the decision of controversies, public and private; and that such as would not stand to their judgment were interdicted from being present at their sacrifices and holy rites, which was taken for a grievous punishment in those days.

It is likewise testified of them, that they were well learned in all natural philosophy, men of moral conversation, and for religion not so grossly ignorant and superstitious as other heathen priests; for they thought there was one only God, and that it was not lawful to represent him by any image; that the souls of men did not perish with their bodies; and that after death men were rewarded according to the life they had led upon earth. They lived likewise in great respect with all people, and ruled their affairs with great prudence and policy; for being governed by a president, who kept his residence in the Isle of Man, they did once every year meet in that place to take counsel together for the better ordering of their affairs, and carried matters with so much discretion, that the said King Cratilinth found it difficult to expel them, because of the favour they had amongst the people.

But that which contributed greatly to the propagation of the gospel in this isle, was the persecution raised by Dioclesian, which at that time prevailed very greatly in the south part of Britain, and brought many Christians, both preachers and professors, into the kingdom of Man, who were all kindly received by King Cratilinth, and had assigned them by him lands and revenues sufficient for their maintenance.

In this isle King Cratilinth erected a stately church to the honour of our Saviour, which he adorned with all necessary ornaments, and called it *Sodorense Fanum*, that is, the Temple of our Saviour; hence it is, says the above story, that the bishops of Man are called *Sodorenses Episcopy*.

So long as this isle remained in the possession of the Scots, the bishops of the isles made that church their cathedral; but since their dispossession, the Isle of Jona had been the seat of the bishops of the isles, and continueth so to this day. In this isle Amphibalus (above-mentioned) is said to have sat first bishop, a Briton born, and a man of excellent piety. He lived long, preaching carefully the doctrine of Christ, both among the Scots and Picts, and after many labours taken in promoting the Christian religion, died peaceably in the said isles. Thus far the learned and good Bishop Spotswood, who in my humble opinion, with all reverence I think, preferred his zeal for Christianity before his judgment in the case above.

There are so many improbabilities in this and the story before it, that I cannot omit to observe some of them. First, Hector Boetius says Amphibalus fled from the persecution of Dioclesian, in South Britain, in the year 280. Whereas Dioclesian did not obtain the empire till the year 286, neither did the tenth persecution arise till the year 302; and Gildas and Polydore Virgil say expressly, that both St. Alban and Amphibalus suffered martyrdom in the year 305; and the general stream of all British writers concur in this martyrdom, neither do any of the Scotch writers mention Amphibalus, in the life of Cratilinth, before Hector Boetius and his followers.

And it is in my judgment almost impossible to conceive, that the Manx nation should preserve no memory of so considerable a blessing as their first conversion to Christianity; besides all their traditions are directly against it. Matthew Paris affirms, that the body of Amphibalus was found at Radburn, near St. Albans, in the year 1178; and many other marks of his martyrdom at Radburn strongly conclude he died for his religion in England, and never fled to the Isle of Man to erect a bishopric, and *Fanum Sodorense*; besides it must appear something wonderful and surprising, that no memory of Christianity, nor ruin of any such church should be found, or so much as mention made of them, at the time of St. Patrick's landing there, which is enough with me to show there is nothing of truth or certainty in the abovesaid story.

Next to the said accounts already taken notice of, Mr. Cambden, my Lord Cook, and Doctor Heylin, all three affirm, that the bishopric in the Isle of Man was erected by Pope Gregory IV. anno 480, in an island near Castletown; whereas the bishopric is sufficiently proved, by the great Primate of Armagh, to be erected by St. Patrick, about the year 447, and the place itself shows there is no such island near Castletown.

And herewith all the ecclesiastical writers of any credit in those ages agree, that St. Patrick (alias Patricius,) was the first that planted the Christian religion in the Isle of Man; and since their ancient, authentic, and national tradition concur therewith, I cannot but allow him to be truly the apostle of the Manx nation, as well as for the reasons following.

First, if I remember my reading rightly, I have met

with it in the curious essays of the great and learned Lord Montaigne, who lived about the time of Pope Gregory IV. or not long after. This pope was said to be a person of great learning, piety, and virtue, and a zealous promoter of the Christian faith, by which he obtained the epithet of Great; who, walking on a time through the market-place of Rome, espied a number of beautiful captive children sitting there to be sold, which induced his compassion as well as curiosity to go up to them, and inquire of those that sold them what country they were of; and being told they were Britons, he then asked if they were Christians, and was answered, no. Upon which he said, it was great pity that such angelical faces should not be made Christians.

In consequence whereof he soon after sent St. Patrick, with twenty more assistants, to preach the gospel, and convert to Christianity the people of Scotland and Ireland; for it does not appear he came into Ireland till the year 441, and Austin the monk had been sent into England before him by the same pope.

St. Patrick with his company, having landed in North Britain, met with great success in their mission; upon which St. Patrick leaving St. Andrew and other learned preachers to pursue the great work of propagating Christianity there, passed over to Ireland, where he found the harvest great, but the labourers too few: whereupon he returned to North Britain, in the year 444, and collecting together some of his former assistants, with some new converts of learned and religious persons, to the number of thirty, he came with them through the north of England, to take shipping at Liverpool for the south of Ireland; and on his approach near that town, the people came out to receive him, and at the place they met him erected a cross in honour and memory thereof, and called it by his name, which it bears to this day.

St. Patrick and his company having rested and refreshed

themselves awhile at Liverpool, took shipping for Dublin, but in his passage put into the Isle of Man, where he found the people, especially the rulers, given to magic; but being overcome and convinced by his preaching and miracles, they were either converted or expelled the island.

St. Patrick and his company going for Ireland, anno 447, left one Germanus, a holy and prudent man, *(ad regendum et erudiendum populum in fide Christi,* says Jocelinus) which, for the honour of the Manx nation, was sixty-nine years more ancient than Bangor, in Wales, which was the first bishopric we read of among the Britons, and 114 years before Austin the monk introduced the Liturgy of the Lateran, and thereby so absolutely settled the business of religion, that the island never afterwards relapsed.

Germanus died before St. Patrick, who sent two bishops to supply his place, Conindrius and Romulous, of whom we have little memorable, but that one or both of them survived St. Patrick, to the year 494, being five years, when one St. Maughold was elected bishop by the universal suffrage of the Manx nation; but by whom consecrated is very uncertain, as also his successors for some ages, which I shall studiously omit, and only acquaint my reader that one St. Columbus is acknowledged by all writers to be the founder of the abbey of Hye, in the Island of Jona, which monastery was the cathedral of the bishops of the isles, who were from that time styled *Episcopus Sodorensis,* from a village called Sodor, adjoining to the said monastery.

But after the Isle of Man was made the seat of the Norwegian race, the bishoprics were united, with the title of Sodor and Man, and so continued, till conquered by the English, since which the Bishop of Man keeps his claim, and the Scotch bishop styles himself Bishop of the Isles, anciently, *Episcopus Insularum Sodorensium.*

I could here enlarge pretty much on the succession of the bishops of this isle, from the time of St. Maughold, yet as it is not certainly known who they were, or in what order they sat, I shall purposely omit them, and content myself with giving you a list of their succession from the time of Goddard Crowman, the first king I have before taken notice of, and so conclude my history of Man, both civil and ecclesiastical, and with the greatest certainty that I have been able to collect from the best writers on this subject.

THE SUCCESSION

OF

THE BISHOPS OF MAN.

How long St. Maughold sat bishop we do not find, only Dr. Heylin says, he was bishop anno 578, of which we have no other certainty, nor of a successor till the year 600.

Whose name was Coranus, tutor to the three sons of Eugenius, the fourth King of Scotland, as Bishop Spotswood informs us. After him the succession appears wholly broken till the eleventh century; yet during this long vacancy many errors arose, and many mistakes were advanced concerning it, which most of our English writers have fallen into without any good ground in history, save that the bishopric of the isles had its beginning about that time, to wit, in the year 840.

In a very ancient manuscript by the Rev. Mr. Henry Jones, nephew to the Right Rev. Dr. Fell, Bishop of Oxford, we meet with an exact succession for above 200 years, which, in the opinion of the learned, was extracted from the roll of the ancient abbey of Rushen in the Isle of Man.

This manuscript, by way of introduction, informs us, that though they had a traditional succession of bishops from the time of St. Maughold, yet they were not certainly known; therefore it was thought proper to omit them, and begin from the time of King Goddard Crowman, as before proposed.

In his reign we meet with one Hamundus, by some written Vermundus, Bishop of Man, and probably was the first bishop styled of Sodor and Man. He was the son of Jole, a Manxman. Matthew Paris says he died in the year 1151. It is not certain by whom he was consecrated, nor his successor, who was one

Gamaliel, an Englishman, who lies buried at Peterborough, in Northamptonshire; and was succeeded by Reginald, a Norwegian. To him the thirds of all the livings in the islands were granted by the clergy, that from thenceforward they might be freed from all episcopal exactions. It is probable that he was the first bishop that was consecrated by the Archbishop of Drontheim, in Norway. His successor was one Christian, a native of the isle, who lies buried in the monastery of Banchor, in Ireland. To him succeeded,

Michael, a Manxman, a person of great merit and exemplary life. He died in a good old age, and was honourably buried apud Fontanus. In the year 1203, to him succeeded,

Nicholas de Melsa, Abbot of Furness. He lies buried in the abbey of Bangor.

After him Reginald, a person of royal extraction, sister's son to good King Olave, was consecrated bishop in the year 1216; who, though he laboured under great infirmities of body, governed his church with prudence and resolution. At last, with an exemplary resignation, he yielded up his soul into the hands of his Creator, and lies buried in the abbey of Rushen. He was succeeded by

John, the son of Hefare, who by the negligence of his servants was burnt, apud Jerevas in Anglia. After him one

Simond, a person of great discretion, and learned in the Holy Scriptures, governed the church with prudence and piety. He held a synod in the year 1239, in which thirteen canons were excepted, most of them relating to the probate of wills, the clergy's dues, and other inferior matters. He died at his palace of Kirk Michael in a good old age, and lies buried in the cathedral dedicated to St. German, in Peel Castle. After him

Lawrence, the archdeacon before-mentioned, was elected bishop, and after great disputes consecrated by the Archbishop of Drontheim, but was unfortunately drowned with Harold, King of Man, his queen, and almost all the nobility of the isle; so that the bishopric continued vacant almost six years, when

Richard, an Englishman, was consecrated at Rome by the Archbishop of Drontheim. This bishop consecrated the abbey church of St. Mary, of Rushen, anno 1257. After he had governed the church twenty-three years, and returning from a general council, anno 1274, he died, apud Langallyner in Copelandia, and lieth buried in the abbey of Furness. In his time the Scotch conquered the island. He was succeeded by

Marus Galvadiensis, commonly written Galloredinus, at the nomination of Alexander, King of Scotland; for which reason it is supposed he was banished by the Manxmen. During his absence, the island lay under an interdict; but at last being recalled, he laid a smoke-penny upon every house, by way of commutation. He held a synod at Kirk Braddan, in which thirty-five canons were enacted. He lived to a great age, and was for many years blind, and lies buried in St. German's church, in Peel Castle. He was succeeded by

Mauritius, who was sent prisoner to London by King Edward I. therefore supposed never to be consecrated, nor put into the catalogue of bishops. In his room was substituted

Allen, of Galloway, who governed the church with great honour and integrity. He died the 15th of February, anno 1321, and lies at Rothersay, in Scotland. To him succeeded

Gilbert, of Galloway, who sat but two years and a half, and lies buried near his predecessor, in the church of Rothersay aforesaid. And after him

Bernard, a Scotchman, held the bishopric three years, and lies buried in the monastery of Kilwining, in Scotland. He was succeeded by

Thomas, a Scot, who sat bishop fourteen years: he was the first that exacted twenty shillings of his clergy by way of procuration, as likewise the tenths of all aliens. He died the 20th of September, 1348. The same year,

William Russel, Abbot of Rushen, was elected by the whole clergy of Man, in St. German's church, in Peel Castle. He was consecrated by Pope Clement VI. at Avignion, and was the first that shook off the yoke of the Archbishop of Drontheim, by whom his predecessors had for many ages been consecrated. He held a synod, anno 1350, in Kirk Michael, in which five articles were added to the former canons. He died the 21st of April, 1374, and was buried in the abbey of Furness. He was Abbot of Rushen eighteen years, and bishop twenty-six years. After him

John Duncan, a Manxman, was elected by the clergy of Man; and going to Avignion was confirmed by Pope Gregory XI. and consecrated *per Cardinalem Presiestium, dudum Archipiscopum.* In his return home he was made prisoner at Bolonia, in Picardy, and lay in irons two years; and at last was forced to ransom himself for 500 marks; so that he was not installed till the year 1376, in which Mr. Jones's account determines he was succeeded (as Dr. Heylin in his Help to English History informs us) by

Robert Welby, anno 1396, who, it is believed, sat twenty-two years, and had for his successor

John Sperton, who is the first bishop mentioned in the Manx records. After him we find no bishop named till the year 1503, in which

Evan, or Huan, was elected by Sir Thomas Stanley, then governor, and afterwards lord; from whence may be observed the clergy's election of their bishops ceased, and became fixed in the house of Stanley, where it remained till the island being purchased by the government, the King of England is become perpetual nominator. This Evan was succeeded by

Hugh Hesketh, as appears by the roll of the family of Rufford, viz. Hugh Hesketh, third son to Robert, Esq. a reverend father in God, the Bishop of the Isle of Man; and *hic jacet Robertus Hesketh, Armiger, qui obit primo die Jan. A. D.* 1490. He was succeeded by

Robert Ferrier, who sat bishop anno 1554, says Sir Richard Baker. He was afterwards removed to St. David's, says Grafton, and was succeeded by

Henry Man, anno 1555, who died 1556, says Dr. Heylin, and was succeeded by

Bishop Salisbury, the year uncertain; whose successor was

Thomas Stanley, son to Sir Edward Stanley, first Lord Monteagle. How long he sat is uncertain, but it appears by record, John Merrick was sworn bishop of the isles, anno 1577. It was he who gave Mr. Cambden the history of the Isle of Man, published in his Britannia. He was succeeded by

George Lloyd, anno 1600, who was afterwards removed to Chester. He had for his successor

Bishop Foster, as Dr. Heylin in his Help to English History informs us. And was succeeded by

Dr. John Phillips, anno 1605, a native of North Wales, who was sworn bishop the same year. He translated the Common Prayer (at this time to be seen,) into the language of the natives; and, Mr. Challoner says, the Bible, though not now extant. A man famous in his generation for his great pains in preaching, his charity and hospitality, even to the meanest of the people. He was succeeded by

Dr. Richard Parr, anno 1635, a Lancashire man, sometime fellow of Brazennose College in Oxford; who whilst he continued in the university (says Mr. Challoner, of his own knowledge,) was an eminent preacher. He was the last who sat bishop before our late unhappy civil wars. Next to him

Samuel Rutter was sworn bishop, anno 1661. He had been archdeacon several years, and governed the church with great prudence during the then late wars. He was a man of exemplary goodness and moderation, and sat bishop till the year 1663. To him I am greatly obliged for his collections and memoirs made use of in my History of the noble House of Stanley, but especially in that ever-memorable Siege of Latham, the defence whereof he had a large share in. After him

Dr. Isaac Barrow was consecrated bishop, anno 1663, and sent over governor by Charles Earl of Derby. He was a man of a public spirit, and great designs for the good of the church; to whose industry is greatly owing all the learning amongst the clergy of Man, and to whose prudence and charity many of the poor clergy owe the bread they eat. This good man, to the great loss of the island, was removed to St. Asaph. He was succeeded by

Dr. Henry Bridgeman, anno 1671. After him

Dr. John Lake, anno 1682, afterwards removed to Bristol. Next to him

Dr. Baptist Levinz, anno 1684, who died 1693, and the see remained vacant five years, when, to the inexpressible benefit of the inhabitants of Man,

Dr. Thomas Wilson was promoted to the government of the church: but, as the life of this bishop is ultimately connected with the state of the island and its history during a period of sixty years, in which all the energy of his capacious mind, and all the virtues of his excellent heart, were devoted to benefit and improve his charge, I cannot pass him over, as I have done others, with a brief notice, believing no particulars of a life so exemplary can be uninteresting to my readers. I shall, therefore, make a large extract from the history of this apostolic divine, as it was published, under the authority of his son, in 1787.

Dr. Thomas Wilson was born at Burton, in Cheshire, September 20, 1663, and, as he himself says, in his diary, of honest parents, fearing God. After a preparatory education in his own country, he was sent to Trinity College, Dublin. His first design on entering at the University was, to devote himself to the study of physic, in which he made some progress; and even after having yielded to the advice of his friend, Archdeacon Hewetson, to dedicate his services to the church, he still continued to pursue, at intervals, the study he had originally set out with, which afterwards proved of essential service to the people of his diocese; and, what was of the utmost importance to Mr. Wilson himself, greatly extended his sphere of usefulness.

He continued at College till the year 1689, when he was ordained deacon; of which event, he, ever after, kept the anniversary, as a season of particular devotion. The exact time of his leaving Dublin is not known; but soon after his return to England, he was licensed curate of New Church, in the parish of Winwick, Lancashire, of which his maternal uncle, Dr. Sherlock, was rector; and here, out of a stipend of £30. per annum, he devoted one-tenth to charitable uses. On the 20th of October, 1690, he was ordained priest, on which occasion he formed certain solemn resolutions, from which he never swerved throughout the course of his life.

The first, that no temptation should induce him to occupy two livings at one time.

2d. That whenever he should obtain a cure of souls, he would, on no account, dispense with constant residence on the scene of his duty.

3d. Never to give a bond of resignation, or to make any contract or promise, merely to obtain church preferment.

It was not long before his religious deportment and amiable manners in private life recommended him to the notice of the Earl of Derby, who, in 1692, appointed him his domestic chaplain and tutor to Lord Strange, with a salary of £30. per annum, to which was soon after added £20. more, for the superintendance of the alms-houses at Latham; on which occasion, he increased the sum set apart for the use of the poor, from one-tenth to one-fifth of his income.

The manner in which he made this dedication is worthy of record. On the receipt of all monies, he regularly placed the portion designed for charitable uses into the drawer of a cabinet, with a note of the value to be kept sacred for the poor; and in this sacred repository, first a tenth, then a fifth, then a third, and, at last, one half, of his revenues were placed: and whenever he deposited the poor man's portion, it was with the same reverence as if it had been an offering to heaven.

Mr. Wilson's resolutions, as before stated, being entered into, from a conviction of their propriety, were ever after considered as matter of religious obligation, from which no motive could induce him to depart; as he fully proved, when, soon after Lord Derby offered him the valuable living of Baddesworth, in Yorkshire, his lordship intending that he should still continue with him as chaplain and tutor to his son; but he refused to accept it, being inconsistent with his resolves against non-residence.

The same regard to the dictates of conscience influenced his whole behaviour, and it was not long before he gave his noble patron a proof that no selfish motives could deter him from pursuing the path of duty, or restrain his zeal in a good cause. In consequence of an extravagant expenditure, and great inattention to his affairs, Lord Derby had become deeply involved, and the tradesmen about his estates were many of them most seriously injured by the state of his accounts. Mr. Wilson beholding with equal concern the ruin of his patron's property, and the distress of his dependants, determined to hazard a respectful remonstrance, which, however, he was fully sensible was a step replete with danger to his hopes of preferment; yet, being unable to dispense with what he considered to be his duty, he waited on his lordship in his dressing-room, and, after a short conversation, left with him a letter, which is remarkable for the simplicity, good sense, and integrity, it pourtrays.* The result of this unusual proceeding was equally honourable to the noble patron, and his upright dependant. The earl, convinced of his chaplain's probity, was aroused to a serious investigation of his affairs, in the arrangement of which he received his most willing assistance, and by the measures thenceforward adopted, Mr. Wilson was made the happy instrument by which the reputation and property of his patron were retrieved, and many of his tradesmen, by this timely arrangement, saved from bankruptcy.

Nor did his zeal and integrity miss of their reward; for, in the ensuing year, the earl offered him the bishopric of the Isle of Man, which had been vacant since the death of Dr. Levinz in the year 1693.

* See Appendix, No. 1.

This offer, however, Mr. Wilson at first declined, believing the charge too great for his talents and strength, and thus the matter rested, till complaint being made to King William, that an incumbent had long been wanting for this diocese; and, in consequence, Lord Derby fearing the patronage would lapse to the crown, if an immediate nomination did not take place, he insisted on his chaplain accepting the preferment; and thus Mr. Wilson was, to use his own expression, *forced into the bishopric.* But however modest might be his estimate of his own abilities, it is certain, the history of human nature hardly presents an example where intellectual worth has been carried higher, or accompanied more completely, by the most admirable Christian virtues. The rules laid down for his self-government at his outset in life, were maintained with undeviating strictness; his considerations were not directed to what would make his sojournment on earth pleasant, but to what would render his transition to heaven certain; and to this great end all his labours for his own conduct, or the benefit of his fellow-creatures, were made to conduce.

To comprehend the nature of the sacrifice he made, when he became bishop of Man, one must take into consideration the state of the country to which he was *banished*, and contrast it with the society he renounced. On the one hand, he beheld a people depressed, and almost brutalized by poverty and neglect, with whose language he was unacquainted, and who were prepared to receive him with dislike and suspicion; and for this hopeless association, he had been compelled to resign the ease, elegance, and distinction, of a nobleman's mansion, where, from the lord to the lowest servant, all regarded him with respect and affection. Happily for Dr. Wilson, the first few years of his residence in the Isle of Man were cheered by the society of a woman, who seems to have been formed on the same model with himself, and to have participated in all his laborious acts of charity with equal interest and readiness. The difficulty respecting the language was of no long existence, he was soon able to deliver his paternal exhortations in their own tongue; and by convincing his flock how much their real good was his so'e object, he secured the affection and respect of the whole body, with the exception only of a very few whom interest or jealousy taught to oppose him.

When he first took possession of the see, he found the residence appropriated to him in ruins, the churches throughout the diocese in a falling state, the clergy sunk in ignorance and vice, the people not merely untaught and rustic, but greatly debased by the illicit trade then almost their sole pursuit, and which naturally led to a commerce with the worst characters of the adjacent countries; whilst the most extreme ignorance of religion, or even morality, pervaded all classes, or rather, the one great class; for, with the exception of the officers sent over by Lord Derby, to occupy the posts of government, the residue of the population were alike subject to the sudden influx of abundance, or as sudden depression of poverty.

The only sources of circulation were derived from fishing or smuggling, and the money thus acquired was almost invariably spent in intoxication, or vulgar dissipation, under the idea, that the same channels of gain were still open to them. It was to correct these fundamental errors, that Bishop Wilson strove to divert their attention to agricultural pursuits; and, as a first and most material step, in concert with the keys, he prevailed on Earl James, in the first year of his succession, to grant the act of settlement already mentioned. Whilst this question was under consideration, the bishop also occupied himself in restoring the dilapidated state of the revenues of the see, and rebuilding his house at Kirk Michael, as well as in repairing the churches, and renewing the discipline of the parochial schools. From the beginning he exacted his tithes, not with severity, but certainly with sufficient strictness;

and this unquestionably from a conscientious design to protect the dues of the church, and not to suffer that which should be set apart for sacred purposes, to be diverted into other channels.

His house he enlarged, and rendered capable of receiving several young men, whom he educated under his own eye, and by his example, in order to have a succession of clergy, who might walk in the way he set before them; and thus he laid a solid foundation for the extension of knowledge, and practice of piety, in the next generation. In repairing the parish churches, he always set the example of a large subscription from his own purse, and exerted his influence where he knew there was ability in others, so as to obtain his end without exactions from the necessitous; nor were his exertions confined to these public acts: by frequent visits, he acquired a patriarchal influence in nearly every family in his diocese, and acquainted himself with the character and circumstances of each individual, to whom he administered aid, counsel, or reproof, as the case demanded; and so tempered his wisdom or severity with kindness and condescension, that he was soon regarded as a ministering angel, and his presence believed to produce a blessing wherever he came. His charity was unwearied; at his door the indigent were sure of relief, for he scrupulously observed the Scripture precept, 'never to turn his face from any poor man,' so that it was said of him, 'he kept beggars from every house but his own.' For a long time there was no medical man in the island, and he was in the constant habit of giving advice and medicines to the sick of all ranks; but when, at length, some persons in that line established themselves there, he willingly relinquished to them the care of the wealthy, but still afforded his aid to those who had nothing but prayers and blessings to give in return.

Soon after his accession to the bishopric, Dr. Wilson was united to Mary, the daughter of Thomas Patten, Esq.

of Warrington, and in the year 1699, she accompanied him to the island. This most amiable woman was, in every respect, the companion best fitted for him, pious, humble, and charitable as himself. By her he had four children, only one of whom (a son) arrived at maturity. The period of his connubial happiness was very short; Mrs. Wilson, at the end of five years, fell into a languishing complaint, in which she lingered nearly twelve months, and then resigned her pure spirit to her Maker.

This afflictive trial was borne as Bishop Wilson bore all the dispensations of Providence. Situated as he was, a greater bereavement can hardly be conceived! he had lost the only one who could participate both in his pleasures and his troubles, and his loss was irremediable; but, notwithstanding his keen sense of the affliction, he knew how to bless the hand that chastised him: he felt like a man, but 'not like one without hope.' His prayers during her sickness, and on her death, are amongst the finest examples of devout resignation; and in his meditations he drew such a character of the deceased, as, while it must have aggravated his regret, was yet calculated to elevate his hopes.*

The annual return of his episcopal revenues in money did not exceed £300. Some necessary articles, and some particular objects of charity, could only be purchased or relieved in specie; but the poor of the island were fed and clothed, and the house, in general, supplied from his domains. Those who could weave and spin, found at Bishop's court the best market for their commodities, where they bartered the produce of their industry for corn.

Tailors and shoemakers were kept constantly at work in the house, to make into garments the cloth or leather† which his corn purchased; and these were distributed as

* See Appendix, No. 2.
† The Manx then generally wore a shoe of untanned leather, laced on the foot, called *Carcéns*.

gifts, or at low prices, according to the measure of their wants, to all who applied for them. He considered himself as the steward, not proprietor, of the revenues of his see, being resolved, from his first accession, not to heap up wealth for his children from a source, which the strictness of his religious principles led him to believe ought not so to be appropriated.* He kept a register of all the poor in his diocese, in which he entered the names and circumstances of his pensioners, and this he called 'Matricula Pauperum.'

During fifty-eight years of his pastoral life, he never, unless visited by sickness, omitted to perform some part of the church duty on every Sabbath day. In the year 1703, he framed those ecclesiastical constitutions, of which it was said by Lord Chancellor King, that 'if the ancient discipline of the church was lost elsewhere, it might be found in all its purity in the Isle of Man." In September, 1708, he consecrated the chapel at Douglas, to which he had been a principal contributor. In 1709, the library at Castletown was finished, derived almost wholly from the same source. In 1711, he went to London, to settle some excise business relating to the lord and people of the island, when he was greatly distinguished by Queen Anne, who offered him an English bishopric, which he declined, because, as he said, he 'felt that, with the blessing of God, he could do some good in the little spot where he then resided, whereas, should he be removed to a large sphere, he might be lost, and forget his duty to God, and to his flock.'

His paternal care of this favoured people appears in the various annual exhortations delivered by him to the clergy, in which it was his custom to comment upon the events of the past year, to admonish the negligent, and encourage the diligent; he insisted strenuously on the duties of visiting and catechising the uninformed, and furnished each

---

* See his Address on this subject to his Children, in the Appendix, No. 3.

parish with books of instruction and devotion; but, above all things, required from his clergy the most scrupulous regard to their own character and conduct, as the only means of giving efficacy to their doctrine.

Nothing could more strongly evince his anxiety on these subjects than the prayers composed by him for the use of all the churches in his diocese, when certain persons lay under sentence of death for violations of the laws. He treated these events as national calamities, and employed his utmost exertions to render the examples thus necessarily made, of public utility to warn and awaken his whole flock. His own deep concern on these occasions must have been to the last degree impressive, and could not have failed to operate forcibly on the minds of the people.

So also on occasions of scarcity, which frequently occurred in those times, he evermore led the sufferers to God. He taught them to endure with patience whilst the chastisement lasted, and when the trial was at an end, he joined them in such fervent thanks as created in his hearers a perpetual sense of the superintendence of providence, and rendered even want and deprivation eventual blessings.

Those who have not lived as I have done on the scene of Bishop Wilson's apostolical exertions, who have not heard his praises, after the lapse of a whole century, still the theme of every tongue, and seen the still unfaded monuments of his benevolence, may be inclined to think these praises are exaggerated; but I may safely appeal to the inhabitants of the Isle of Man, to say, whether I have not curtailed and omitted numberless instances of his piety and charity.

It is with infinite pain that I have now to change the scene, and from exhibiting the man of God in the delightful performance of his duty, followed by the praises and love of his people, and secure in the respect of all ranks, to describe him as persecuted, insulted, and even *imprisoned*. Whether his extraordinary piety, combined with his deserved popularity, had excited the jealousy of his contemporaries in office, cannot now be known; but it seems more than probable some such predisposing cause must have existed, as the alleged ground of quarrel between him and Governor Horn appears so trifling, that it is hardly possible to believe it should have been suffered to disturb the peace of a man, whose exemplary character had at that time secured him the applause of persons of the first distinction in all parts of Europe.

A story is current in the island, which offers a kind of solution to these difficulties, but being unnoticed by the historian of Dr. Wilson, or any other writer since his time, I can neither venture to insert as an unquestionable fact, nor can I wholly pass over what is universally believed, where every particular relative to the bishop is preserved with religious care.

It is said (and in this particular the author of his life concurs) that when he took possession of the see of Man, he found the revenues in a state of dilapidation; the tithes in particular had been suffered to lapse from the neglect of former incumbents: and a practice had crept in of wholly reserving the estates of the principal civil officers from this species of taxation; which exemptions, founded only on custom, were termed prescriptive rights, and at length came to be set up as indefeasible. The first efforts of the bishop for the improvement of the impoverished revenues of his church, were directed against these powerful opponents.

In the prosecution of this matter, much animosity was engendered on both sides; and there are some documents extant which certainly bear out the relation. That a man of the bishop's upright and independent spirit should have set himself to abrogate claims merely founded in power on one side, and admitted from weakness on the other, is very highly probable; that he should also have gone resolutely to the source of the evil, is consistent with his whole course of acting and living; but that he should have conducted this matter with the asperity sometimes ascribed to him, I find it difficult to believe. According to the ecclesiastical laws of the island, a process may be commenced in the bishop's court, which does not even require a hearing on both sides, or a notice to the defendant; and on an exparté statement, an order *may* pass against a person complained of, which if not implicitly obeyed, subjects them to imprisonment during the pleasure of the court, or till an appeal is accepted to the metropolitan. And it is said, that under authority of this law, (certainly existing, but not often acted upon,) Bishop Wilson, in consequence of the resistance of the then Clerk of the Rolls to the payment of his tythe, issued his precept, and committed him close prisoner to the dungeon at Kirk Germain. In confirmation of this statement, a petition appears on record from the Clerk of the Rolls, complaining of such treatment, and praying to be heard in person against the demand; to which petition the answer, signed by the bishop's own hand, is, *that such hearing was not customary, nor would be granted.*

In what manner this affair ended I have not been able to ascertain; but as most of these prescriptive rights were annihilated, in all probability the bishop obtained a victory, as in justice and reason he ought to have done: for the iniquity of assessing the poor and exempting the rich must be obvious to all.

In the present times, when the indefeasible rights of man are so well established, perhaps we may wish that what it was perfectly just and proper to do, had been done with more regard to those rights. We are naturally shocked at the idea of claims, however well founded, being arbitrarily established; and, perhaps, we must also admit, that if there was a blemish in the character of Bishop Wilson, (and what human creature is without one,) it consisted in an attachment, approaching to bigotry, to the canons of the church. In exacting conformity to ecclesiastical laws, he followed both the spirit and the letter. It was enough that the church had decreed a point to render even debate on the subject a sacrilege in his eyes. He shrunk with horror from every question that might by possibility disturb the faith either of himself, or his flock: in his dread of the incursions of infidelity, he even excluded discussion.

It is well known that he suspended a clergyman in the island, for hazarding a doubt, in one of his discourses, whether the power of granting absolution for sin had really devolved from the apostles to their successors in the ministry.

But after all, these mistakes, if such they were, sprung from a mind zealously devoted to the cause of genuine religion. Dr. Wilson had settled his belief on conviction, as his whole course of acting through a long life evidently proved. He knew the consequences of agitating doubt in ignorant minds, such as he had to govern: he saw that to give efficacy to his doctrine, he must follow the example of his Saviour, and "teach as one having authority;" and according to the character of the times in which he lived, he could admit of no compromise. Controversy was not then, as now, under the control of moderation, or even good manners; it was a species of warfare, in the prosecution of which, all means, whether of insult or injury, were considered as lawful weapons; and such in all probability had been the conduct of his opponents in the difference arising on the subject of tythes. In the lapse of time all that is not upon record is lost, and we see only a severe infliction, without knowing any of the aggravation that led to it, or the circumstances which might make it necessary. One thing, however, is obvious, that had the bishop exceeded his authority, the means of obtaining redress against him were open and easy, and that this was never attempted. The use he made of the improved revenues of his see are also a proof, written in unfading characters, of the disinterested purity of his motives; and at any rate the course of retaliation adopted against him, if such it was, was wholly unjustifiable, as being founded neither in law or equity; besides which, the number of years that had elapsed from the time when Dr. Wilson established these offensive claims, and the changes which had taken place in the governing power, leads one to doubt whether the extraordinary persecution he afterwards underwent could have originated in this source.

The history of this affair, as it may be gathered from his life, is as follows: In 1719, Mrs. Horn, the wife of the governor, having some quarrel with one Mrs. Puller, she carried her resentment so far as to charge her opponent with a criminal intimacy with one Sir James Poole, then also resident in Castletown; and had so much influence with the Archdeacon Horrobin as to prevail on him to refuse the sacrament to the supposed offender, on account of this accusation. Mrs. Puller, mortified and exasperated by this public disgrace, had recourse to the mode pointed out by the ecclesiastical constitutions to establish her innocence, namely, by oath; which she and Sir James Poole tendered before the bishop, with compurgators of the best character: and no evidence being produced by their accusers to establish the charge, though repeatedly called on to this purpose, they were in consequence cleared of the imputation, and sentence passed against Mrs. Horn, as inventor of the calumny, for which she was required to ask pardon of those she had traduced: but, far from complying with this moderate requisition, the governor's lady peremptorily refused obedience, and openly expressed the utmost contempt both for the bishop and the censures of the church. For this indecent disrespect to the laws, which her elevated situation rendered the more offensive, she was in her turn banished from the altar, till atonement should be made. Notwithstanding which, the archdeacon, out of pique to the bishop, or for some other unworthy motive, received her to the communion.

An insult to himself the bishop would have had no difficulty to forgive, but disobedience to the church he could not consistently overlook; and after some further discussion, he was compelled to suspend the archdeacon; who in a rage, instead of referring the matter to the Archbishop of York, the proper judge in ecclesiastical affairs, threw himself on the civil power, where he was assured of support in his contumacy.

In the interim, the bishop had appointed the Rev. Mr. Ross to officiate in the chapel at Castletown, during the archdeacon's suspension; but the governor refused to deliver the keys to him, and kept the chapel shut up altogether. On which the bishop made a strong remonstrance at the Tynwald court against this entrenchment on the spiritual authority. This document, which is dated June 25, 1722, being addressed to the governor at the Tynwald,* was not noticed but at the conclusion of the meeting; and when nearly all the keys and most of the council had retired, Captain Horn, with those who remained, made an order, *in the name of the whole*, that the bishop should be fined £50, and his two vicars £20 each, for illegal and extrajudicial proceedings in suspending Archdeacon Horrobin. And on the 29th of the same month, on their refusal to pay the penalty, they were all three committed to Castle Rushen. The laws of the island must have been in a most indeterminate state, when such proceedings as these could be carried into effect, on a sentence actually disavowed by nearly all the persons pretended to be concurring in it, and of which no previous notice had been given to the defendants, to afford them an opportunity of rebutting the charges brought against them.

The concern of the people on this insult being offered to

---

* See Appendix, No. 4.

their beloved pastor, amounted to agony. They assembled in crowds round the prison walls, and it was with infinite difficulty they were prevented levelling the governor's house with the ground; nor was it preserved at last but by the exhortations of the bishop, who being permitted to address them through a window of his prison, entreated their forbearance and submission, telling them he would "appeal unto Cæsar," (meaning the king,) "and had no doubt he would vindicate his cause, if he had acted right." But though he restrained them by his influence from open violence, nothing could allay their anxiety. All business throughout the island was at a stand, one sole object attracted the attention of the whole community, and nothing but personal and almost daily conviction of his safety, could satisfy the individual apprehensions of his flock, who resorted from all parts in hundreds to the walls of the castle; nor would they depart without his benediction and counsel.*

With what sensations governor Horn must have beheld these scenes of public distress and gratitude, it is not difficult to conceive; but it is wonderful that it should have produced no effect on his conduct; for so far was he from relaxing any part of the persecution to which he had subjected these divines, that he actually detained them two months; and during that time dictated every possible aggravation of their sufferings, refusing admittance either to friends or servants, and treating them in all respects as persons confined for high treason.

The case meanwhile was fully stated by the bishop in a petition to the king in council, which was, however, dismissed on the ground of informality, inasmuch as it should have been addressed to the Earl of Derby; but it was recommended by the law officers of the crown, that the

* The bishop afterwards declared, that he never governed his diocese so well, or instructed his people with such effect as from the walls of his prison.

bishop and vicars should deposit the fines as a means of procuring their release, under an assurance that such compliance should not prejudice their appeal. Accordingly they did pay down the money; and being then set at liberty, they immediately repaired to England to prosecute the affair before the proper tribunal.

In a subsequent petition, the bishop states that his reasons for not appealing to the lord of the isle, in the first place, were, that as the prosecution against him was conducted by the earl's attorney, he did suppose it was with his lordship's concurrence, more especially as the fines, if legally assessed, would have belonged to his lordship also.

That the bishop judged right in believing the matter was to a certain extent countenanced by the earl, is rendered evident by what followed; and the only justification, or rather apology, to be offered is, that Lord Derby must have been deceived by misrepresentations, which, however, ought not for a moment to have counterbalanced the high and well established reputation of the bishop. However, on finding it necessary to carry his appeal through this channel, the bishop and his vicars went into Lancashire, and repeatedly presented themselves at the mansion of the earl, who, nevertheless, refused them all access to his person, nor would he even examine into the nature of their complaint; but after keeping them in attendance from August to November, he at last peremptorily refused to accept the appeal on any terms. On which they were obliged to resort to London, and offer a third petition to the king.

The Attorney General then gave a regular notice to Lord Derby of the proceedings, and demanded from him if he had any knowledge of the affair, or any thing to object against the appeals being entertained. To which his lordship returned an answer in substance as follows:

"That not having had any previous intimation of the proceedings from any of the constituted authorities in the

Isle of Man, he could give no answer as to the complaint; but that he believed the persons complained of to be honest and well-meaning men; and had no doubt the matter in the bishop's petition was misrepresented."

The result of this iniquitous business, after two years' prosecution, attended with heavy expenses and much personal vexation, was, that the whole proceedings were declared to be illegal, and the fines were in course reversed; but for recovery of damages against the governor and officers, or even of costs of suit, no provision was made: but these matters were to be referred to a fresh suit at law, to which the bishop had no inclination to resort. All personal offences or losses he could easily forgive and overlook; his sole object had been to establish the discipline of the church, and having succeeded in that, he had no further resentment to gratify. The suspension of Archdeacon Horrobin was taken off by him after proper submission; but whether Mrs. Horn submitted to the terms enjoined, I have never been able to discover. I conclude, however, that the bishop would not relinquish a point of such importance to the established discipline of the church.

One cannot contemplate the issue of this extraordinary proceeding without sensations of regret, that the principal actors in it should have escaped without due punishment. Nor can I help reverting to the case of Captain Christian, wherein a course so decidedly different was pursued by the court of England. In his affair an irregular appeal was received in the first instance, though offered by a person* having no personal interest in the prosecution; and on that petition a reprieve was granted. In a subsequent stage, the judges who had passed an illegal sentence were *fined* and *imprisoned*, and full restitution made, with all *costs* and *charges* to the heirs of the sufferer. But here, in an

---

* The deemster Christian, who had fled to England to avoid being a party in the judgment.

instance of admitted injustice and tyranny, exercised on a man rendered sacred both by his function and the virtues of a long unblemished life, the court declares itself unequal to the task of redressing his grievances, beyond the reversal of a paltry fine, and leave all the rest as they found it, with hardly a slight reprimand to the offenders. In considering this outrage, a natural comparison arises between the times when such misconduct could be so passed over, and the present, when notwithstanding the violent cry raised against existing defects in the government and breaches of the constitution, I think no one will deny, that if such a scene was enacted in one of our remotest dependencies, and on the person of the most obscure individual, it would raise a clamour which nothing but the fullest redress to the injured, and punishment of the delinquents, could pacify or allay.

Bishop Wilson felt the consequences of the rigours he had undergone during the remainder of his life, having contracted a rheumatic disease from the dampness of the prison, which disabled the fingers of his right hand. The expenses also fell very heavy on him, being in the whole more than £500; of which he received £300 in a subscription, set on foot without his knowledge, to assist in carrying on the cause.

In the year 1739, the clergy of the island were thrown into great trouble by the death of the Earl of Derby, who leaving no issue, the lordship of Man devolved to the Duke of Athol; and by this event they were nearly deprived of their subsistence. Their livings consisting of one third of the impropriations, which had been purchased from a former earl, in the episcopate of Dr. Barrow; an estate belonging to the Derby family in Lancashire having been collaterally bound as security for the payment of the annual returns. On the separation of the island from the earldom, the Duke of Athol claimed the impropriations as an inseparable appendage to his estate and royalty. The deed of conveyance was unfortunately missing from the records, nor could any title be made out either to the original purchase or the collateral security.

Under this alarm the clergy would have taken a very small sum in lieu of their claims; and the bishop mentions in a letter to his son, how much they were troubled to find proper persons to serve in the ministry; people being entirely discouraged from bringing up their sons to the church. But at length, by the unceasing industry and perseverance of the diocesan and his son, the original deeds were discovered to have been lodged in the Rolls Chapel, London; and being immediately exemplified under the great seal of England, the security of the impropriations was established to the great relief of the parties concerned.

In 1740, a severe scarcity occurred in the island, where in fact the corn raised being always far short of the consumption, whenever (as it happened at that time) an embargo was laid on the English ports, great necessity was sure to ensue. The bishop distributed his own grain as far as it would go, and bought up an additional quantity at a high price, to sell out at a reduced one, but all his efforts were inadequate to relieve the pressure of distress. To increase the calamity, an epidemic disease broke out, and as he was the *only physician* in the island, his bodily fatigues must have been incessant. In this deplorable state, a petition* was preferred to the king in council, by the bishop's son, (who was chaplain to George II.), that the embargo might be taken off to a certain extent: a supply of corn was, at length, obtained just in time to save the whole people from starvation. The Duke of Athol also exerted himself for their relief, and received due acknowledgment from the keys on the occasion.

In 1743, the bishop wrote a letter of thanks to his

* See Appendix, No. 5.

majesty personally, for the distinguished honour he had conferred on his son, in making him a prebend of Westminster.* The bishop's apostolic character had, at this time, secured him the veneration of all ranks; and the most exalted personages in various parts of Europe bore testimony to his virtues. In the Isle of Man, the people were so strongly persuaded that a larger portion of the blessings of heaven attended on him, that they never began their harvest till he did, hoping to participate, through him, in these advantages: and if by chance he passed near any field where they were at work, their labours were suspended for a moment, whilst they asked his benediction; and then renewed, under an increased conviction, that for one day, at least, they would be prosperous.†

At the advanced age of eighty, he gives the following account of his daily labours in a letter to his son.

"I bless God I am pretty well. I preached on Palm Sunday; administered the sacrament on Easter Eve; preached and administered the sacrament on Easter Day at Peel; the next Sunday at Kirk Michael; and last Sunday at Jurby, when I performed the whole service."

In 1744, he purchased some land, which he added to the living of Jurby. In 1755, his solicitations, added to those of his son, obtained a renewal of the royal bounty to the clergy, which had been suspended for several years.

He continued to ride on horseback till the year 1749. In 1751, he wrote a letter to the new governor, in which he apologized for his neglect of personal attendance, under

---

* See Appendix, No. 6, for the letter to the king, and also one to his son, on the same occasion.

† The same reverential regard obtained even in the great city of London, where, during his last visit, crowds would flock around him, with the cry of "Bless me, too, my lord."

the plea of his *great age:* indeed, the scene of his earthly existence was now drawing to a close; and with what delight he must have contemplated the prospect of transmission from time to eternity, may be partly conceived, when we review the events of a life uniformly devoted to the service of God, and the good of his fellow-creatures. The immediate cause of his death was a cold, caught in walking in his garden in very damp weather. His end was easy and tranquil; it was like his life, devoted to prayer and praise, till he fell asleep to wake in heaven.

Words are inadequate to paint the anguish of his flock, when thus deprived of their beloved pastor. He was attended to his grave by the whole population of the island, without a single exception, unless of those who, by age or sickness, were incapacitated. The tenants of his nearest demesnes were appointed to bear him to his last earthly home; but at every resting place a contest ensued amongst the most respectable persons present, and happy were they who could perform this last sad office for their friend and benefactor. He was interred in Kirk Michael churchyard, at the east end near the chancel, and over his grave a square tomb-stone was placed, surrounded by iron rails, on which is the following inscription:

On the sides,

"Sleeping in Jesus, here lieth the Body of THOMAS WILSON, D. D. Lord Bishop of this Isle, who died March 5, 1755, aged 93, and in the 58th year of his Consecration."

At the ends,

"This Monument was erected by his Son, THOMAS WILSON, a native of this Parish, who, in obedience to the express commands of his father, declines giving him the character he justly deserved."

"Let this Island speak the rest."

On the decease of Bishop Wilson, the patronage of the see being vested in the Duke of Athol, his grace paid a compliment to his memory, most honourable to himself. From a conscientious desire that the benefits effected by the late excellent incumbent should proceed under the auspices of his successor, he waved his right of nomination, and, disregarding the many claimants who were, no doubt, looking up in hopes of a prize, now rendered both valuable and honourable, he referred it to the bench of bishops, requesting them to point out a man worthy of wearing the mitre which Bishop Wilson had adorned.

In consequence of which request, Dr. Mark Hildesley was unanimously recommended by them, and appointed by his grace, being consecrated Bishop of Man, April 25, 1755. On coming to his diocese, his sentiments were thus expressed:

"I know it is sometimes said, that 'a person succeeds with disadvantage to an office which has been filled by a predecessor of remarkably eminent qualities.' I must take leave to think the reverse as nearer truth; at least, with respect to the instance I am about to refer to, namely, my coming after the great and good Dr. Wilson to this see of Man; forasmuch as I see many excellent things done and established to my hand, in regard to the government of the church, besides the example which, by the traces he has left, his lordship still lives to show, and which I will endeavour, as far as I am able, to follow, though I am sensible it must be '*non passibus nequis.*'"

The first great work Dr. Hildesley sat himself to complete was, the translation of the Scriptures into Manx, begun by Dr. Wilson, who, at his own expence, had printed the Gospel of St. Matthew, and prepared the other Evangelists, and the Acts of the Apostles; and this, with the assistance of the clergy, he was happy enough to finish. It might, indeed, be truly said of this good man, that he had caught the mantle of the prophet as he ascended to heaven, though he had but just completed the great work above-mentioned, when he was called to give an account of his stewardship, having often been heard to declare, that he only wished his existence might be protracted till the Scriptures were finished in the native language; and it is extremely remarkable, that he received the last part of the Bible from his publisher on Saturday, November 28, 1772, on which occasion he emphatically sung his *Nunc Dimittis* in the presence of his whole family; and next evening, after family prayers, he read a lecture on the uncertainty of human life, observing, that many people were in a moment deprived of their senses and existence; and thus, in a prophetic manner, foretelling his own decease, for, on the following Monday, he was seized with a stroke of the palsy, which deprived him of his perception. In this situation he lingered till that day week, when he died, and was buried according to his own directions, by the side of Bishop Wilson, that he might be united in death with that man whose example he had endeavoured to imitate whilst living.*

On the death of Dr. Hildesley, the Rev. Dr. Richmond obtained promotion to the Isle of Man. But on the period of his episcopacy I take no pleasure in expatiating; the unbending haughtiness of his disposition formed so decided a contrast to the characters of his predecessors, that he

* When Dr. Hildesley was at Scarborough, in 1764, the following lines were stuck up in the Spa room, which, being taken down by his sister, were found amongst his papers after his death, with these words written on them by the bishop: " From vain-glory in human applause, *Deus me liberat et conservat.*"

If to paint folly till her friends despise,
And virtue till her foes would fain be wise;
If angel-sweetness, if a godlike mind,
That melts with Jesus over all mankind—
If this can form a bishop—and it can,
Though lawn were wanting—Hildesley is the man.

excited a general sentiment of aversion in the minds of his people, which must have defeated the efficacy of his doctrines, however pure. He died, and was succeeded by

Dr. George Mason, who sat till the year 1785. The last part of his life was disgraced by a scene of necessity, and derangement of circumstances, utterly inconsistent with his station. In his hands were placed the funds subscribed towards building the church dedicated to St. George, on an elevation above Douglas; and by his insolvency and death, the persons employed in that erection were actually deprived of the sums due to them, to their great injury, and, in one or two instances, their complete ruin.

The last incumbent was, the Rev. Claudius Crigan, a man of simple and unostentatious manners; but, from the absence of all energy of mind or character, not very well calculated to sustain his dignity, or embellish his office. He sat twenty-eight years, and then resigned his life and his see, without exciting any considerable regret in the minds of his flock.

The present bishop is a gentleman of distinguished rank and polished manners; he is a son of the late highly respectable and Rev. Lord George Murray, bishop of St. David's. At the death of Dr. Crigan, the bishop elect being under the age at which, by the canons, he might assume the pall, the see was held unoccupied for twelve months.

The church of Man is governed under a bishop, by an archdeacon, two vicars general, and sixteen ministers; the militia under the governors, by three majors and eighteen captains of parishes; the towns by the four constables; and the civil constitution by two deemsters, six coroners, seventeen moars or bailiffs, with several inferior officers under them.

The Bishops of Man, besides their spiritual jurisdiction, are barons of this isle. In all trials for life they may assist in the temporal court till the sentence. They hold courts in their own names for their temporalities. If any of their tenants are tried for life, they may demand them from the king's court, and try them by a jury of their own tenants; and in case of conviction, the lands they hold are forfeited to the bishop.

The arms of the bishopric are upon three ascents, the Virgin Mary standing with her arms extended between two pillars, on the dexter whereof is a church in base, the ancient arms of Man.

The archdeacon is the second spiritual magistrate. He has, in all inferior cases, alternate jurisdiction with the bishop; and many other privileges, as well in temporals as spirituals. He holds his courts either in person or by his official, as the bishop does his by his vicars-general, which are always two, one for each division of the isle, and are in the nature of chancellors to the bishop; these with the registers compose the consistory court, and have under their jurisdiction seventeen parishes.

There were formerly many chapels in the isle, and there are now in each town one standing, as also one in the centre of the land dedicated to St. John, near which, on a little hill, they hold their Tynwald court, or public assembly, at which their laws are promulged on every midsummer-day, as being raised with several ascents for the different orders of people, and is indeed a pretty curiosity.

But, above all, the abbeys seem to have exceeded the ability of the country, among which the abbey of St. Mary, of Rushen, was the chief. It consisted of twelve monks and an abbot, who at first were meanly endowed, and lived mostly by their labour, but in process of time they had good revenues. The buildings are very handsome, the rooms convenient, and the chapel larger than any thing (the cathedral excepted) in the island. It was called the daughter of Furness, which is said to be the mother of this and many other abbeys in the Isle of Man.

In the records thereof is found, that one John Fargher was Abbot of Rushen and deputy governor; and in a piece of timber in Kirk Arbory, which separates the church from the chancel, one Thomas Radcliffe was Abbot of Rushen.

These abbots were barons of the island, held courts for their temporalities in their own names, might demand a prisoner from the king's court, if their own tenant, and try him by a jury of their own tenants, as the steward of the abbey lands may do at this day.

The Prioress of Douglas was a baroness of the island, and enjoyed the same privilege. The priory was said to be built by St. Bridget, when she came to receive the veil of virginity from St. Maughold. The situation of the nunnery is much the pleasantest in the island.

There were likewise the friars minors of Beemaken, and a small plantation of the Cistertian order in Kirk Christ lez Ayre, but neither of these had baronies annexed to them.

There were likewise several foreign barons, as beforementioned; but few or none of them appear now, nor have any lands or tenants to represent.

Thus I have given my readers the history, constitution, and settlement of this little state in all its branches, civil, military, and ecclesiastic; with all the subordinate officers necessarily employed therein, by which the people in church and state are to be governed; with an historical account of their kings and bishops.

A CATALOGUE

OF THE

GOVERNORS OF THE ISLE OF MAN,

Since Sir John Stanley's time, till the year 1741,

WITH THE

NORTH AND SOUTH DIVISIONS.

———

JOHN Letherland, Lieut.	A. D. 1417
John Fasakerley, Lieut.	1418
John Walton, Lieut.	1422
Henry Byron, Lieut.	1428
Note.—I find no record from this time, till the year 1492	
Peter Dutton, Lieut.	1496
Henry Radcliff, Abbot of Rushen, Deputy	1497
Randolph Rushton, Capt.	1505
Sir John Ireland, Knight, Lieut.	1508
John Ireland, Lieut.	1516
Randolph Rushton, Capt.	1517
Thomas Danisport, Capt.	1519
Richard Holt, Lieut.	1526
John Fleming, Capt.	1529
Thomas Sherburn, Lieut.	1530
Henry Bradley, Deputy-Lieut.	1532
Henry Stanley, Capt.	1533
George Stanley, Capt.	1535
Thomas Stanley, Knt. Lieut.	1537
George Stanley, Capt.	1539

Thomas Tyldsley, Deputy 1540
William Stanley, Deputy 1544
Henry Stanley, Capt. 1552
Thomas Stanley, Knt. Lieut. . . . 1562
Richard Ashton, Capt. 1566
Thomas Stanley, Knt. Lieut. . . . 1567
Edward Tarbock, Capt. 1569
John Hanmer, Capt. 1575
Richard Sherburn, Capt. 1580
Cuth. Gerrard, Capt. 1592
Thomas Martinier, Deputy 1592
 Note.—1591, Richard Aderton was admitted and sworn lieutenant under the captain, by my lord's directions, for all martial affairs.
The Hon. William Stanley, Capt. afterwards Earl of Derby 1593
Randolph Stanley, Capt. 1594
Sir Thomas Gerrard, Knt. Capt. . . 1596
Cuth. Gerrard, Deputy 1596
Thomas Gerrard, Knt. Capt. . . . 1597
Robert Molyneux, Deputy 1597
Cuth. Gerrard, Capt. 1599
Robert Molyneux, Deputy 1599
Robert Molyneux, Capt. 1600
John Ireland and John Birchal, Governors, jointly by patent from the king. 1609
John Ireland, Lieut. and Capt. . . . 1610
Robert Molyneux, Capt. 1612
Edward Fletcher, Deputy 1621
Edward Fletcher, Governor . . . 1622
Sir Ferdinand Liege, Knt. and Capt. . . 1623
Edward Fletcher, Deputy 1625
Edward Holmewood, Capt. . . . 1626
Edward Fletcher, Deputy 1627
Edward Christian, Lieut. and Capt. . . 1628
Evan Christian, Deputy 1634

ISLE OF MAN. 95

Sir Charles Gerrard, Knt. Capt.	1635
John Sharpless, Deputy	1636
Radcliff Gerrard, Capt.	1639
John Greenhalgh, Governor	1640
Sir Philip Musgrave, Knt. and Bart.	1651
Samuel Smith, Deputy Governor	1652

Note.—That my Lord Fairfax made commissioners for the governing of the isle this year, viz. James Challoner, Robert Dinely, Esq. Jonathan Witton, Clerk.

Matthew Cadwell, Governor	1653
William Christian, Governor	1656
James Challoner, Governor	1658

AFTER THE RESTORATION OF THE KING.

Roger Nowell, Governor	A. D. 1660
Richard Stevenson, his Deputy	1660
Henry Nowell, Deputy for one part of the year, and Thomas Stanley for the other part	1663
Bishop Barrow, Governor	1664
Henry Nowell, his Deputy	1664
Henry Nowell, Governor	1669
Henry Stanley, Governor	1677
Robert Heywood, Governor	1678
Roger Kenyon, Esq. Governor	1691
Colonel Sankey, Governor.	
The Hon. Capt. Cranston, Governor.	
Robert Maudesley, Esq. Governor	
Capt. Alexander Horn, Governor.	
Major Floyd, Governor.	
Thomas Horton, Esq. Governor.	
The Hon. James Murray, Esq. Governor	1741

THE NORTH DIVISION.

Kirk Patrick,
Kirk German, } Dedicated to those saints.
Kirk Michael.
St. Mary of Ballaugh, a Parsonage.
St. Patrick Jurby.
Kirk Andrew's, the Archdeaconry.
Kirk Bride, dedicated to St. Bridget, a Parsonage.
Kirk Christ Lez-Ayre.

THE SOUTH DIVISION.

Kirk Maughold, dedicated to St. Maughold the third bishop.
Kirk Lonan, dedicated to Lomanus, said by the tradition to succeed St. Maughold in the bishopric, the son of Tygrida, one of the three holy sisters of St. Patrick, and thought to be the first Bishop of Trym in Ireland.
Kirk Conchan, dedicated to Concha, sister to St. Martin, Bishop of Tours, and mother to St. Patrick.
Kirk Braddan, which signifies a Salmon in the Manx language.
Kirk Marrown, dedicated to that saint.
Kirk St. Anne.
Kirk Malew, dedicated to St. Lupus.
Kirk Arbory, dedicated to St. Columbus.
Kirk Christ, Rushen.

Review of the State of the Island under the dominion of the House of Stanley—Excessive Alarm excited by the revestment in Great Britain—the revival of Prosperity and general amelioration of Character and Manners resulting from a better order of things—Prejudice against the Duke of Athol, whence it originates, and how maintained.

HAVING brought the history of the island down to the time when it underwent its last great change, I shall endeavour to give a summary view of the condition in which the Manx people stood, when the power of the house of Stanley was extinguished.

As I have before observed, the population had been essentially reduced by the Scottish usurpation, and the inhabitants were levelled to a class of mere peasants, who, at the time the Stanleys came into possession, were too poor to emigrate, and too ignorant to effect their own improvement. Their new lords, therefore, claimed an indefeasible right in the whole landed property, and appear to have considered the people in much the same point of view, that a Russian noble regards the vassals on his estates, as creatures existing only to cultivate lands for his benefit, in which they had, individually, neither right or interest. In this state of humiliation, the Manx remained with little variation for three centuries, employing themselves in fishing during the short season the herrings were on the coast, and for the rest of the year devoted to complete idleness, except the trifling garrison duty exacted from each, whilst the women performed the task of cultivating just so much land as, on the closest calculation, would supply the wants of the family, and pay the lord's rent. They dwelt in mud huts, without doors or windows, merely serving the single purpose of defending them from the inclemencies of the weather. There was at this time an essential difference between the Manx and the Scottish Clans, inhabiting the out-isles, formerly associated under the same government, and, probably, then actuated by the same habits and manners.

In those isolated spots, though the land belonged altogether to one chief, yet were his interests so bound up by participation and relationship with those of his dependents, that his superiority seemed to be reflected back, and to give to the whole community an elevation proportioned to his own. On the contrary, the Lord of Man, for many ages, came amongst his people, but to coerce their persons, or to subtract from their little gains: in comparison to him, they were a distinct and inferior race of beings, who could only gaze on him in his elevated sphere, as a meteor or a comet, likely to endanger or alarm, but without a promise of advantage to mark his track. So circumstanced, they had quietly taken the evil with the good, neither stimulated by comparison, nor encouraged by hope, till about twenty years before Bishop Wilson's time, when a new channel was opened by a band of adventurers who came from Liverpool, and settled themselves in Douglas, for the avowed purpose of carrying on an illicit trade; and by the advantages they held out, they soon induced ships to and from the East and West Indies, as well as those engaged in the Guinea trade, to touch at the island, where they found a ready market for part of their cargoes, which were afterwards conveyed in Manx vessels (and by those means eluding the custom dues) into other countries, as well as Great Britain and Ireland.

The profits attending this nefarious traffic were soon perceived to be so large, that the natives, awakened from their stupor, resolved to participate with the strangers. The lord of the isle also, deriving advantage from certain small duties paid to him, was little concerned to suppress it; and the people, already trained up to the sea, and inured to hardship, were well calculated to encounter the dangers of such an employ. But, in a pursuit of this kind, it is obvious the morals of the nation must be put to extreme hazard: it was impossible a commerce, founded on trick and fraud, could be prosecuted, without an entire surrender of principle; and the conviction that such was the case, gave to the good Bishop Wilson, as may be easily imagined, the most lively concern. In a letter to his son, dated in 1742, he says,

"Our people are mightily intent upon enlarging the harbours at Peel, Ramsay, and Douglas; but the iniquitous trade carried on, to the injury and damage of the crown, will hinder the blessing of God from falling upon us."

He earnestly strove to divert their awakened activity into another channel; but, in this particular, all his influence could impose no restraint. The gains and profits were obvious and present, the injury done to a government whose relationship they scarcely admitted was founded upon abstract principles, which they had a difficulty, as well as disinclination, to comprehend; and it became evident, that only the strong arm of power could extirpate this nest of plunderers. On this ground, the revestment of the island in the crown of Great Britain was proposed, and carried into effect, as we have related, greatly against the wishes of its former possessors; and yet their reluctance bore no comparison to that with which the change was regarded by the natives. This feeling was also considerably aggravated by the secrecy observed on the part of the Duke of Athol or his officers, in relation to the treaty whilst pending. It appears by evidence given in before the English commissioners in 1792, that the first news of this intended sale was only a slight rumour, which reached the island in January, 1785; in consequence whereof, a requisition was made to the governor to convene the keys, with which he did not comply; that, in the month of March following, the proceedings in Parliament becoming a matter of notoriety, and when, in fact, the consent of the duke and dutchess had been given to the transfer, a second petition was presented for assembling the legislature of the island, which was at length granted; and, in consequence of this meeting, two gentlemen* were deputed by the keys to attend Parliament on behalf of the Manx, accompanied by a merchant as agent for commercial affairs.

To have thus transferred a nation and its inhabitants, without the compliment of informing them of the change about to take place, appears a stretch of arbitrary power hardly reconcileable with our ideas of civil liberty. It is true, that when complaint of this disregard to their claims and feelings was made to the duke, he expressed some surprise, and declared he *had given* direction to one of his officers to make the matter known in the island, whilst it was yet undetermined. This officer, when applied to, alleged his obedience to the order; but, on further investigation, it came out, that he had only acquainted the governor, and between these two gentlemen the secret had rested till the whole was effected, and remonstrance had become equally vain and useless.

Soon after this event, an act passed both houses of Parliament, not merely calculated to root out the illicit trade, but imposing such severe restrictions on the regular commerce of the island, that the people, previously alarmed and agitated, were now driven to such despair, that they believed their ruin to be complete; insular property sunk to the lowest state of depreciation, and nearly all who had the means of removal, began to entertain the idea of emigration, when, as a last effort, three other commissioners were dispatched to England, to represent the miserable

* Mr. Moore and Mr. Cosnahan.

condition of the inhabitants, and endeavour to obtain some redress of their grievances.

Happily, this last remonstrance was attended with success; some clauses of unnecessary severity in the act complained of were repealed, and certain encouragements held out to the fair trader, which opened a brighter prospect, and effectually relieved the public mind. From this time, the character and situation of the Manx have been gradually improving; the advantages of being governed by a great nation, instead of a petty lord, is universally felt. Those who had already accumulated large gains from the contraband trade, were, by the change, obliged either to sit down upon the lands they had acquired, and turn their thoughts to agriculture, or to embark their capital in regular commerce. Very few sunk back into the state of apathy formerly indulged. Industry, though ill-directed, had been awakened; some luxuries, too, had crept in, which, though not always beneficial to individual character, are still, up to a certain height, universally productive of national advantage.

But whatever pursuits were superinduced, the herring fishery, supported by ancient habits and early association, was regarded as the chief good; and to this pursuit, requiring neither talent nor labour, the mass of the peasantry still confined their hopes and exertions; on which account, agriculture, with its moderate returns and permanent advantages, was yet almost entirely neglected.

The Duke of Athol, in making a sale of the island, had reserved all his feudal rights as lord of the soil, with certain other profits coming under the same description. But the enmity excited in the minds of his late subjects was too active a principle not to produce continual resistance against these claims, which, no longer backed by sovereign power, were met by every species of opposition; so that it became necessary in 1790, to resort to Parliament to establish his mutilated rights, which was accordingly done by the duke, who further complained, that the sum given to his ancestor was greatly beneath the value of the revenue ceded to the crown. His petition, therefore, went to obtain an additional compensation, and also to establish those manorial rights, which, being unnecessary to the purposes for which the revestment was made, were never intended to be disturbed.

On this petition much contention ensued; the general feeling was averse to the first article; the keys petitioned against that clause which affected the insular rights; and, at length, after severe debate, the bill was thrown out.

The duke being thus left even in a worse situation than before, renewed his attempt in 1791, when a case was presented to the privy-council, containing such strong allegations, that commissioners were appointed to visit the island, and make a thorough investigation, both as to the particulars in dispute, and also into the general state of the revenues, produce, and trade.

The result of this inquiry proved, that great part of the duke's complaint was well founded; that the sum of £70,000 given for the cession had been calculated on a revenue ill-managed and unfairly collected; consequently falling much short of what, under a better system, it might have produced; and that, in other respects, the property meant to have been reserved to the noble complainant was unnecessarily crippled.

In consequence of this report, a fresh bill was offered in 1805, on which the former contentions were renewed in both houses. Many members asserted, that the duke had received full compensation for the Isle of Man in its then state; and that if by the fostering care of the British government the revenue had been increased, it was no reason why the late possessor should call for farther remuneration. It was asserted, that the last Earl of Derby had farmed his own receipts to a merchant of Liverpool for £1000 per annum. And it was observed, that if such a precedent was set up, with equal justice might any man, who had neglected his estate and sold it for a depreciated value, demand an additional compensation of the next possessor, when he should, by his industry or skill, have improved and restored the dilapidated property.

On the other hand, the friends of the duke maintained, that the loss sustained by him and his family, might, at a moderate computation, be estimated at £620,000; a sum so enormous as to excite the ridicule of opposition. But at length, *being supported by ministry*, the affair was decided, the manorial rights clearly ascertained and established, and an additional sum of £3000 per annum out of the consolidated fund bestowed on the duke and his heirs for ever.

This success renewed the ancient grudge of the people against the Athol family. In the year 1798, the duke had accepted the post of governor of the island, an office, as it appears to me, much below his rank, and which, by constantly keeping alive the recollection of his former supremacy, ought to have been painful to his feelings: nevertheless, when he first assumed the government he was received with every sentiment of respect; the people were disposed to regard him as a fellow-sufferer with themselves, by the act of his ancestor, and hoped that his interest would still be exerted in behalf of his natural dependents. As such, on his arrival the natives, forgetting their usual apathy, flocked around him, took the horses from his carriage, and drew him to his house, amidst the loudest acclamations. But this popularity was of short duration: whilst the bill above-mentioned was depending, the people were *instructed* to believe, that its object went to the entire annihilation of their property, which it was represented the duke, in imitation of one of the Earls of Derby, meant to seize into his own hands. A prejudice once sown, especially by a popular leader, is difficult to eradicate, in proportion to the grossness of the soil in which it has taken root; and the extreme ignorance of the mass contributed to establish a belief, which, to this moment, is not wholly done away; many of the landholders still asserting, that such a scheme *was* on foot, but that by *some* means, (which they neither understand, nor can explain,) it was defeated through the interference of certain individuals, who, from thence forward, have been regarded, without justice or reason, as the protectors of Manx independence; whilst the duke has invariably to encounter either the strongest marks of aversion, or at best a silent and contemptuous neglect. His acts, many of them highly beneficial to the community, are viewed with suspicion, and to the utmost of their power the legislature set themselves to negative and defeat all his propositions. Most people wonder that, so circumstanced, his grace does not resign an office in which he is so ill understood, and from whence he can derive neither honour nor profit: but perhaps the maintenance of his private rights are bound up to a certain extent in the exercise of his power as a governor; and in addition to that consideration, he has extensive influence in the appointment of officers in the different departments, which are usually filled up through his patronage, by persons connected with, or dependent on, his family, generally to the exclusion of the natives, whose jealousy is very properly excited by this preference shown to foreigners, who, on the other hand, feeling their obligation to the duke, are strenuous supporters of his power, and serve to compose a little court, and maintain a faint appearance of state during his short visits to the island.

Tour round the Island, commencing at Douglas—Description of that Town and Neighbourhood.

BEFORE I enter on general subjects connected with the present state of the island, I think it may form a very proper ground-work to draw a short sketch of the country itself. The scenery of the Isle of Man, except on the north side, where it is better wooded, has no great beauties; there is nothing to elevate or astonish, and not much to admire: the mountains are of too tame a character, and too frequently covered with fog, which, as a native poet says,

"Sits like a night-mare squat on Mona's breast,"

to give pleasure, except to an imagination strongly tinctured with Ossianic scenery; such may here find all the varieties of tint and form that enraptured the mountain bard, but they will still languish for the bolder features of his scenery. The highest elevation rises so gradually, that its effect is lost to the eye; there is hardly a bold or abrupt precipice throughout the whole, except in the rocky scenery round the coast, which can only be surveyed from the sea; the interior is cast in the same mould with its inhabitants, and a sort of quiet mediocrity characterises the whole. The country is intersected by streams, which, though scarcely more than rivulets, serve to diversify the scene; and the water is every where pure and excellent, totally free from the brackish taste usually prevailing in the vicinity of the sea, and, as has been found on experiment, admirably adapted to the use of the manufacturer as well as for domestic purposes.

The course usually pursued by travellers is to make a

tour round the coast, on which all the towns and villages are seated, the interior being chiefly divided into small farms, or abandoned to the undisturbed dominion of heath and gorse. The high roads are tolerably level, and capable, with a little more attention, of being made excellent. The town of Douglas, from various causes, has a pre-eminence over all the others, both in trade and population, though it is not the seat of government; but as it is the point at which nearly all visitors first arrive, I shall begin my description in that quarter.

The approach to this place by sea presents a most imposing aspect. On turning either of the heads that form the semicircle of the bay, which is of considerable extent, the eye takes in at once a variety of objects calculated to raise fairy hopes of the interior. In the centre stands the free stone palace of the Duke of Athol, called Mona Castle, magnificent from its size, if not from its architectural beauties. The hill behind this mansion is planted and cultivated, so as to draw forth and embellish all its natural advantages, though the space devoted to this purpose, not exceeding five or six acres, bears no proportion to the size of the dwelling. At a short distance is a neat and elegant villa belonging to Colonel Stewart; and in addition to these several modern houses, at different elevations, overhang the bay, and give an air of modest opulence and comfort to the whole. In a recess at the south side rises the town with a handsome pier, and a light-house, of classical elegance, presenting a new proof of the capriciousness of taste in the human mind, these two being planned and erected by the same artist, who built the chaotic mass above-mentioned for the Duke of Athol. The whole bay is two miles across, and is sheltered from all winds except the north-east; both its points are rocky and dangerous, and in the middle is a bed of rocks called "Connister," on which, in the stormy season, many vessels find their destruction.

It is unfortunate when the first glance at a place excites expectations, which every succeeding view must damp and dissipate. Those who arrive at Douglas on a fine day can hardly fail to find the pier covered with groupes of white-robed damsels, full of gaiety and spirit. They will cast their eyes with delight on the villas which surround or overhang the bay. If the time is evening, they may probably be greeted with the sound of military music from the parade; and the combination must naturally lead them to anticipate an entrance into a Mahometan paradise, peopled with houris. But this lovely vision will only last till they have ascended the stairs opposite to the custom-house; from that moment they must thread their way through a labyrinth of narrow dirty streets, and prepare to encounter the usual variations of dirt and neglect; for certainly nothing can be more inconvenient or disagreeable than the internal arrangement of this town, where the divisions form angles which would defy the skill of the best charioteer of ancient or modern times: no part is flagged, nor is it well lighted, except in the vicinity of the harbour. The whole forms a triangle, the longest side extending from the ridge to the pier; but as the buildings are now rising in every direction, this shape will soon be lost; nor is it indeed even now so clearly defined as it was a few years back. The pier is in length five hundred and twenty feet, its breadth forty: it is handsomely paved with free stone. At the distance of four hundred feet it suddenly expands fifty feet to the right: this part being raised forms a semicircle to which there is an ascent by a flight of steps. And in the centre of the area is the lighthouse, according to the opinion of nautical men, more to be celebrated for its beauty than utility; being situated considerably within Douglas Head, and so nearly on a level with the town, that its light is often confounded with that of the neighbouring houses.

The harbour is esteemed the best dry one in the Irish

channel, and admits vessels of considerable burthen, at high water, close to the quay. The customhouse is the best building in the town, and conveniently situated for business. It was erected during the prevalence of the contraband trade, by one of those persons who had realized a considerable property in that pursuit; but in the panic following the revestment of the island, he sold it much under its value to the Duke of Athol, by whom it has been devoted to its present use. Till very lately all the houses in Douglas were low and ill-constructed, crowded together without regard to convenience or uniformity; but latterly several new streets have been constructed in the suburbs, well situated for comfort and accommodation, in which the houses combine some degree of elegance in the exterior, with considerable attention to internal convenience.

The act of the legislature, taking away the protection from foreigners, has been more severely felt in Douglas than in any part of the island, this being the spot generally preferred by visitors of this description; and in consequence many houses are at this time uninhabited, and the shops have lost that animated appearance of business formerly visible in them: but yet as all the imports and most of the exports pass through this port, there is still a considerable trade carried on, and a degree of bustle perceptible on the quay, that keeps hope alive, and leads the inhabitants to look forward to the renewal of past prosperity from some other source. The shops afford a good assortment of articles of necessity and convenience; but it is the practice to mix various branches of trade in one receptacle, particularly linen-drapery, grocery, and hardwares, which is not favourable to the condition of the stock. One of the principal traders in the town of Douglas deals in the following incongruous list of commodities—millinery, mercery, liquors, wines, grocery, linen-drapery, stationary, ironmongery, salt, shoes, tobacco, snuff, brushes, brooms, mops, perfumery, hats, hosiery, herrings, and coals.

The assembly-room is spacious, but neither elegant nor even neat; yet the balls are well attended, and the young people dance to their two fiddles with as much hilarity as if the apartment was illuminated by Grecian lamps, or adorned with velvet hangings. A theatre was erected a few years since; but the encouragement given being insufficient to induce good performers to make even temporary visits, the building has been diverted to other purposes.

Amongst the most promising establishments are a public library and reading room; institutions so necessary to the improvement of society, that they deserve in all places the highest support, and the most careful superintendence: but in this, as in many other instances, too much party spirit prevails, and in consequence the advance has not been equal to the commencement. The president, the committee, and the secretary, have been occupied with private differences, when they should have been debating only on the best means of promoting the good of the society, and therefore the collection of books is neither so large nor so well chosen as it might have been, considering the time which has elapsed since the formation, or the funds subscribed. There is now only one printing-press* in the island, from whence a newspaper issues weekly; but it is the vehicle merely for advertisements. In Douglas is a small chapel dedicated to St. Matthew; but the place of worship most frequented is a new church, a little above the town, which is neatly finished, and where the pews let at a very high rate. The parish church, called Kirk Braddan, is at a distance of two miles. There are, besides these, a Methodist meeting house, a Presbyterian chapel, and also one for Catholics.

A Lancastrian school, and a house of reception for the poor, ought to be mentioned with praise. Both owe their

* Since writing this, another has been established.

rise to voluntary subscriptions, to which those persons, whom the natives are too fond of distinguishing by the term *strangers*, have been much the largest contributors. Formerly, the poor of Douglas, as is still the case in all other parts of the island, were partly maintained by a collection, which is made every Sunday in the different churches after the morning service, when the wardens go round from pew to pew, and though none of the donations are large, yet it is very unusual for any one to refuse some trifle. In country places, where the persons claiming parochial relief are not numerous, these alms have been found tolerably adequate to their support; but in the towns, though the collections were much larger, yet they fell very far short of the wants to be supplied; and this deficiency it was the custom to make up by domiciliary visits of the paupers themselves, who usually on a Monday morning made a progress in a body from house to house, to the great annoyance of the inhabitants, who were literally besieged by a body of claimants not easily to be either satisfied or dispersed. The establishment of a public kitchen in Douglas has completely relieved the housekeepers of that town from this weekly visitation: to support this institution each family subscribes according to inclination or ability, and the whole is conducted under the vigilant and judicious superintendance of the high bailiff of the town, to whose exertions the plan, excellent as it is, first owed its rise. Those poor persons who, from sickness or infirmity, are unable to attend at the regular meals are provided with food at home, the others take their shares at a common table, and some few reside in the poor-house altogether. The whole number receiving daily aid are about a hundred persons.

The Lancastrian school has also been an essential public benefit, and a very visible improvement has taken place in the children of the poor since its institution. Establishments of the same kind, but on a smaller scale, have been set on foot in Ramsay and Castletown; from whence it may be hoped, that the blessings of education, which not many years since were unattainable even by the higher ranks in the island, will now be extended to the lowest. The last public buildings which I have to notice are the hot and cold salt water baths. These, which are not yet quite finished, will be of inestimable utility to valetudinarians, and no doubt tend to increase the resort of visitors from the opposite coasts during the bathing season.

The post office for the island is in Douglas, where all letters are brought from Whitehaven, and thence forwarded to the other towns. The packet sails from England, wind and weather permitting, every Monday night; and after a stay of three days is again due for the opposite coast.

The lodging-houses are very numerous in this town, but there are few inns, and only two of any pretensions; in these the accommodations are good, and the difference between their charges and those made at English hotels is so great, that it induces many persons to give a preference to Douglas, for a temporary visit during the summer, especially as the sands are well adapted for bathing, and proper machines in waiting. The markets are abundantly supplied; but for a scale of prices, &c. I shall reserve a page at the conclusion of the work.

The Duke of Athol's house or castle, as it is the first object which strikes the eye of the traveller, and the most considerable for magnitude in the island, must not be passed over with the slight notice already taken of it. It is an erection faced with free-stone, on a plan so extraordinary, that it has puzzled persons, much better skilled in architecture than I pretend to be, to decide what class it belongs to. The mansion is a perfect square. On a line with the back front extends a string of offices, forming *one* wing under a colonnade, and thereby giving an air of deformity to the whole. The principal front recedes a little in the centre, for no reason but to countenance the erection of a modern balcony with a light iron railing, to contrast the Gothic columns running up in the other parts of the building. The windows are much too narrow, and the grand saloon, which is of magnificent dimensions, is completely spoiled by a row of small lights, like the windows of an attic story, passing over the cornice and principal sashes; besides all, the eye is offended by a line of battlements, above which rises a pointed and slated roof, giving a direct contradiction to the armed pretensions of the front; nor is this the worst error in judgment, for, amidst an assemblage of chimneys, roofs, cornices, and carved work, springs up a round Gothic tower, with long *sash windows* between the loop-holes, the only visible use of which strange excrescence is to sustain a flag-staff, whence the colours are occasionally displayed.

The domain around the mansion is on a scale of littleness exciting continual astonishment, since there could be no cause why the lord of the whole island should fix on a spot so circumscribed, that the dwelling appears completely crowded under the hill, or rather gives an idea of having slid down in some violent concussion of the earth.

The terraces, walks, and gardens, would hardly suffice to exercise the taste of a citizen, who had to plan out his parterre and paddock for a country box at Islington; and the whole is so much elbowed and incommoded by neighbouring villas and cottages, that it can be compared to nothing more appropriate than the noble owner himself, descending from his elevated station as Lord of Man, and submitting to jostle and associate as *deputy* with those officers over whom he ought to have held sovereign sway. The cost of this building, with all its defects, is said to have been upwards of £50,000; a large sum to expend on a mere monument over departed greatness.

Tour continued—Castletown—Derby Haven—The Calf—Peel Town and Castle—Ramsay—Lazey, and the Road returning to Douglas again.

FROM Douglas to Castletown, which is the regular route, the distance is ten miles. The road lies past the seat of Major Taubman, called the Nunnery, from the ancient structure formerly occupying the same site; but of which not a vestige remains, except a gateway still supporting the old bell, but now forming an entrance to the stables. The gardens and grounds have some beautiful features. For many years the whole has been without a rival; and travellers, finding nothing else to admire, have lavished more praise than it deserves on this spot, which certainly has many advantages in point of situation; but the scenery is disfigured by the erection of small houses, a mill, a warehouse, and even by two bleachfields, evermore spread with linens of different shades, all which are directly in front of the mansion. The house is not more than a decent country seat, whose whitened walls are curiously finished by a cornice and bordering of deep red stone. Above the nunnery the road commands a view of a rich valley, in which stands Kirk Braddan; and over all rises the lofty mountain of South Barrule. On the left is the delightful little villa belonging to Major Tobyn, standing in the midst of a farm so neat and well cultivated, that the whole presents a scene of judicious and profitable improvement, combined with domestic comfort and beauty, which attracts continual admiration. Half way to Castletown, on the right, is Mount Murray, belonging to a nephew of the Duke of Athol; and from hence the mountain scenery runs up in a variety of barrenness, including Snawfel, Penny Pont, and North Barrule.

Kirk Santon, a small church, lies on the left; and about a mile from thence are several druidical vestiges, being stones elevated and placed in a circular form. Following the direct road, you arrive at Balla Llonay Bridge, usually called the Devil's Bridge, which is said to be the scene of his satanic majesty's frequent exploits; on which account it is with extreme reluctance the natives venture over it after dark.

Balla Salla is the largest and most populous village in the island. The river and scenery are particularly beautiful, and some remains of Rushen Abbey still adorn the banks of the stream. This retreat was founded by Olave, King of Man, in 1104; but the church, though begun at the same time, was not finished or consecrated till 1257, though it had in that long interval served as a burial place for several of the royal family. The monks were twelve in number, besides the abbot. They practised great austerities, wearing neither shoes nor linen, nor eating flesh. In 1192 the recluses removed to Douglas, but in four years they returned to the abbey. In 1316 this place was plundered by Richard de Mandeville, who carried off the treasure to Ireland; and it was finally suppressed with the monasteries in England, in the reign of Henry VIII. but whether by the Lord of Man or by the King of England, I have not been able to discover. The site and remains of the abbey are in the possession of Mr. Moore, whose father, when first deemster, built a handsome house on the spot, and converted some remains of the monastery into out-offices.

From Balla Salla to Castletown, a distance of only two miles, the road is greatly beautified by some flourishing thorn hedges, which are cultivated with great attention on the estate of George Quayle, Esq. These were, a very few years since, the only specimens of this ornamental fence in the island.

Although tradition has handed down no authentic

account of the antiquity of the four principal towns, yet there is reason to believe that Castletown, or, as it was originally called, Rushen, is the most ancient; and that it may have been nearly coeval with the castle, though the surrounding buildings, not being framed like that for duration, must have been many times renewed since the first formation of the town. All those now in existence appear to have been raised within the last century, except one, now the George Inn, but formerly the abode of the lieutenant, and of the lord himself when on the island.

The venerable castle demands particular attention; it was erected in 960 by Guttred, the second Danish prince in succession from King Orry. This building, which is remarkable for solidity, bears a strong resemblance, and was probably constructed on the same plan with the Castle of Elsineur, in Denmark. It is of a figure not easily described. A sort of stone glacis runs round the keep, and includes some other buildings now fallen to ruin. This glacis was added by Cardinal Wolsey, during the time that he was guardian to Edward, Earl of Derby. Within the walls are some convenient and partly modernised apartments, appropriated to the use of the lieutenant governor, and also a large court-room devoted to public use. On the walls are three confined buildings where the records are kept, and the business of the rolls-office is conducted. There are also two rooms sometimes granted as an indulgence to persons confined for debt; but the great mass of unfortunate persons of this description, have hitherto been crowded together in three apartments set apart for that use; whilst felons were confined in the interior of the keep, in chambers so ruinous, that it was a great impeachment of the humanity of the government to commit any one on mere suspicion to such dungeons. Within the last year, however, great alterations have been commenced in the internal part of the castle; all of which is undergoing a substantial repair, and rooms of different dimensions are planned out, where the miseries of incarceration will be alleviated by some attention to the convenience and accommodation of the sufferers.

The streets of Castletown are regular and airy. In the centre is an open space or square, around which are several very excellent houses, and at one end a neat and well appointed chapel. The keys have a house appropriated to their use; but it is a mean building, unsuited to the station held by this branch of the legislature. The free school of this town is considered as a very beneficial institution: it owes its rise to Bishop Barrow, who founded it in order to secure a succession of students, who should be properly educated for the ministry. The qualification required in the master is, that he should be a clergyman, and have taken his degrees at one of the universities; and the endowment arises from a sum given by Charles, Earl of Derby, being the profits of a former vacancy of the bishopric. Dr. Barrow also obtained several contributions, with which he purchased part of the impropriations; and he gave two valuable estates of his own in the island, called Hango Hill and Balla Gilly, all which are applied to the maintenance of four students, who previously to their admission must give security either that they will enter on the ministry when their education is finished, or repay the money expended on them. After leaving the academy, the young students have a stipend per annum till they obtain promotion in the church.

Castletown being the residence of the lieutenant governor, and usually also of the southern deemster; and as all law proceedings are conducted there, it must be considered as the metropolis of the island; and though not so flourishing in its trade, or so gay from the influx of strangers, as its rival, Douglas, yet it affords, in the opinion of many, a much pleasanter retreat to persons unconnected with trade, or those who prefer a quiet social intercourse to a mixed society. The only public place of amusement here, as in the other towns, is the assembly room; but there is the usual routine of card playing, tea drinking, and morning visits. The gentlemen have a reading room; and, of late, a literary society has been set on foot, which it is to be hoped will before long give to the general association a higher tone. There are not many shops in Castletown; and the access by sea is so difficult, that trade to any extent can never be carried on there, as most of the supplies must necessarily be landed at Douglas.

The Isle of Man bank is established in this town, and is indeed the only house in the island which carries on the banking business unmixed with other concerns.

About a mile and a half across the sands is the isthmus which joins the peninsula, called Langness Point, to the shore, and by its bend on one side forms an excellent and secure creek, called Derby Haven, where are the remains of a round tower, built by the Earl of Derby in 1603. This was no doubt a commanding point, and much better calculated to repel an enemy than Castle Rushen, which, indeed, has always been nearly inaccessible by sea, owing to the dangerous and rocky bay before it. Near the fort at Derby Haven are the ruins of a church, by some supposed to have been a cathedral. It is now used as a place of interment for Catholics.

About two miles west of Castletown is Port le Moray; and a little beyond that Port Erin, a romantic secluded bay, offering an excellent harbour. On the beach is a small village composed of huts of fishermen, with here and there a little cottage villa of a superior description. Near this place are the Giant's Quoiting Stones, as they are called, being large masses of unhewn slate standing erect; and a little further is a barrow, called Fairy Hill, very generally believed to owe its rise to the labours of those visionary beings, but, in reality, thrown up in commemoration of Reginald, King of Man, who was slain in single combat by Ivar, in 1248.

From Port Erin it is usual to make the passage to the small island called the Calf, always an object of curiosity to visitors; the distance from which place is three miles. The circumference of the Calf is computed to be five miles, including an area of six hundred acres. A very small part of this surface is converted into arable land, but the whole forms a fine sheep-walk. It is the property of the Duke of Athol, and by him leased to a farmer of the name of Gurley, who has erected a convenient house in the centre of his domain, in which he resides, with his wife and two or three servants, who are the only inhabitants of this isolated spot.

It is very properly tithe-free, having the benefit neither of church nor minister. Except in the garden of the farmer, there is not a tree or shrub on the whole island. Rabbits abound every where, and are a great source of profit to the farmer in the spring of the year. The Calf is also the resort of immense numbers of sea-fowl, who form a most striking and picturesque scene from the water, sitting in innumerable tiers, one above another, on their nests in the clefts of the rocks, where the silence and security of their situation must efface every recollection of their vicinity to their enemy, man, and recal the idea of those first ages of the world when birds and beasts were allowed to multiply their numbers, and possess their domains unrivalled and undisturbed. The scenery is uncommonly bold and beautiful, especially when thus adorned by its white-breasted inhabitants.

This islet is said to have been, at different times, the retreat of two hermits. The first, in the reign of Elizabeth, imposed on himself a residence in this dreary solitude, as a penance, for having murdered his mistress in a fit of jealousy. The other was one Thomas Bushel, who made it his abode in the time of James I. in order to try the experiment how far a life of severe abstinence would promote longevity. What is called Bushel's house is now in ruins; it bears the outline of a small building, apparently consisting of two rooms, situated on the highest ground, and within a few yards of a perpendicular rock.

Whether this extraordinary ascetic died in his melancholy retreat, tradition gives us no certain information; but there is a place called Bushel's Grave, on the top of the adjoining rock, from whence we are led to suppose that he did so.

This cemetery is most curiously constructed in the form of a cross, containing two cavities six feet long, three wide, and two deep. Immediately on the edge is a wall of stone and mortar, two feet high; the whole is roofed and slated, but except the before-mentioned application of this repository to the purpose of sepulture, no probable conjecture has been formed of the use or design for which it was constructed. The rock itself is only accessible on one side, and is called the Eye or Burrow: it adjoins the Calf at low water, but at high water there are forty feet of intermediate sea.

Besides this point, there are two lofty triangular rocks, springing abruptly from the water, the highest of which rises one hundred feet; and in the narrower channel, between the Calf and the main land, is an islet named Kitterland, which affords herbage to a few sheep in summer.

Leaving Port Erin, the road to Peel lies through the pretty village of Kirk Arbory, so called from the number of trees formerly flourishing there, of which not a vestige now remains. From hence we have a near view of the mountain called South Barrule; and on the opposite side are the lead-mines of Foxdale, the working of which has, of late years, been relinquished, though the belief of their intrinsic value is still maintained by many well-informed persons. On the left is a mountain-torrent, falling from a perpendicular rock of about thirty feet, which the inhabitants have agreed to honour with the title of a cascade. At a short distance is Kirk Patrick, a church erected in 1710, by the exertions and benefactions of Bishop Wilson, who, besides giving £100 to better the endowment, presented the pulpit, reading-desks, communion-table, &c. &c.

Not far from hence is the most romantic and beautiful spot in the island, a valley called Glenmoi. It is a deep and rocky glen, well wooded, through which runs a rivulet, murmuring over its stony bed, and in one part forming a delightful fall of from thirty to forty feet. The northern bank is almost perpendicular, covered with luxuriant ivy, intermixed with holly; the south side exhibits a rich plantation of ash, chesnut, and hazel. As the valley winds considerably, all foreign objects are necessarily excluded, and the whole has an air of the most pleasing solitude.

Peel, which was originally called Holm Town, is twelve miles distant from Douglas, and eight from Castletown; it is more remarkable for its ancient than its present rank.

In the feudal times, this town must have derived consequence from its vicinity to the castle; and when the smuggling trade was at its height, Peel was a station of importance, but it is now little more than a narrow and dirty fishing town. The population is estimated at twelve hundred people. The bay abounds with excellent fish, and on this coast the herrings have, for many years, been taken in the greatest abundance. Peel Castle stands on a peninsula about one hundred yards west of the town; at low water it is joined to the main land by a stone wall, shelving to the top. Formerly, the approach was by a flight of steps, but time has rendered them nearly useless, and travellers now make their way to the ruins by clambering over the rocks.

Till the revestment of the island in the British government, this fortress was garrisoned by native troops in the pay of the lord, who usually gave them English officers; but, at the sale of the royalty, the armoury was cleared of the matchlocks and other ancient weapons, the garrison reduced, and the whole has been suffered to fall into a state of incurable ruin. The remains, however, have yet an imposing appearance, the walls are still flanked by towers, and the outline is pretty well defined; it encloses an irregular polygon of two acres. The building was originally composed of a sort of red slate, winged and faced in many parts with red stone. Almost in the centre is a square pyramidical mound of earth, each of its sides facing one of the cardinal points. The admeasurement of this elevation is seventeen yards, and it is surrounded by a ditch five feet and a half broad, but of the use for which it was designed, no account is extant; it is conjectured either to have been an eminence whence a commander might harangue the troops, or with more probability, the burial-place of some great personage.

In this fortress, two eminent persons have been imprisoned at different times; the one Elenor, wife to Humphrey, Duke of Gloucester, in the reign of Henry VI., the other, the great Earl of Warwick, who, on one of his reverses, was banished to the island, and detained in the custody of this garrison.

Within the castle walls are the remains of two cathedrals, one dedicated to St. Patrick, and believed to be the first Christian church erected here; the other, inscribed to St. Germain, and built about 1245. This last is described by several ancient authors, particularly Waldron, as having been richly ornamented, and abounding in monumental inscriptions; but, if it ever was so, the page of history has been more lasting than even memorials of stone and marble, for, at present, not a trace of these embellishments is discoverable to the most curious research. It is completely unroofed, and only occasionally used as a cemetery. Bishop Wilson was the last diocesan enthroned in this cathedral.

Underneath is the ecclesiastical prison, constructed with all the gloomy severity of Monkish times: it is a vault eighteen feet deep, of which the roof is formed by thirteen pointed arches, supported upon short pilasters, only twelve inches above the ground. The bottom is extremely rough; and in one corner is a well, or spring, which must have made a deplorable addition to the natural humidity of the place, where neither light nor air is admitted, but through a small window, deep set in the wall at the east end.

Waldron also says, in his account of this place, that there were other cells under the two churches, adapted to the purpose of punishment, in some of which the wretched inmates could neither sit nor lie down, and that their seclusion in these dens of horror depended on the nature and enormity of their offences, and on the will of their judges. In these days of civilization, who can reflect without astonishment on the cruelty that could inflict, or the patience that could endure, such aggravated tortures both of body and mind. But though these severities have never been exercised since the reformation, yet one cannot hear without wonder, that the other part of the ecclesiastical prison was tenanted so lately as in the days of the excellent Bishop Wilson, who, in more than one instance, consigned offenders to that miserable abode for various offences against the church, particularly the non-payment of tithes, and even in some cases without a hearing. Indeed, the power of the clergy in the Isle of Man has always had an arbitrary character, and even to this day the sentence of the bishop, or vicars general, is decisive, nor does it admit of bail: there is no alternative between prompt submission or imprisonment.

Three miles from Peel is the celebrated Tynwald mount. Its appearance is pleasing from the neatness with which its singular form is preserved, and venerable from its antiquity, and the interesting purposes to which it is entirely dedicated. It is a circular barrow, of moderate height, formed into a pyramid of three circles, the lowest being about eighty yards in circumference, and the top not more than seven feet in diameter. On this, when the legislative assembly is collected, a canopy and chair are placed for the lord, or his deputy; and the different officers, clergy, and keys, take their respective stations below him, whilst the surrounding area is filled with the people. Near the mount stands St. John's Chapel, from whence, after prayers and a sermon, the several persons forming the Tynwald court, move in procession to the mount, the ancient formulæ being still observed; though from the great change of circumstances which has taken place since the origin of the institution, the ceremony is so completely divested of the dignity of former days, that it excites little attention, and hardly now affords a holiday-gaze to the mob.

The first part of the road to Ramsay from St. John's lies through a deep and solitary glen, of two miles in length, containing in all that distance only one miserable cottage, and one stunted oak. It is a most hermit-like solitude, steep, lofty, barren, and desolate. In the bottom runs a narrow rivulet, above which, the road is cut on the side of the hill. Leaving this dingle, you approach the pleasant village of Kirk Michael, a place rendered interesting to the admirers of superior goodness, as having been the home-scene of Bishop Wilson's active benevolence for more than half a century. I could scarcely forgive the traveller who, on entering the precincts of this parish, did not pay his first visit to the modest stone that covers the earthly remains of so much excellence.

The church is in the midst of the village, of which the chancel was rebuilt after the death of his father, by Dr. Wilson, son to the bishop, who was born at Bishop's Court, and all his life took a warm interest in the affairs of the island, and, by his purse and influence, rendered many very essential services to his countrymen.

Near the church-yard is an upright stone, of great antiquity, on which are chiselled various devices of horses, riders, dogs, and stags; on the upper part is a warrior, with his spear and shield; on the edge are some runic characters, which are thus variously translated by different antiquaries. Sir John Prestwich asserts, that the words form the following sentence:

"Walter, son of Thurulf, a knight, right valiant, Lord of Frithu, the Father, Jesus Christ."

Whereas Mr. Beaufort, with equal confidence, reads the inscription thus:

"For the sins of Ivalsir, the son of Duval, this cross was erected by his mother Aftridi."

There are some other monumental relicts, which make a better appearance in description than reality, being almost defaced by time.

In this parish is a pile of stones, called Cairn Vial, probably raised in commemoration of some contest, or of some eminent chief buried on the spot.

A mile from Kirk Michael is the palace (as it is called by courtesy) of the Bishops of Man. It is a moderate-sized building, well wooded, and standing in the midst of some excellent land, in an improved state of cultivation. The present diocesan is repairing and enlarging the house, and by the interest he takes in agricultural pursuits, will probably afford a beneficial example to the neighbourhood, and stimulate their exertions.

There are many barrows in this part of the country, which, in early ages, was frequently the scene of bloodshed and contention, most of the northern invaders having landed at Ramsay. Governor Challoner had several of these tumuli opened, but found only a few urns of clay, and in one, some bones, which had apparently passed the fire.

Two miles north-east of Kirk Michael is the village of Ballaugh, one of the most populous in the island, some manufactories for coarse hats being established there. In this parish is still a good deal of boggy land, intersected by the Currah drain. The farmers have a great advantage in being near marl-pits, which, used as a manure of late years, has been employed to the manifest improvement of the lands. Two miles from Ballaugh is the church of Jurby, almost at the point of land bearing the same name. The church-yard is on very high ground, and affords an extensive view over the channel to the opposite coast. A cross road leads from hence to Kirk Bride, situated five miles from Ramsay, and two from the Point of Ayr.

Between Kirk Bride and Ramsay is Kirk Andreas, a rectory and archdeaconry, of which the old church has within a few years been replaced by a new one. Near an ancient seat called Balla Hurry, is the encampment formed by the troops of Oliver Cromwell. The situation is well chosen, it is surrounded by a wide fossé, and has a bastion at each corner, the internal square being sufficiently sunk to secure the soldiers from the fire of the enemy.

The approach to the town of Ramsay lies over a stone bridge of three arches, which crosses the Sulby river. The town is small and irregular, but derives a slight degree of importance from being the seat of justice for the northern district. There is a pier which runs out a few hundred feet to sea, and is terminated by a light-house; the bay is spacious, and the anchorage good, but the harbour, from neglect, has become nearly useless, and will only afford shelter to vessels of very small burthen. The country about Ramsay, as well as the neighbourhood, is far superior to the town; the former being in a high state of cultivation, and chiefly inhabited by native families of considerable respectability, amongst whom a pleasant association is kept up; nor do they so decidedly exclude strangers from all participation in their hospitality, as is sometimes done in other parts of the island.

Provisions are considerably cheaper here than at the southern side, and it is also asserted that the land is much superior, and affords greater promise of advantage to the farmer; against which, however, I should fear the want of an immediate and certain market must be more than a counterpoise. Many apple orchards flourish here in great luxuriance, and thorn or quickset hedges, on most estates, have superseded the stone wall so common in the south.

In proceeding from Ramsay to Maughold you leave the lofty mountain, North Barrule, on the right. Maughold head is a bold promontory, beneath which, under some moss-clad rocks, is a deep spring, much celebrated for its medicinal virtues. These waters were supposed to derive additional efficacy, if drank sitting in the chair of the saint, which still remains near the well.

This point, and the adjacent village, take their name from the venerable person who was there cast ashore, and who, as tradition informs us, made himself a dwelling on the spot where he landed; and where his exemplary piety, and the uncommon severity of his life, attracted such universal reverence, that his solitude was soon invaded by a number of votaries, who, desiring to shelter themselves beneath the protection of his sanctity, or to profit by his example, soon raised a town in his immediate neighbourhood, which became one of the most populous in the island. Of the truth of this legend no evidence remains, except the uncommon dimensions of the church, which greatly exceed those of any other place of worship in the country; and the circumstance of its standing in a space of five acres of consecrated ground, which certainly implies a larger population than that by which it is at present surrounded. Near this church-yard is a pillar of clay slate, on which the figures are so rudely executed, and withal so much defaced, that it offers a full license to fancy, to ascribe the original design to the most opposite subjects. Some say it is intended to depict the birth, passion, and crucifixion of our Saviour; others discern in it a clear and distinct configuration of the visit of St. Bridget to St. Maughold, when he invested her with the veil. For my own part, I can only wonder at the ingenuity that can discern, in such an heterogeneous mass, a likeness to any thing in heaven or on earth; and I feel rather inclined to think, that the artist employed his chisel under a conscientious recollection of the second commandment.

Passing on towards Laxey, Snowfield rears its venerable head, and invites the traveller to a view which, for its extent, is unrivalled in Great Britain, of which empire this mountain is said to be the exact centre; and a great part of which may be distinctly seen from the top of it. Of Ireland you behold the Arklow mountains, the high point of land on this side the bay of Carlingford, and the hills behind Strangford; of Wales, the towering Snowdon and great Ormshead, besides a long line of mountains; of England, part of the coast of Cumberland and Lancashire; and of Scotland, all the high land between Dumfries and Port Patrick. Whilst the Isle of Man itself forms the home view, and is spread out like a map beneath your feet.

Laxey is a village of little trade, composed of about thirty houses, the retreat of fishermen; but the glen is deserving of notice, for the romantic beauty of its scenery. It is well planted with trees. About half-way up are some copper mines, from whence no great advantages have as yet been derived, though they are occasionally worked. A little way up the valley is a flax spinning-mill, belonging to Messrs. Moore's, of Douglas. Kirk Lonan, the parish church, is a mile from the village. At some distance on the road to Douglas are twelve stones placed in an oval form; just without the oval are two others, six feet high, one of which is cloven from top to bottom. The whole are erected on a mound of earth, elevated four or five feet; in the centre of which is an excavation seven feet long and three wide. The natives have connected several supernatural tales with this spot, but they give no rational account of its origin: most probably the whole is a remnant of Druidism.

Ken Droghead is a village rather more than two miles from Douglas, of which the parish church is dedicated to St. Onca, the mother of St. Patrick, though the name is usually corrupted to Conchan. This neighbourhood has been held up of late years as an example to the rest of the island, on account of the great and visible improvement effected here by different agriculturists, to which its vicinity to Douglas, and the facility of obtaining manure, have no doubt contributed.

Having now completed the circuit of the island, I have only to notice the inland parish of Maroun, which offers no extraordinary particulars to record. It is intersected by a road leading to St. John's. Nearly opposite to the parish church are the walls of a chapel, called St. Trinnian's, said to have been erected in consequence of a vow made by a shipwrecked mariner; and its present ruinous state is ascribed to the malice of the demon by whom this unfortunate had been persecuted, who being restrained from any further personal injury to the sufferer, amused his revenge by throwing off the roof of the new building.

Agriculture—Its great Advance of late Years in the Isle of Man—Scale of Population at different Periods—State of Buildings—Advantages possessed by the Manx Farmer over those of neighbouring Countries—Roads—Manure—Notice of some particular Improvements effected by Individuals.

THE agriculture of a state, whether large or small, must ever form an interesting consideration, connected as it is with all that relates to domestic ease and independence. Its pursuits have a character different to almost all others, in this money making and money spending world. The returns of the farmer, ere they can be ensured, must be sought by a combination of industry, patience, and ingenuity; qualities tending to improve the character of the mind, whilst they are employed to embellish and enrich the surface of the land. If to the wisdom which enables him to discern the best means, he does not add coolness to pursue his end, he has little chance of ultimate success; and if unremitting care and practical economy are wanting, he will still find himself at a distance from the goal. These are very different characteristics to those which commerce demands, in whose service wealth and luxury too frequently become the reward of mere enterprise, whilst the unobtrusive and moderate trader is left to pine over disappointed hopes and fruitless efforts. The pursuits of the farmer have this essential advantage, that if the returns are slow they are in a moderate degree certain; and meanwhile, the health both of body and mind may be benefited by a profession, which, in a peculiar manner, protects its members from contamination of morals, and leads them to look up to that Providence, whence only they can derive their success. The farmer more than any one feels, or ought to feel, his dependence on a superior power, awaits his visible operations in the kindly return of the seasons! he claims his bounty in the fruitful shower! and if he thinks at all, he must acknowledge, that though he may plough and sow, it is beyond his might to ensure any increase.

Again, I conceive that in this class the great virtue of benevolence is a more active principle than in those whose employments shut them up in a shop or at a desk! The wants of the labourer must ever be visible to his employer: it is his interest to encourage industry and suppress immorality: and it is seldom you see the bustling female who superintends the domestic concerns of the farm-house or yard, forget the sick wife of the cottager, or refuse those little aids which, though hardly missed from her large stores, are yet of infinite benefit to those whose means are limited to the measure of daily wants, without any provision of increased comforts for the hour of sickness.

Perhaps this view of peace and goodness, combined with industry, will in England be regarded as drawn from the old school, when farmers moved contentedly in their own sphere, and fulfilled the duties of it, with scrupulous integrity and satisfied humility; when they took their turn at the plough, whilst their wives and daughters exercised their sensibility in the care of the poultry and pigs, and their ingenuity at the spinning wheel; before the possessor of a hundred acres thought it requisite that his sons should be dashing sportsmen, or his daughters accomplished *young ladies*; and before every thing was given to speculation and theory, and nothing to practice and industry. If this primitive state of things is no longer held in deserved esteem in the wealthy and luxurious state of Great Britain, there is no reason why it may not be restored or preserved in the Isle of Man, where the science is in its infancy, where success may yet crown the persevering endeavours of industry, and both respect and honour attend its progress.

In pursuing this subject, I cannot follow a better or more scientific guide than John Christian Curwen, Esq. president of the Workington Agricultural Society, of which the Isle of Man formed a branch, from the year 1809 to 1813. This gentleman being much connected with the country, and having framed his annual reports, on the state of the agricultural interests, upon actual inspection, and great local knowledge, must have been a sufficient judge of the subject: and I trust this general acknowledgment of his authority will supersede the necessity of noticing the particular passages which I may give even in his own words.

Having commented on the great neglect of this useful science, which subsisted during the earlier times, and on the particular causes whence this inattention to the internal interests of the island originated, I shall only now endeavour to show the progress that has been made under a better system of government, in the last twenty years. At the time of the revestment, nearly all the farms were occupied by native landholders, who cultivated small portions of their estates, and submitted the residue to the undisturbed dominion of heath and gorse. The first advances, as might naturally be expected, took place in the neighbourhood of the four towns, with the exception of those domains occupied by Bishop Wilson, who first raised large supplies of corn, and made extensive plantations, now flourishing in their prime and beauty, a lasting memorial, amongst a thousand others, of his judicious skill and care. That his example to a certain extent did produce its proper effect, is proved by the consequences; because, from that era, those seasons of excessive scarcity, which, previous to and even during his life, so frequently recurred in the island, have never been felt with equal severity.

But for the present highly-improved state of the country, the Manx are certainly indebted to the spirited exertions, and superior practice taught them by those of their fellow subjects, whom they are too fond of separating from themselves by the offensive designation of strangers. It is those strangers who have ascertained the grateful nature of the soil! called forth and applied the various species of manure, which nature, with abundant liberality, had for ages offered in vain to native indolence or prejudice; and by these means have transformed a sterile heath into luxuriant corn fields and verdant pasture.

To the same class of visitors may also be ascribed the revival of planting, which, if it proceeds a few years more as rapidly as it has done in the last twenty, will render the legend of the naked valleys, and unclothed hills of Man, as incredible to future ages, as we now consider the record which describes the Druids in their groves, or an army in ambush under shelter of a forest.

Early writers all concur in representing the soil as extremely unfertile, in which account Sacheverell, Rolt, and many later authors agree, without inquiry or examination: since, the present appearances evince, beyond dispute, that the defect lay not in the lands but in the cultivators. It is a truth, that small as the population was forty years back, they got most of their wheaten bread in a manufactured state from Cumberland, from whence vessels trading to Ireland brought it out, and disposed of it at sea to the Manx boats, then constantly hovering about in pursuit of their established trade. Wheat was then hardly raised in the island, and even so late as 1798, when Feltham wrote his tour, he asserts that this grain could not be cultivated with advantage in the island, being from the nature of the soil, and other predisposing causes, liable to the smut in such a degree, as to discourage all attempts to introduce it. This error is now fairly corrected by the large crops raised since that time of the cleanest and best quality, as the returns from Liverpool market will prove. The generality of land, in a good situation, well cultivated, will give of oats forty to fifty bushels per acre, of barley the same, and of wheat twenty-five to thirty.

Formerly!—and when on this subject I use that word, to prevent repetition I desire to be understood as meaning within twenty or thirty years. Formerly the instruments of husbandry were so few, that scarcely twenty carts were to be found in the whole island, and the farmers had no mode of carrying their corn but in kreils fixed on the horses' backs.

In the year 1642, Governor Greenhalgh made an ineffectual attempt to introduce the use of lime as a manure; and having built a kiln, it soon circulated as an article of news, that the deputy was actually engaged in a project to burn *stones* for the improvement of the land. The people hastened in crowds to witness the result of this wonderful process, and probably not without some strong doubts of the worthy governor's sanity: when, however, they beheld these masses perfectly reduced by the action of fire, they eagerly resolved to profit by an example, from whence they expected the most beneficial consequences must ensue. *Earth-pots*, as they were termed, were raised in all parts of the island, in which, without reference to quality, every kind of stone, flint, slate, or pebble, were indiscriminately subjected to the same process. For the ill success attending this *judicious* attempt they had an infallible reason to produce, founded on a belief that the governor had intelligence with the faries, by whose agency *his* minerals were turned to a powder, whilst those of his cotemporaries were only condensed to a greater degree of hardness.

Of this curious fact many evidences remain, and quantities of calcined stones are frequently found in different parts, which have either been left in heaps, or used to fill up drains.

A clear idea of the little profit derived by proprietors of very large tracts of land from their possessions, may be obtained from a list of the implements in possession of a person who occupied at least four hundred acres of his own estate; for the cultivation of which he had, according to Mr. Curwen's information, one plough and one harrow. In abundant years, the estate produced bread-corn (that is, oats and barley,) for the family; in failing ones, not that: and the cattle depended on the gorse and furze, with which the land was covered, both for food and shelter. The same estate is now let to a thriving tenant, for a rent of £800 per annum.

Nor is the reign of prejudice and ignorance yet wholly at an end; they have still a strong hold in the minds of some of the natives, and at the time I write there is a tract of excellent land, within three miles of Douglas, held by the proprietor, and surrounded by farms in such a state of cultivation as must awaken emulation, if that sentiment was not completely smothered; yet the owner of this place is so bigoted to his ancient habits, that if out of three hundred acres he can raise enough to supply the instant wants of his family, and retain seed for the coming year, he thinks he has done all that foresight and industry can require. The females spin their own wool and flax for clothing; and at the end of the season they are well satisfied to behold the whole returns consumed, comforting themselves with the hope that there is more coming in. As to a possible failure of their returns, they never calculate on such an event; nor does the future provision for a large family disturb the equanimity of their minds, believing, with primitive simplicity, that sufficient to the day is both the good and evil thereof. The estate, by the laws of the land, must descend to the next heir; and for the rest of the progeny, during the lives of their parents, they will live at home in unthinking and inactive stupidity, and at their death must turn out, as a matter of course, with no provision but their own labour for support. For all which improvidence, as we should call it, the present proprietor has an unfailing apology and reason, viz. that his father did so before him; that he himself has enjoyed the estate as his due; and his brothers, who were brought up with him, are now in extreme old age, spending the remains of their strength as daily labourers on the roads, or in the neighbouring farms.

But these instances of neglect are becoming every day less frequent, and Mr. Curwen ascribes the change to the advance of trade, the great resort of settlers from other countries, and the excessive increase of luxury and taxation in Great Britain. The years of scarcity, also, have had here, as elsewhere, their beneficial effects; the great profits made by some farmers inducing a general spirit of speculation and improvement, which, in ordinary times, it would have taken many years to excite; whilst every tax imposed by the Parliament upon Great Britain operates as a bounty upon Manx agriculture. In all cases, the advance has been commensurate with these causes, as appears from the following comparative statement.

And first, as to the population. Mr. Curwen says, that at the commencement of the last century, the number of inhabitants on the island was under ten thousand; in 1755, he computes them at fifteen thousand; in 1777, only twelve years after the revestment, the numbers had increased to twenty thousand: they are now estimated thirty-five thousand. That this scale is absolutely correct, I am not quite assured. Bishop Wilson wrote a short history of the island some years before his death, which took place in 1755; and certainly no man had better means of ascertaining the real state of the country: he then calculated the population at twenty thousand.

In 1795, the Duke of Athol observes, in his case submitted to the privy council, that the king, by the revestment, has acquired an increase of thirty thousand subjects. It usually turns out that round numbers are inaccurate, but it is a fact, admitting no dispute, that a great and rapid increase has taken place of late years.

Another visible change appears in the buildings; every where the mud-walled cabin and thatched roof are giving place to erections of brick or stone with slated tops. In 1790, there were but four breweries in the island; at this time there are more than thirty, and many of them individually doing more business than the whole collectively at that time. So lately as 1807, three butchers supplied the town and neighbourhood of Douglas, and these only opened their stalls on the market-day: there is now a constant supply of meat exhibited by at least twelve competitors. Mealmen and hucksters were recently unknown in the towns, and many consequent inconveniences were felt by private families, who had to seek their corn in large quantities at the farmers, and thence to carry it through the whole process of grinding, and manufacturing for use.

But the most beneficial improvement has been made in the cultivation of garden produce for the market. Ten years back, a cart loaded with vegetables for sale was surrounded as a prodigy, and never seen except when some of the neighbouring gentlemen collected the refuse of their gardens, and sent it for general distribution; whereas now, many acres round the different towns, but particularly Douglas and Castletown, are cultivated for public use, and the markets are almost overstocked with vegetables, and the common sorts of fruit.

Another evidence to the progress of agriculture appears in the quantity of clover and grass seeds imported: at present the gross annual amount exceeds £1000 in value; twenty years past they did not reach to £20, and even within five years not to £500. In producing these various benefits, the institution of an agricultural society has been of essential service, for which measure the inhabitants are wholly indebted to Mr. Curwen, though their efforts are no longer conducted under his auspices; and it is to be feared, that they may languish in future for the want of some such spirited and experienced leader. In one of his reports he mentions, with very natural exultation, that when he attended an annual meeting at St. John's, in 1810, the assemblage of gentlemen and farmers greatly exceeded his expectations, whilst the interest and spirit which marked the proceedings, evinced the impression that was made upon the public mind, and proved that the views of the society referred to objects connected equally with the profits of the landed proprietor, and the good of the public at large.

A very material advantage appertains to the Manx farmer, in his freedom from all poor's rates, as well as other taxes, the poor being wholly maintained by voluntary contribution. Land rent has certainly risen, particularly near the towns, to its full value; but should the present depreciation of farm produce continue, it must necessarily fall. The soil, though neither very luxuriant nor of great depth, yet makes generally a grateful return, if frequently renewed or stimulated by manure; and this operation is much facilitated by the abundance of wrack or sea weed* thrown up on the sands, which has been found for a single crop to answer every purpose produced by more substantial manures; and the easiness with which lime is procured by water carriage round the coast is highly favourable to exertion. Mr. Curwen observed with pleasure and surprise, how much the cultivation of green crop had increased between the years 1809 and 1812, when he made his last visit.

Till lately, the importation of sheep was limited to one hundred annually from England; by the interference of Mr. Curwen the number has been increased to five hundred; and he confidently asserts, that the manufacture of woollens will ere long be the staple commodity of the

---

* Sea weed does not answer so well in compost of soil or mould only, the decomposition being less rapid; but it is admirable with stable-dung, or even with straw, either of these promoting immediate fermentation, but in no case will it combine with lime.

island. Only one establishment for this purpose exists at present, which is conducted with skill and spirit, and I believe amply rewards the care and industry of its proprietor,* who is also a very considerable planter, and in all his undertakings exhibits a patriotic, independent, and active mind, equally beneficial to the country, of which he is a native, and honourable to himself.

The quantities of grain cultivated in the last few years have been such, as to supersede the necessity of importing that article, notwithstanding the increased population. The rate of labour is as yet very moderate, being much under that established on the opposite counties of Cumberland and Lancashire. Potatoe crops are now well understood; cleaning the land is very strictly attended to by many farmers, and from its obvious good consequences will doubtless soon become the general practice. Improvement of live stock has, of late, been an object of emulation amongst the graziers, and there are several dairy farms, admirably managed, in various parts of the island.

The small breed of horses, for which the Manx, in common with the out isles, was once famous, is now almost extinct; but there is no deficiency of such as answer well for purposes of husbandry, and even those for the saddle are of late much improved. But although, in the particulars I have mentioned, much has been done, it is nevertheless indisputable that much yet remains to be effected, and the impartiality I have promised demands a fair statement on both sides. One of the greatest impediments to successful exertion in agricultural pursuits, is found in the state of the public roads. In the vicinity of Douglas, and also near to Castletown and Ramsay, these have been put into a much better state than they formerly were; but in many parts of the island they are in a most deplorable condition, and sadly increase both the labour and expence of

* Mr. W. Kelly.

the farmer. The great error seems to consist in the manner repairs are attempted, which is simply by carting a few loads of stones wherever a deep hole or rut calls for such a supply, and leaving it to the action of carriages to crush or level them, instead of following the mode adopted in England of spreading and binding the solid material with a layer of earth or gravel. It is generally admitted, that the funds appropriated to the maintenance of the high roads are abundantly sufficient, if they were placed under due superintendence; but it generally happens, that the overseers are men little acquainted with the proper methods of performing their duty, and besides that, they have usually distinct occupations and private concerns, which fill up their whole time, and render it impossible they should perform their duty to the public so fully as they ought to do.

The herring fishery is another impediment to farming. At the time when an increase of hands are most wanted by the cultivator, he is left wholly to the aid he can derive from feminine assistance, by which alone he is to cut and carry in his harvest, whilst hundreds of stout young men are awaiting the arrival of the fish in listless idleness, or dissipating their *expected* gains in drunkenness; for such is the infatuation which the "herring fever" (as Mr. Curwen styles it) produces, that some weeks before the time it is expected to commence, and the whole period after it has begun, even on days when the weather or other causes prevent all possibility of fishing, they will on no account, not even for an hour, embark in any other pursuit. No one in their senses would recommend that the fishery should be relinquished altogether; on the contrary, it must be admitted, that the pursuit is a most essential benefit to the island, and causes an influx of money, which gives life to every occupation. But I am warranted, by the concurrence of the best informed persons, in saying that it is ill-conducted, and that one half the men, who are at present engaged in it, would, under proper regulations, take as much fish as the whole number do at this time. The difference to the agriculturist of the additional hands thus obtained, at the season of harvest, is evident, as well as the increased profit to individuals, since the advance on the price of manual labour, at this season, holds out as fair a return as can be derived from the fishery, all expences and extravagances included.

But if the male part of the population are irretrievably devoted to gathering in the harvest by sea, it is but justice to say, that the females endeavour, by the utmost industry, to supply their place on shore. Nothing can exceed the activity and cheerfulness with which they undertake and effect labours apparently exceeding their physical strength, particularly in reaping, thrashing, &c. Another great fundamental inconvenience exists in the want of an established market for disposing of farm produce. At present the grower, having no certain sale for his crops, must lose much time in seeking customers, before he can raise money for his rent or current expences; and the prices, in these cases, are too often arbitrarily regulated by the measure of his wants, rather than by the value of his commodities. Some adopt the mode of exporting their produce to Liverpool, or Whitehaven, where the returns may be more certain and prompt; but these are subject to severe drawbacks, from the risk at sea, and the heavy charges of freight and factors.

With the grazier the case is still worse: fat cattle can never be shipped without incurring great danger of deterioration from a lengthened voyage; and in the island, the consumption is too small to encourage extensive speculations in this line, nor are the butchers willing to give even such prices as their returns would fully warrant; this has been so much a subject of complaint, that some farmers have even opened shops to retail their own meat, of whom only one has found the plan either practicable or advantageous. There is no doubt, however, but a little public spirit and unanimity would overcome this impediment, if the principal farmers would unite here, as in other places, to establish a regular market for corn and cattle: buyers would soon arrive from the opposite coasts, and then the prices also would be fixed by general agreement.

I am not aware of any other material disadvantage which the farmer has to encounter in this island, that can in any degree counterpoise the peculiar benefits held out, except one, which is indeed of serious importance, but to which I cannot help thinking the wisdom of the Manx legislature will ere long apply a sufficient remedy. I speak of the laws as they are now constituted; first, with relation to persons not natives of the land; and next, as they regard the landlord and tenant. But on this subject I shall expatiate more at large under the proper division.*

If those heroes who have depopulated nations are allowed still to occupy a distinguished place in the history of states and empires, surely, in a confined space like the Isle of Man, which is too small a theatre for magnificent actions, we may be allowed to celebrate those who have, to the extent of their power, exerted themselves to benefit and improve the little circle within their influence; and to my humble conception, there seems to be at least as much praise due to the conqueror of sterility as to the depopulator of nations. In the first class of those, coming under the former description, no one can deserve more honourable mention than the tenant of Ronaldsway, near Derby Haven, whose farm exhibits a scene of neatness and superior cultivation greatly to be admired. His vicinity to a lime-stone quarry, and the quantity of wrack deposited at his very door, are sources which, as he applies them, must produce wealth to him, and benefit to the community. Mr. Faulder is also unrivalled in the extent and excellence of his stock, and is the farmer of whom I spoke before, as

* See Laws.

having successfully undertaken to retail his own meat. From his stores Castletown is abundantly supplied with animal food. The superiority of his mode of feeding is obvious, from the article he offers to the public; and, in fact, there is so much integrity and judgment in his proceedings, as well as a spirit and activity, that all are ready to allow his success, great as it is, is only commensurate with his exertions and deserts. There are few persons, however, who could at once embrace so many objects of speculation, as are encountered by the ardent spirit of this gentleman, who, besides supplying all the bodily wants of his neighbour from his dairy, his shambles, and his granary, has actually undertaken to cultivate the minds of the rising generation; and for this purpose he has established an academy, where, under the care of a tutor, he receives about twenty pupils, besides his own numerous progeny.

One of the best dairy farms is occupied by a gentleman of the name of Dunlop, who is remarked for the uncommon beauty of his stock, the extent of his crops, and the general air of success and abundance which follows his operations.

Mr. Curwen says of the north side of the island, that it offers much the greatest facilities for farming; the ground is in a state of nature; the means of enriching it are at hand; exertion, capital, and industry, are alone wanting to cover with luxuriant crops that surface which, at present, yields little or nothing. The truth of this estimate is about to be proved. Several spirited settlers have, of late, fixed their abode in that district, and amongst them the present bishop, who takes a lively interest in all agricultural concerns; but, as yet, the improvements are too new to be entered upon record, and it is only in the neighbourhood of Castletown and Douglas that we can form an estimate of the capabilities of the soil.

Hitherto I have spoken only of persons who rent the lands of others, and consequently have a *present* advantage to draw from their exertions. But there is another class lately sprung up amongst the natives, with whom profit is a subordinate consideration; and where the chief attention is fixed on ornamental husbandry amongst these, a general taste for planting seems to prevail. The seat of Major Taubman is an example very likely to have excited this spirit. The trees there of an old growth are uncommonly fine, and the whole scene, as we have before observed, forms an agreeable contrast to the barren hills by which it is surrounded.

Several other places embellish the neighbourhood of Douglas, and give fair promise of future beauty, though none, with the exception of Mona Castle, can be classed above the rate of middling gentlemen's houses in England; yet they diversify the face of the country, and their small lawns and paddocks, spotted with clumps of new planted shrubs, will soon form a very pretty scenery. It has been the work of time to efface a prejudice generally entertained, that the vicinity to the sea would be completely unfavourable to trees; but the contrary has at length been decidedly proved, wherever the experiment has been fairly made. Perhaps no kind of improvers are more easily checked than planters; their efforts must always be disinterested, since the real benefit or comfort can only be reaped by posterity; and it should, therefore, be attended with some degree of certainty, to compensate for its distance. Nor is it fair always to ascribe failures to a radical defect either in the soil or situation. Trees, injudiciously managed, either from neglect or ignorance, might equally as well perish in the finest parks in Great Britain, as on the most sterile mountain in the Isle of Man; and it is most true, that an unsuccessful attempt in a place where all eyes have been fixed on the result, with an inward inclination to believe it would not answer, has an effect to repress similar endeavours, when, if the real source of the disappointment was taken into the account, it might rather stimulate than paralyze their hopes.

It is well known in the island, that an English gentleman, of considerable property, bought an extensive tract of mountain-land in the interior, not less than fifteen hundred acres; and when he cast his eyes over the wide-spread domain, his imagination pictured such a fairy vision of beauty and fertility, as entirely overcame the sobriety of his judgment. In his first speculations, he promised himself a mansion embowered in groves, fields, white with his ever-increasing flocks, roads, rivers, canals, and bridges. He calculated not merely on supplying the wants of a paltry thirty thousand inhabitants in food and clothing, but actually extended his philanthropic views to the starving nations of the arctic circle, who were to be rescued from the dominion of want and cold with the surplus of his abundant stores.

In less time than ordinary abilities, with ordinary means, would ask to reclaim a heath or a bog, and turn them into arable and pasture land, he undertook to have forests waving, and rivers flowing, through the whole compass of his property; and no sooner had his active mind overcome one difficulty in speculation, than he conjured up others to resist and to conquer. I forbear to dwell on his proposal for importing the musk oxen, on which he expatiated at an agricultural meeting, with all the warmth of his character, as replete with offered benefits to the community, and only attended by two or three trifling obstacles, the first of which was founded in the difficulty of importing these animals, and keeping them alive when imported; the other he thought still less consequential, being merely the possibility that prejudice *might* revolt from the taste of musk beef.

Projects so patriotic and extensive deserved a better fate, and I grieve to record their evaporation in complete disappointment. The trees, it is true, were planted with an unsparing hand, and the sheep, purchased from an overflowing purse, combining the choicest breeds, selected from all parts of Great Britain, and the greatest pains were exerted to insure their safe arrival. So far all was hope and exultation; the natives assembled in crowds to view these precious treasures—to admire the plaids of the Highland shepherds, who came from the Cheviot Hills to guard their fleecy care; and they believed the owner of such wealth and such wonders must be almost as great a man as their far-famed Prince Mananan, with his fogs and his fairies.

Whilst the summer smiled, the sheep grazed on the fragrant heath, and the young plants took root unmolested; but, alas! no sooner did winter assert his reign, than all was want and dismay; for, till the snow actually bespread the ground, the necessity of providing for such an astonishing event had never entered the thoughts of this admirable projector. For a while the animals preserved their existence by browsing on the buds of the infant plantations, and the tops of the young firs; but these were soon destroyed, and with them all hope of future shade or shelter. Next the sheep fell victims to disease; and, lastly, the promises of philanthropy, with the visions of speculative profit, all sunk together in irretrievable ruin. Happily, however, this failure, instead of annihilating the hopes of our mountain-laird, has only turned them into another channel: he is now eagerly bent on the cultivation of flax, to which his whole domain is to be subjected; and he waits only till he has tried the effect of a new invention for dressing this article, before he will erect a factory, build a town, cover the mountain with artificers, and supply all Europe with linen cloths. There is so much vivacity of genius, such a grasp of benevolence, and such genuine public spirit, in all these designs, combined as they are by the gentleman in question, with repeated acts of solid use to this community, of which he is an acknowledged benefactor, that those who witness their failure must still respect the source whence they originate; and that charity must indeed be cold, that does not wish him success, though the faith must be strong that can hope it.

Much expectation of beneficial example was excited in the friends of Man, when Colonel Mark Wilkes, a native of the island, and a gentleman well known in the higher walks of literature, returned from the East Indies with a fortune, earned by uncommon talents judiciously applied, and promised his countrymen to devote the residue of his days to the peaceful pursuits of agriculture. Unfortunately for the Manx, his talents were too well known and appreciated to admit of this seclusion; his services were again demanded in the government of St. Helena, whither he returned in the year 1812.

Colonel Wilkes is erecting a mansion in the Isle of Man, on an extensive scale, though I cannot help thinking, if it had been conducted under his own inspection, a better taste would have been displayed, especially as the farmhouses, offices, and cottages, built by himself upon his estate, are raised on plans so chaste, as to add much to the rural beauty of the scenery, and form a decided contrast to the cumbrous mass appointed for his own future habitation. In the short space of three years, that part of the country belonging to Colonel Wilkes has been converted from a barren waste, not worth half-a-crown an acre, to luxuriant arable and pasture land, great part of it letting at £2.

There are, doubtless, many other individuals in the island, who may justly claim distinction as improvers in this valuable science, but it would be tedious to general readers to dwell longer on the subject. To sum up the whole, I believe it is universally admitted, that a great, and for the time, an astonishing progress has been made; that the approaches of insular distress are nearly fenced out; and that the few obstacles which remain must shortly give way to the awakened spirit of inquiry, industry, and emulation now prevailing in the country.

Herring Fishery, and Trade in general.

THE herring trade being the staple commodity must be first noticed. It has hitherto been considered as an established fact in natural history, that the appearance of the herring on the different coasts of Europe in the summer season was in consequence of migration. Their progress from the cold regions of the north has been detailed with singular precision; they have been marshalled in large bodies, or sent out in detachments, as the fancy or information of Zoologists dictated; but late inquirers strongly question this progress from distant parts, and rather incline to the belief that the herring, like the mackarel, is in reality at no great distance during the winter months from those shores which it frequents in the season of spawning, inhabiting only the deep recesses of the ocean, or plunging itself in the soft mud at the bottom; but that at the vernal season it quits the deeper parts, and approaches the shallows in order to deposit its spawn in proper situations.

The reasons given by Dr. Block are chiefly these: that it is physically impossible this fish should traverse so many thousands of miles in so short a time; that in one or other part of Europe herrings may be found all through the year: on the coasts of Swedish Pomerania from January to March; in the Baltic sea, and many other places, from March to November; about Gothland, and also on the coast of France, from October to December. The fishermen of Scarborough scarcely ever throw a net in any season of the year without finding herrings among their fish.

But by whatever means, or from whatever cause, they are conducted by the hand of Providence to the different coasts on which they are periodically seen, no where can their arrival be welcomed with greater avidity than at the

Isle of Man, where a new spirit seems to inform the population as soon as the fishery commences. Between four and five hundred boats, usually of sixteen tons burthen each, and without decks, are employed in this service. These are manned by two seamen and four countrymen, who come from their inland habitations at this season, which commences about the end of July, and continues through the month of October. The nets are buoyed up by inflated bags of dog-skin. The produce of a boat is commonly divided into nine shares, one of which appertains to each fisherman, the owner of the boat takes two, and the proprietor of the nets one.

The fishing is very frequently interrupted: the least appearance of a change in the weather hurries them instantly to port. Indeed, the boats are by no means calculated for encountering a storm, or even a severe gale; and some deplorable accidents, which have happened in former seasons, are still remembered as warnings against encountering similar dangers. Nor are they solely restrained by fear from constant exertion, dissipation being quite as frequently a bar to their pursuits. A very successful night is almost sure to be followed by drunkenness, and consequent inability to attempt a repetition of their good fortune. They are also scrupulously careful not to leave the harbour on Saturday or Sunday evening. Tradition has preserved a story, that in former times they had a custom only to except Saturday from the pursuit of business, but that with the setting sun of the following evening it was the practice to put to sea. On one of these occasions a tremendous gale, accompanied by thunder and lightning, signals of divine vengeance, dispersed the boats, a great part of which were speedily buried in the waves, the remainder took shelter in the recess of an impending cliff, and before morning were overwhelmed by its fall. The warning has been accepted by the inhabitants of Man, who in this respect, at least, are careful not to intrench upon the Sabbath-day.

The view of this little fleet at sea on a calm day is highly beautiful. They always throw their nets in the night; and on their return to the harbour next morning, children and women are employed to convey the fish to the several receiving houses, where the operation of salting is immediately performed, as much of the excellence of the herring is thought to depend on the speedy performance of this process. The Dutch and the Scotch, (in imitation of them,) have adopted the practice of salting the fish on board the vessels, and of throwing overboard at sunrise all that remain fresh; but in this island they proceed on the old plan. The fish are rubbed as soon as brought in, and left in heaps till the following morning, when they are regularly packed in barrels, with a layer of salt between each row. Those designed for red herrings are differently treated; they are first piled up with layers of salt for two or three days, after which they are washed and hung up by the gills upon small rods, placed in extensive houses built for the purpose, where the rods are suspended in rows from the roof to within eight feet of the floor; underneath are kindled wood fires, which are kept constantly burning till the fish are sufficiently dry and smoked, after which they are barreled for exportation.

The number of herrings annually cured in the island is subject to considerable variation, but is calculated at an average of between eight and ten millions. The present price of fresh herrings varies from ten to twenty for a shilling; and for those that are cured, two guineas the barrel is the average price. A barrel contains about six hundred.

Formerly premiums were given to the owners of successful boats, and certain bounties upon all that were exported to foreign lands; but both are discontinued.

The chief exports from the island, besides herrings, are strong linens and sail-cloth, but in no large quantities, there being but one factory for making these articles, and that on a small scale. Considerable supplies of grain have of late years been sent to Liverpool, with butter, eggs, fowls, bacon, and some other trifling matters. There is, as I observed before, a manufactory of woollens, but these are eagerly bought up for home consumption as fast as they can be finished. Some years back an attempt was made to establish a mill for cotton spinning; but after the erection of the works, the proprietors made a rather late discovery, that the exportation of the article to Great Britain was prohibited, and after some ineffectual endeavours to convert the works to other purposes, the whole were suffered to go to ruin: nor do I imagine that manufactories on a large scale can ever answer here under present circumstances. England usually allows a large drawback on manufactured goods, which in their raw state are subjected to heavy duties, in order to preserve her trade in foreign markets. The population of the Isle of Man, considering the fishery, is not at all too abundant for the existing occupations of the country; or if it were, the vicinity to the manufacturing counties of England, where labour is always rewarded with high wages, leaves no chance of competition for any insular establishments, except for the internal supply.

For some years past the inland trade has been much more flourishing than it now is. Since the non-protection act there are, particularly in Douglas, more shops than customers; but it is to be hoped this will revive again, or indeed very serious consequences may be apprehended. At all times the balance of trade is greatly against the island; but this has hitherto been counterpoised by the income brought in from other countries through the medium of persons settling here; and now that this source is closed up, the distress for want of a due circulation is very severely felt. Gold coin is hardly ever seen, silver is also very scarce, the copper being peculiar to the country is more stationary: fourteen-pence Manx makes one shilling British. To obviate this great want of a currency, the merchants and shopkeepers issue cards of five shillings, two shillings and sixpence, and one shilling each, nominal value; these are in the form of promissory notes, payable on demand in British coin; but they are found to be attended with so many inconveniences, and such great risk to the public, that it is at present under contemplation of the legislature to make some regulations on this subject, and probably before long the British government will grant an issue of Manx coinage.

Some of the principal merchants in Douglas also circulate guinea notes; but the only regular bank established in the island is at Castletown, and the notes and cards of this house, from its known stability, obtain a natural and decided preference. The whole establishment is conducted on a scale of liberality very honourable to the proprietors and advantageous to the public, though it is often regretted that the gentlemen concerned in it have not established a branch at Douglas, where the great commerce is carried on for the whole island.

The imports are all kinds of manufactured goods, chiefly from Liverpool; coal from thence, and from the ports in Cumberland: wine from Oporto and Guernsey, from whence also they get geneva and brandy: rum must pass through an English or Scotch port. Since the year 1765, the contraband trade has been nearly annihilated; the little that is now done in that way is supposed to be by coasting vessels; but the custom-house department is so admirably conducted under the vigilant superintendence of the present collector, that it is generally believed the revenue is quite as well protected as at any of the ports of Great Britain.

The shops in the different towns have much the appearance of general storehouses, each one exhibiting an aggregate of articles not always calculated for combination; nor can I give the dealers in general, particularly the natives, the praise of civility, or a desire to accommodate.

Persons accustomed to the obliging manners of English tradesmen, are in general much disgusted with the air of inattention and disrespect so prevalent here, especially in those who have realized some property, or as it is usually termed, got a little above the world.

Some of the existing laws* are considered as great obstacles to traffic with other countries, or even to an extended trade amongst themselves. On one hand, the stranger is exposed to imprisonment and sequestration of property for the smallest sum, whilst the native is protected from incarceration for the largest. The want of regular bankrupt laws also tends to cripple the efforts of the trader; and in many respects the fundamentals of commerce are neither understood nor acted upon, especially in what relates to credit and punctuality in money dealings : but all these defects, I think, are in a course of rapid improvement. Every day brings with it a visible enlargement of ideas, and as the disadvantages are felt they will be overcome.

The manufactories for internal consumption, besides that already mentioned for woollen cloths, are breweries, soap and candle manufactories, and tanneries. The brewer and malster are combined in one, and all these being free from duties of every kind, must necessarily leave an open field for great profits, especially as the prices of the articles manufactured are nearly as high as in England, where they are subject to such heavy charges, and in consequence one would expect that large fortunes would be speedily realized by those entering on these concerns ; but I believe, especially of late years, that the numbers engaged are rather too many for the consumption, and the payments of the publican and others too irregular to admit of the full advantages to be expected.

There are few shops, and not many houses occupied by

* See Laws.

the lower orders, where spirits are not sold either in large or small quantities. The smuggling trade introduced habits of intoxication, which still prevail to an extent the most lamentable; and nothing but a heavy duty, producing a consequent advance of price, will probably counteract this evil tendency.

Most of the small farmers and cottagers still spin their own wool and flax, and get them made into cloth by village weavers, there being generally one or two looms in every parish. These practices are favourable to economy, and encourage domestic industry, whilst they preserve the simplicity of the peasants.

The Revenue—Exports and Imports.

THE revenue under the lords, proprietors, arose from a duty on exports and imports, a rental on all lands, amounting to £1400 Manx currency, from manorial rights and fines, a few fees, and certain prerogatives, by which the lords laid claim to all waifs and strays. In the time of the last Earl of Derby, the customs were estimated at £2500 per annum. The public expenditure at the same period was £700. In the course of the last century smuggling had increased so much, that the annual returns of trade were supposed to be at least £350,000, whilst the value of seizures was not more than £10,000, so that the profits to those engaged in it must have been enormous; and the Duke of Athol having a small duty on imports from this and other sources, procured for his share an annual surplus of nearly £6000 British. An abstract of the clear revenue derived from the island by the lord, for ten years previous to the revestment, states the average yearly amount to be £7293.

The revenues given up to Great Britain were only those of the customs and herring dues, amounting to £6547, for which the sum of £70,000 was allowed. After the revestment, all the old duties were repealed, and the following new ones levied.

To be imported from England only, and there entitled to the usual Drawback, to be landed at Douglas only, in the Isle of Man.

	DUTY. s. d.	QUANTITY.
British spirits	1 0 per gal.	50,000 gal.
Rum	1 6	30,000
Bohea Tea	1 0 per lb.	20,000 lb.
Green Tea	1 6	5,000
Coffee	0 9	5,000
Tobacco	0 2	120,000
Coals	0 3 per chaldron.	

From Foreign Ports.

Hemp
Iron
Deal Boards
Timber
} at 5 per cent. ad valorem.

French wine £4 per tun.
Any other wine £2 per tun.
Foreign corn, having been first imported into England, and had a bounty allowed, 10 per cent. ad valorem.
Any goods, wares, or merchandize, not specified in this Act, imported from England or Ireland, 2 per cent. ad valorem.

Flax
Flax seed
Yarn } except only from Great Britain. } Duty free.
Ashes
Fish and flesh
Corn

Linen cloth of British or Irish fabric
Hemp
Hemp seed
Horses and cattle
Utensils and implements of agriculture } Produce or manufacture of Great Britain or Ireland in English vessels only. } Duty free.
Bricks and tiles
Trees, sea shells, and lime
Soaper's waste
Packthread and cordage
Salt
Boards
Timber
Hoops

Colonial goods entitled to a bounty on importation into England.
English or colonial iron, in rods or bars, from Great Britain in British vessels. } Duty free, but subject to entry at the custom-house, under a penalty of 15 per cent. ad valorem.

All linens to be landed in the Isle of Man must be exported from Great Britain or Ireland.

Glass and woollen goods from Great Britain.

Tea, coffee, spirits, tobacco, glass, coals, silks, salt, and wine, must, on no pretence, be exported from the island.

It being found that, in consequence of the suppression of the contraband trade, the harbours had been neglected and become ruinous, the old duties were repealed, and the following levied:

Harbour Dues.

	PER ANNUM.	
	s. d.	
Herring boats,	10 0	Not a new duty, but a modification of the old one
Any ships belonging to his majesty's subjects in ballast, only putting into the harbour	0 1½ per ton.	
The same with cargo	0 2	
The same, if repaired there, an additional sum	0 1	
Foreign ships in ballast	0 2	
Ditto with cargo, not breaking bulk	0 3	
Ditto breaking bulk, additional duty	0 2	
Ditto anchoring in any of the bays	2 6	
On all spirits and wines imported, per tun	2 6	
Tobacco, per cwt.	1 6	
Tea, per cwt.	2 0	
Coffee, per cwt.	1 0	

Foreign goods not specified, 10 per cent. ad valorem.

British goods not specified, salt excepted, 5 per cent. ditto.

At this time the expenditure of the island exceeded the revenues, and in consequence the following additional duties were imposed in 1780.

Rum, 6d. per gallon, making the whole duty 2s.

Tobacco, 1d. per pound, ditto 2d.

Hemp, iron, deal, boards, and timber, from foreign parts, 5 per cent. ad valorem, making the whole 7½ per cent.

French wines, £4 per tun additional.

Other wine, £2 ditto, ditto.

The duties on tea and coffee were withdrawn, and the following substituted.

		s.	d.	
Bohea Tea		0	6	per lb.
Green Tea		1	0	
Coffee		0	4	

The allowance of British spirits being more than the demand, were reduced from fifty thousand gallons to forty thousand; and the allowance of rum increased from thirty thousand to forty thousand gallons, thirty thousand to be imported from England, and ten thousand from Scotland.

The importation of wine in any vessel of less value than seventy tons burthen was prohibited.

No goods, fresh fish excepted, were allowed to be exported from the Isle of Man without a warrant from the custom-house.

In 1790 the importation of British spirits was prohibited, but instead of them were allowed, ten thousand gallons of brandy, subject to a duty of 3s. per gallon; ten thousand ditto of geneva, ditto 3s. ditto.

To be shipped from England to Douglas only, in casks containing not less than one hundred gallons.

The annual allowance of tobacco having been reduced from one hundred and twenty thousand pounds weight to forty thousand, was increased to sixty thousand.

All wine was subjected to an additional duty of £8 per tun, making, with the former duty, £16 for French wines, and £12 for other wines, and to be landed at Douglas only.

Hops, entitled on exportation from England to a drawback of the whole duty, were made subject to a duty of 1½d. per lb.

Since this period little variation in the duties have been made. All goods of limited quantity must be imported under license. The collector of customs is obliged to give one month's notice of the expiration of licenses, and take in for fourteen days all petitions for new ones. If such of the petitioners as are natives require goods equal to the quantity limited, they have the preference over foreigners; if they require a greater quantity, the licenses are granted in rateable proportions. The counterfeiting a license subjects the offender to a fine of five hundred pounds; and taking a fee for one, subjects the collector or officer to a penalty of fifty pounds.

From the sale of the island to the year 1792, the expenditure was fully equal to the revenue; at that time commissioners were sent over to examine into the state of the country, as well as to ascertain whether certain allegations of the Duke of Athol were well or ill-founded. In the course of their inquiry, they discovered that the custom-house department was in a state of entire disorganization: their memorial on this subject states, that the system of management is ill-digested, incomplete, and unfit; of which, amongst others, they adduce the following proofs. That persons, wholly ignorant of the duties and practices of their several departments, are appointed to stations of the first importance, without any previous instruction or preparation.

That even the obvious precaution of furnishing them with written or printed rules for their government had been neglected, nor was any source pointed out whence information could be derived, or any security given or required, for the due performance of the duties of the office, or the proper application of the trust reposed in them; no inquiry was ever instituted as to character, so as to exclude those who had been formerly in the practice of the illicit trade, nor was there any check or control among the different officers, by which error or misconduct might be discovered or punished.

It was also, at that time, the practice to bestow various offices (not easily combined) on one person. The receiver-general, though an officer of the highest authority, had never been in the island from the time he took the oaths, when he remained a few days, leaving the whole execution of the duties to a deputy, who was, as he acknowledged, completely without any instructions to define the objects, nature, and extent of his office. His practice was to receive the duties, and transmit them through the agency of a lawyer in London to his principal, and he did not actually know where this last resided, or how he might make application to him directly; nay, that he had even at different times required directions in his proceedings through the agent, but had received neither instructions nor answer.

Various other instances of neglect, equally striking with these, are pointed out, and strongly reprobated in the Report; and, as it appears, with the fullest effect, for very soon after the whole system was revised and altered, most of the existing officers displaced or otherways provided for, and the present establishment arranged, to the entire extirpation of the illicit trade in the island. The office of receiver-general was given to the collector of customs at Douglas, and the whole revenue of the island placed under his superintendence and control.

This extensive power, which he has now held many years, is universally allowed to be exercised with the strictest integrity as well as moderation; and the gentleman who holds it, though closely connected with the house of Athol, is pronounced, by the unanimous concurrence of all parties, to be eminently qualified by principle, knowledge, and prudence, for the station he occupies. No stronger proof of the excellence of the plans now adhered to can be adduced, than the improved state of the revenue. According to the report before quoted, the amount of custom dues in 1790 was £3006 8s. 11d. he expenditure same year £3272 2s. 2d.; whereas, in 1792, Mr. Pitt stated in the House of Commons, that the revenue of the island had risen to the gross sum of £12,000 per annum! at which time a farther compensation of one-fourth of this amount was granted to the Duke of Athol, and his heirs for ever.

The public services, for which internal taxes, continual

or occasional, are levied, are of four sorts: Building or repairing of churches, building of bridges, making and keeping high-roads in order, and the maintenance of the clergy. In respect to churches, each parish is obliged to bear its own burthen; not, however, to the extent of building, without a special act of Tynwald: but for repairs, the parishioners are convened by the churchwardens, and the money required levied upon the inhabitants in proportion to their rental.

The same mode is observed for building or repairing bridges. The high-road fund is derived from a tax upon every retailer of ale or spirits; a small rate upon lands and houses, leaving an option to pay in money or service; a tax upon dogs; and all fines incurred for public offences, or contempt of court: by these means a sum of about £1000 per annum is obtained for making and repairing the roads.

The clergy derive their income in part from the tithes, which are divided into three portions, one belonging to the lord, one to the bishop, and the other to the parochial minister. The incumbents have also a glebe, and a royal bounty of £100 per annum, to divide amongst the poorest, which was obtained by Bishop Barrow in the reign of Charles II. One-third of his share of the impropriations was purchased by the same worthy prelate from the lord proprietor, by collections made through his interference, which were settled to increase the revenues of the church, and for the establishment of a free-school at Castletown.

The tithes are divided into great and small; these are sometimes taken in kind, but more frequently commuted, and hitherto upon very easy terms. There was formerly a tithe upon all fresh fish, upon ale brewed, and also a tithe of twopence annually upon every man engaged in any occupation, though he only exercised his calling three times in the year.

The Laws—House of Keys—Civil Officers, Juries, &c.

THE laws of the Isle of Man are, at this time, a constant subject of insular dispute; by one party, they are represented as a mass of folly and corruption; by the other, as models of the most perfect jurisprudence. The truth, probably, in this, as in other speculative cases, lies in a medium between the two opinions.

From the time of the revestment, the legislation being protected by that act from all foreign interference, few corrections or alterations have taken place. The ruling powers, divided by internal and personal contention, have suffered the public good to lie dormant. Even in the boasted constitution of Great Britain, the watchful eye of legislative wisdom is ever open to discern and correct mistakes or encroachments: how, then, can it be supposed that a code, springing out of feudal customs and an arbitrary government, should require neither amelioration nor improvement in the long interval of sixty years? for, if nothing else demanded inquiry in all that time, still the persons employed in the exercise of power should have been subjected to some inquiry as to their proceedings; and if not the principle, at least the practice, of the legislature demanded investigation.

For a small population thinly scattered over the island, without manufactories or commerce, few laws were requisite, and the memory might be supposed fully competent to record all that was absolutely necessary.

Except the natives, none had any interest or concern in them. In such a community, whose time was wholly occupied in the provision of mere necessaries, fraud, force, or avarice, had no latitude for disturbing the peace of society; and the trifling differences which sprung up, were willingly referred to the deemster, and settled by the traditionary laws, or, perhaps, more frequently by his supreme will and pleasure, without reference to precedents of any sort.

So little form was used in those appeals, that, according to the statute-book, the deemster's presence alone, whether in the field or house, walking or riding, constituted a court; and the plaintiff meeting his opponent, when this officer was in view, might drag him *vi et armis* to an instant tribunal, and setting his foot upon his enemy's, there hold him till the cause of quarrel was decided. In such a proceeding, depending more on strength of body or lungs, than on questions of right and wrong, there was certainly more brevity than dignity; but one thing seems to have been well established, and that was, the infallibility of the judgment, which could come to such post-haste decisions, and give them the respectable name of laws.

The office of deemster is of much greater antiquity than the origin of the house of keys, and I conclude, was derived from that of the chief druid, who, in the earliest times, and in all countries, where this sect flourished, combined the rank of priest and magistrate. But the council of wise men is also of druidical institution; they were formerly called *taxi axi*, from the Celtic word *Teag asag*, which, according to Dr. Campbell, implies druidism, or elders and senators. In more modern times, this assembly has taken the name of the Keys, which last term Bishop Wilson ascribes to their knowledge of the jurisprudence of the country, and their unlocking the difficulties thereof at their pleasure.

The numbers of this council were not always twenty-four, they had been referred to as a legislative power when only twelve: in one of the old statutes I find it also recorded, *that their existence was wholly at the will of the lord, without whose consent none are to be.* This decision, which is stated to have been from the deemsters, in answer to a question of Sir John Stanley, second lord of Man, was exceedingly ill received; and though it was recorded in the statute-book, and consequently left there for law, was yet virtually rescinded almost as soon as made. The original form of election is no where mentioned, but immediately after the above declaration, such was the ferment it excited, that it was thought prudent on the part of the deputy-governor Byron, to grant the people a share in the election. Accordingly, in 1422, he sent out his precept to the six sheadings, directing them severally to elect six men, out of which six he chose four to represent their respective districts, and these made up the twenty-four keys, by whose advice and concurrence at that time, several laws and regulations were made.

Why this mode of election has not been preserved, or how the people have lost a right so invaluable as that of choosing their own representatives, is not explained; custom has, however, completely abrogated this privilege, and the *practice* now established is, that when a vacancy happens, the remaining members elect two persons, one of whom receives the approbation of the governor, and thenceforward retains his seat for life, unless he vacates by voluntary resignation, accepting a place in council, or is expelled by the vote of the majority for some high crime or misdemeanor. What mode would be adopted, if the governor disapproved of both the nominations, is not settled, nor, I believe, has the case ever occurred. The keys cannot assemble without a summons from the governor, and his mandate dissolves the sitting without delay or demur. This body, when collected, with the lord proprietor, his deputy, and council, constitute a Tynwald court, whose accordance is absolutely essential to every legislative act; but since the revesting of the island in the crown of Great Britain, before it can obtain the force of a law, every decree must be confirmed by his Majesty, and ultimately proclaimed in the English and Manx languages before the people at the Tynwald hill.

In the separate meetings of the keys, the number of thirteen is required to form a house. They elect their own speaker, who holds his office for life; and they decide by a majority. The qualifications of a member are to be of full age, that is, twenty-one years, and to possess landed property in the island. Non-residence, or even being a foreigner, are no impediments to election. Their privileges were of more value in the feudal times than at present, they being exempt from all duties and services to the lord, and free to kill game in any part of the country. To charge a key with misconduct in the performance of his duty, subjects the offender to a penalty, and loss of ears. This body have always possessed the confidence of the people, and though self-elected, seem never to have abused their power. The office is attended with much trouble, and no emolument; but it is every day rising in consideration, and though, formerly, little respect attended the individuals, at this time, a member of the keys in the Isle of Man is regarded by his compatriots as a representative of the Commons is in Great Britain. This increase of consequence takes date since the revestment, and is chiefly founded on the systematic opposition shown by this house to every act or proposition of the Duke of Athol, by which they soothe and augment the aversion of the people to that nobleman, and keep alive, often without a shadow of reason, the suspicion entertained of his motives and designs.

A late writer has observed, "that were the keys once corrupt, they must continue so for ever, the very nature of their constitution being such that it could never be purified:" but, with submission to this author, I think differently. Corruption in a small legislative body, like the one in question, would carry its remedy with it. A few acts of oppression, in the improved state of Manx population, would awaken them to an inquiry into their rights; and, it is more than probable, would restore the original form of democratic election.

The chief civil officers are the governor, and lieutenant-governor, one of them being chancellor ex officio; the two deemsters, or judges, one presiding in the southern, the other in the northern division (these must necessarily be natives;) the water-bailiff, the high bailiffs, one in each town; the coroners, who are six in number, and preside separately over the six sheadings or districts, into which the island is divided, each having under him a deputy-coroner, or lockman.

The council consists of the following persons: the bishop, the receivers-general, the water-bailiff, attorney-general, clerk of the rolls, and the archdeacon.

All the lands of Man formerly belonged to the lord, and the occupiers could neither sell nor alienate without his consent; they were termed the lord's tenants, and were subject to the payment of a fine or rental, which was fixed by the setting quest from year to year. This system had been somewhat relaxed, and the holders came to be regarded as customary tenants, and some of the estates to descend from father to heir for a time, which had given an idea of individual property. But, in 1648, we find an attempt was made by James, Earl of Derby, to seize all the tenures into his own hands; and to effect this, he offered, on a quiet surrender, that he would make a grant to each individual of a lease for three lives, or twenty-one years. This proceeding gave rise to a warm contest, but the dispute remained unsettled till 1703, when it was finally arranged by the interference of Bishop Wilson, and the strenuous representations of the keys. At this time (in 1703,) commissioners were appointed, by whom the lord's dues were incontrovertibly fixed, and the inheritance of their property assured to the people, on the payment of the rents and fines so settled. In 1777, another act was passed by Lord Derby, confirming the first act of settlement, by which, estates on the death of the owner were declared to be the right of the eldest son, or if no son, of the eldest daughter. A man cannot devise an estate of inheritance otherwise than in the direct line, but purchased property he may dispose of by will. If he dies intestate, the whole falls to his heirs at law, saving the widow's right, which is half the real and personal estate of her husband, whether he make a will or not. Of the entailed estate, the widow only enjoys her share for life, which afterwards reverts to the heir; but of personal property, she has power to devise one half by will amongst any of her children, even those of a former marriage, and in the life-time of her husband; and these children can claim their respective shares on the death of either parent, as soon as the said children attain the age of fourteen years.

The whole island was formerly divided into six hundred quarter lands, but at present the number is seven hundred and fifty-nine; all other estates appear to be allotments out of, or encroachments upon these. All wrecks belong to the lord, if not claimed within a year and a day. Mines also are his by his prerogative. Game belongs exclusively to the lord, and the laws were formerly very severe against encroachers, but these have now become nearly obsolete.

Besides the trial by jury in common law and criminal cases, there are various juries impannelled on other occasions. In cases of loss, trespass, or robbery, previous to any other proceedings, juries of inquiry must be summoned, who have power to examine all parties who may, by possibility, have knowledge of the facts to be inquired into; they may even tender the oath to the suspected person, and their refusal to accept this purgation is considered as presumptive proof of guilt. Upon the verdict of this first jury, subsequent process is founded.

Fodder juries are also a very curious institution. If any person gives notice to the coroner that a gentleman, farmer, or cottager, has a larger stock of cattle than his apparent means can support, he is obliged to summon four men of the same parish, three of whom must be farmers, who are to make inspection what grass or fodder the said persons have provided for their cattle, as well in summer as in winter, and to make a true report in writing to the next court; and if it should appear that such provision is not sufficient for the cattle, an order is granted to the coroner to sell off so much of the stock as exceeds the quantum of provender, and to deliver the price to the owner. The law even enjoins the said juries to take special care that the needful fodder is actually in present possession, and by no means to admit the evasive excuse of a dependence for supply upon others.

Marriages may be contracted by banns or license: aliens cannot marry till they have been three months resident in the island. Marriage is, in fact, considered here as an act of partnership, giving no exclusive right to property. A man who marries an heiress, enjoys only one-half of her lands during his life: if she dies without children, and he continues unmarried, the same law invests the female with equal rights as to property of inheritance during her widowhood; but of his acquired possessions, she has power, even during his life, to devise one-half to any child of her own, and this will is in force immediately on her decease. No man or woman, being married, can sell or lease but by mutual consent. If a man marries a second wife, having issue by his first, the second takes only one-fourth part of his estate of inheritance; nor can any will or deed of gift invalidate these singular rights, except by the joint act of both parties; yet the husband incurs the same liability respecting his wife's debts as in England.

In the Isle of Man, children arrive at the age of majority when they have completed their fourteenth year, so far as relates to personal property, to which they then become entitled, and are also liable to debts thenceforward contracted by them; but must attain the age of twenty-one before they can enter in possession of landed estates, or make any disposition by way of sale.

A marriage contracted between the parties, within three years of the birth of a child, renders such child legitimate, if the character of the female is otherwise unimpeached. A woman convicted of adultery loses her wife's or widow's right, and is entitled only to such alimony as the ecclesiastical court thinks proper to allow.

Executors may proceed in the ecclesiastical court for the immediate recovery of debts due to deceased persons; and their decree having once passed, and the order given out, subjects the defendant to instant imprisonment, till satisfaction is made by payment in full. On the other hand, no claim can be enforced against the effects of the dead under a year and a day; or if they had any money transactions out of the island, the law allows to the heirs or executors the extended term of three years, for the settlement of the whole concerns.

The mode formerly adopted for making proof of a demand for or against the estate of the defunct, was very curious: the person charging or denying such debt was obliged to visit the grave of the deceased, with two witnesses, and stretching himself at length on the same, with an open Bible on his breast, he there pronounced a solemn oath, which, in the absence of other proofs, was accepted as positive confirmation or denial of the matter in dispute: but this process was abolished by Bishop Barrow.

As to the penal laws,* their defects being admitted, and the code at this time under the actual consideration of the legislature for the express purpose of amendment and elucidation, it would be useless to enlarge on their present state; and it is to be hoped, when the promised alterations do take place, a stricter police will be established, and the impunity now afforded to crimes, for want of definition in

* For the new Penal Statutes, see Appendix, No. 7.

the existing power, will no longer remain a just subject of complaint.

There is one particular, which seems to have escaped observation, and yet calls imperiously for attention, which is, the manner of conducting coroner's inquests, in cases of sudden deaths, and the slovenly style in which they proceed when summoned.

To prove that this charge is not unfounded, I shall select two anecdotes from the number that have fallen under my observation. In one case, the captain of a Norwegian vessel, after receiving a considerable sum of money, was found dead without any previous illness! The cause assigned was intoxication, but attended by circumstances so suspicious as at any rate to demand a strict investigation; great part of his money had disappeared, and the body immediately after death turned entirely black, and exhibited many symptoms inducing a belief that poison had been administered. On this matter no inquiry took place, or if any, certainly not with the assistance of any medical man. The other affair was yet more extraordinary. A man, wholly unknown, being found in the river apparently drowned, an inquest was taken, and the verdict to this effect being given, he was consigned to the care of the undertaker, when, behold, on stripping the body, it appeared that his throat had been cut, and the neckcloth replaced, all which, with perfect sang-froid, the foreman of the jury declared, he had no doubt the deceased had done himself; so that there was no need to revise the former decision, on account of these new circumstances.

Comments on the State of the Laws, with some Cases adduced in Proof of the Assertion that they require Amelioration.

I AM aware, that the contents of this chapter will be so entirely local, that it will afford little to amuse, or interest, the general reader; but as the facts I mean to state have recently occurred, and the ill consequences attending the abuses of the laws, which I am about to point out, are felt or acknowledged by all, I think it my duty, as an impartial historian, to hold them up to public view, in the belief which I entertain, that this negligence of fundamental principles has, perhaps, originated in the want of a fair statement, or it may be in the very nature of the society, as it was constituted previous to the non-protection act.

I am very ready to admit, that whilst impunity from foreign claims existed, the frequent resort of unprincipled and extravagant persons demanded an extraordinary degree of coercion in the debtor and creditor laws of the island, to protect the natives from encroachment and injury; and that it was, under these circumstances, equal justice to grant immunities to one class, and hold up severe penalties against the other: but now that this protection is done away, and that both the trade and agriculture of the island loudly demand an increased population to revive their drooping vigour, it must be an obvious policy to grant equal privileges to the settler and the native. None are likely to visit this place in future but persons of moderate fortunes, and consequently of habits consonant to their property. If such are to be exposed to the harassing effects of the laws, as they now stand, a very short trial would suffice to make them seek a retreat elsewhere. To illustrate my assertion, I need only adduce a few instances, which are recent and too well known in the island to be controverted.

And first, in matters of debtor and creditor, the Manx laws, with regard to a native, prohibit personal imprisonment, but with great justice subject the whole property of the debtor to the claims of his creditor. This exemption from personal suffering has certainly, in some cases, been diverted to purposes of fraud; the native has been known to make false assignments, or to turn his effects into cash, and then, under cover of the law, to set his creditors at defiance. But as no human institutions are perfect, the impossibility of entirely guarding against the ingenuity of knavery, can never be brought forward to abrogate a principle, which the enlarged views of society causes at this time to be adopted into the jurisprudence of nearly all trading countries; and it is probable, a modification of the bankrupt laws of England would be the best defence against the frauds complained of. But this it is not my concern to determine; all I have to do is to point out the errors that exist, and leave the legislature in its wisdom to correct them.

With regard to strangers, as our fellow subjects from Great Britain and Ireland are invidiously termed, the case is wholly different; actions on a simple affidavit of debt subjects the person to incarceration, and the effects to sequestration; and that, not merely to the value demanded; but the law, as it now stands, authorizes the constable to take possession of *all* the property of the person arrested, to hold it till the question of right is decided, and then to sell, not to the amount of the debt only, but the words of the statute are, "that he is to sell the whole effects, and first paying a year's rent if due, and the servants' wages for the same time, then to satisfy the creditor with all costs and charges, and *afterwards* to deliver the overplus to the right owner." No words can be requisite to point out the injustice of such a system, by which, on a disputed account, a person might be thrown into prison, his trade ruined, his effects wasted, and his family starved, whilst the matter was under discussion; and which, according to law, cannot be decided under four months; and if, on the issue, the creditor only succeeds in establishing a small part of his demand, before the sufferer can be released, he must wait the sale of property, ruined, perhaps, by mismanagement, or, it is not unlikely, remain for life in prison, on a deficiency created by the measures adopted against him. Another strong feature appears in the principle on which bail is conducted. The law obliges the stranger who wishes to contest an unjust demand, to give *Manx* bail; and, as if this was not throwing sufficient difficulty in the way, it also provides, that such bail becomes to all intents and purposes liable for so much of the debt as, on investigation, shall be found due to the claimant, from which liability he is not exonerated, as in England, by the surrender of the debtor to gaol.

But as facts speak more forcibly than arguments, I shall adduce some recent occurrences in illustration of my statement. In one case an English farmer having given offence to a native with whom he had been in habits of strict intimacy, he was arrested without any previous notice, or even the formality of demanding a settlement. The demand, on which the action was grounded, originated in a running account between the parties, and the real balance due was a mere trifle. The action, however, was taken out for the full sum that appeared on the books of the plaintiff; and as he was a man of extensive connexions, and the other a stranger, no one chose to offend the native by becoming bail, and consequently the farmer, who was also an innkeeper, was hurried to prison, his farm-work stopped, his house shut up, and all his affairs thrown into confusion, as indeed was the design of the plaintiff, whose object was to harass, and, if possible, ruin his adversary; and although after six months' incarceration he was released upon bail, and that finally a judgment was given, reducing the demand of his adversary more than two-thirds, yet was this tardy and insufficient act of justice a very poor recompence to a man, who returned, to find his farm unseeded, his stock and crops wasted, his trade fallen into other hands, and his whole affairs in a state of irretrievable ruin, though at the moment of his arrest all had been prosperous and easy. Can it be wondered at, that his spirits sunk under the affliction, and in a short time he fell a victim to the malice of his persecutor.

Another, and somewhat similar instance, occurred in the town of Douglas, only that in this case the misfortune resulted purely from the state of the laws, without premeditation or design. A petty brewer was arrested and imprisoned for a demand of £140, by the administrators of a deceased merchant, who founded their charge, as they themselves acknowledged, simply on a conjecture that a quantity of barley, of which no account was to be found in the books of the deceased, must have been sold by him to this brewer, *because* they were known to have dealings together, and *because* the said brewer was believed to be of a character likely to take advantage of any neglect or omission on the part of the merchant, in order to evade payment. On no better grounds than these, this action was maintained through four months, during which the man lay in prison, his wife and child were reduced to absolute want! his stock of beer entirely spoiled! and his trade, depending wholly on his personal exertions, completely annihilated. At the end of that time it turned out, that the only claim which could be proved against him was for £3. And the only justification attempted to be set up, in extenuation of proceedings so harsh and oppressive, was founded on the previous character of the sufferer; an apology which can never be admitted as sufficient, since it is obvious, that what was done in this case might just as well occur again to any other person, at the pleasure of a vindictive creditor, or indeed of no creditor at all; and assuredly to sequester effects upon a doubtful point, to deprive a family of support, and subject property to arbitrary removal and injury, as well as to detain the body of the debtor, is utterly inconsistent with all the principles of justice!

But that such, notwithstanding, is the law of the land, I have the authority of one of the highest legal officers to assert. A question having been submitted to him, in the case of a person incarcerated for a debt of two hundred pounds, (the debtor having effects on the island in farm produce and stock to at least the value of £1200,) whether his family might subtract so much from the bulk of grain and other articles as would support them till the matter came to a decision? The answer to which was a positive and unqualified negative, with a declaration, that pending the question nothing must be touched, the whole being virtually under arrest, and subjected to the demand.

Unreasonable as these proceedings may appear, they are yet exceeded by the existing law, or perhaps I should speak more accurately if I was to say, the existing practice, between landlord and tenant: to which, however, both natives and strangers are equally liable. A landlord, immediately on payment of one year's rent, or within fourteen days after it becomes due, can arrest the property on the premises for the ensuing year. This is done by the coroner for that sheading, who takes a jury of four persons to value the effects; and as the law provides, that if such effects when sold do not realize the valuation, the said jury are compellable to pay for them at the prices affixed, it may therefore easily be imagined, they will take good care to make ample allowance for contingencies. If the property arrested is growing corn, or hay grass, the farmer is restrained even from cutting or carrying it: at the harvest all he has a right to do is to give notice to the proper officer, who is enjoined to use due diligence to protect the grain. Few farmers, however, could be very easy under the exertion of this second hand *diligence!* Meantime an attempt to sell any part of the property, or in any way to alter the state of what is so arrested, (though it shall be proved to be with the intention of applying the proceeds to pay the rent,) subjects the tenant to imprisonment, from which he can only be released on giving bail to *double the amount* of the current rent. To dwell longer on this would be absurd; the bare statement is fully sufficient, borne out as it is by a recent case well known in the island, and which I have no doubt will awaken attention, and may probably procure redress.

Perhaps no maxim can be more true than that to comprehend an evil in its full extent, we must be in some way exposed to its operation or influence; for on no other ground can we account for the jealousy evinced by the Manx legislature in guarding the personal liberties and privileges of natives, and the complete indifference exhibited by that body on the same subject as referring to strangers. To such a pitch, indeed, has this coercive spirit been carried, that an insolvent act, though loudly called for in the island, and even recommended by the interference of the House of Commons of England, was withheld and opposed in all its stages; nor, I believe, would it ever have been granted, had not a very plain intimation been given, that if such a measure for the relief of the unfortunate did not originate with the insular government, the British Parliament would exert their own authority in the cause of humanity. In consequence of this hint, and its being warmly supported in the house of keys by Mr. Curwen, then member for Carlisle, and also one of the keys, who declared, if it failed there he would move it in his place in England, the act at last did pass, by which a prisoner, after an imprisonment of one year, might be released on the usual conditions of a complete surrender of effects; but the term of this act being limited to two years, is now nearly expired. It is remarkable that, by the Manx laws, a debtor has an allowance of only 3s. per week from his creditor, on delivering up his whole effects, or I should rather say, after his property has been taken from him; which allowance is eventually to be added to the original debt. Whereas a person confined under a criminal charge, receives 1s. per diem during his imprisonment, and retains his effects; so that it should seem, in the eyes of this legislature, the crime of poverty is estimated as deserving much more severe punishment than is inflicted on breaches of the law; more especially as it is a rare thing to see the heaviest offences visited with any other penalty, except a temporary incarceration. Even in a case of murder, and that pretty well proved, the verdict returned being manslaughter, the criminal escaped with only three weeks confinement,* whereas I have known a debtor languish in Castle Rushen eight years after he had relinquished the last remnant of his property.

* I allude to the case of one *Coax*, who was indicted for the murder of his wife; and on whose trial, before the late deemster Lace, it appeared, that he had perpetrated this crime with so much deliberation as to wait the heating of a poker, with which he struck the blows which occasioned her death; yet was the verdict such as I have recorded above.

*Comments on the actual State of Society in the Island—
Characteristics of the Natives—The Clergy—Methodists.*

Having now given as full an account of the history of the island as my materials will allow, and impartially pointed out the local disadvantages a stranger may have to encounter, I must descend from the character of an historian; and in order to form a more accurate "*chart du pays,*" it will be needful to introduce both anecdote and individual character, as far as they may serve to illustrate the present state of society and manners, and enable my readers to judge how far I am correct in the assertion with which I set out, that the island offers a favourable retreat to persons of small fortune, and moderate habits.

In the minds of those who have thought of this place at all, a strong prejudice has hitherto existed against it, as a mere asylum where debtors might elude the claims of their creditors! That the protection hitherto granted by the laws of the island has, in many instances, invited the unprincipled and extravagant to a temporary residence, cannot be denied; but it is equally true, that in various cases it has afforded a retreat, where by the practice of economy those affairs have been retrieved, and debts paid, which had the individuals been subjected to imprisonment, with its attendant disadvantages and expenses, never would have been effected: but at present the question in all its bearings may be laid aside as of no farther importance.

The insular legislature, influenced by a requisition from the British government, have thrown open a door to the recovery of foreign debts; and the consequences of this act are, for the present, most seriously felt in the island, where the sums brought in by strangers increased the circulation, and gave the necessary stimulus to commerce and agriculture; but these very circumstances concur to form a most favourable era for the introduction of those to whom, I am of opinion, the island presents advantages no where else to be found in the United Kingdom.

In Great Britain, by the inroads of luxury and the tremendous increase of taxation, existence is absolutely denied to that class which formerly constituted the middle rank; whereas in the Isle of Man, these are precisely the persons best calculated to harmonize with the manners and customs of its inhabitants, in whose character habitual economy forms a very leading trait. By the vast increase of trade and commerce in England, and the consequent influx of wealth, things have completely changed their names, whilst their natures have undergone no alteration. Prudence is now degraded into parsimony, and prodigality has assumed the honourable title of liberality; but as in this isolated spot it has frequently happened, that people have had to contemplate the result of this transposition of terms, divested of the glare attending its progress, as whilst the place afforded an asylum to the debtor, they too often found, that those who fled from the consequences of extravagance on one side the water, brought the same habits of expense and disorder to the other; and as such characters are usually actuated by a sovereign contempt for those little minds who limit their expenses within their means, the legitimate fruit of this combination of profusion and scorn was distrust and aversion. Hence it has become a rule that the stranger, who would live well with the natives, was compelled to adopt their customs, and above all things found it requisite to avoid every *appearance* of profusion. When it is considered how much we are the creatures of example, and how many foolish things are done for no better reason than because others do them, or to evade the suspicion of poverty, the value of this remarkable feature must be duly appreciated.

It has been alleged that the Manx people are illiberal and inhospitable; but I speak from experience and observation, when I assert them to be neither one nor the other. Those characteristics I have enumerated, as generally belonging to the refugees settling here, and the high airs usually assumed by them, certainly prevented any degree of intimacy between two sets of people, whose arrangements were totally dissimilar. Nor would it have had any effect in producing unanimity, had the Manx hazarded their morals by an attempt at assimilation. But it does not follow that the same aversion to extend the circle of society, would operate to the exclusion of persons more consonant to themselves. I believe the very contrary will be the case, and that a short time will suffice to root out all prejudices on this subject. Meanwhile, in the Isle of Man, no sacrifice is exacted to ostentation. There is no scale of expence established, to which all must conform, who would preserve a respectability of appearance. The simple assertion, "I cannot afford it," is accepted as both reasonable and honourable; and those whose current expences are completely bounded by their income, occupy a more advantageous station in the eyes of their contemporaries, than those who, to make a great show, go not only to the extent of their means, but keep their credit also on the full stretch.

Another advantage, particularly to young housekeepers, is, the entire absence of luxuries; the markets offer few temptations, and the shops very little beyond articles of necessity. Here are neither public places nor gaming tables, even tavern meetings are little frequented, and the possibility of extravagance hardly exists. When to this is added the entire freedom from taxation, it must be evident, that a very narrow income, with tolerable management, may support a family in this island, to whom it would hardly give food in Great Britain.

Another particular most favourable to the maintenance of economy lies in the habits of the house-servants, who, being usually trained up in Manx families, have no idea of that expensive scale of rights and privileges, which has crept in by combination and sufferance in other countries; but it is a necessary caution to those who would profit by the established customs, to warn them that they must not attempt to mix the native domestics with any others; and that they must make themselves acquainted with, and steadily enforce the established practices of the country. The servants have, in general, but a limited knowledge of their duties, but with a little instruction prove useful and active. The regular times of hiring is at May and November, for the ensuing six months. If the persons hired absent themselves from their service within the term of engagement, they are liable to imprisonment; if dismissed by the hirer, the full wages must be paid: these are moderate, and vary according to the abilities of the subject.

It is universally allowed, that no class have a greater influence in forming the character of society at large than the clergy, and I shall enter on this subject with great pleasure, as it relates to those of the Isle of Man, whom I consider as deserving the most honourable mention. To the indolence, carelessness, and even irreligion, too often exhibited in persons holding the office of ministers in England and Ireland, it is, I believe, universally admitted, much of the ordinary vices of the lower orders of people may be ascribed. The remark is trite, but not the less true, that a precept has little influence, when example takes a contrary direction. The graces of elocution, the charms of learning, the finest taste in the choice of discourses, can never counterbalance the mischiefs effected by a negligent or immoral pastor; his Sunday lectures can have no weight, whilst his weekly practice carries him through the haunts of vice and dissipation. Happily for this island, the inhabitants cannot, from experience, appreciate the veracity of this maxim amongst the whole order of Manx clergy, though some may be deficient in learning, and even in that elevated strain of piety so necessary to give full efficacy to the doctrines they teach. Yet I will undertake, without fear of contradiction, to say, there are few, if any, striking instances of dereliction from their duties, and that, generally speaking, the established habits of the whole body are consonant to the best rules of orthodoxy.

When Bishop Wilson first settled in the Isle of Man, he found the clergy sunk in ignorance, and not remarkable for propriety of conduct; he speedily saw the necessity of striking at the root of an evil so extensive in its consequences, and he began by establishing a seminary under his own roof, where, with unwearied pains, he trained up future candidates for the ministry. The benefits of this excellent plan are not yet exhausted, the pupils of his pupils are still alive to propagate the blessing.

If the Manx clergy are a little deficient in the exterior polish of those attainments derivable from a college education, they are, at least, preserved from the contagion of vices too often attendant on a superior course of instruction, and retain a simplicity of character, and correctness of manners, more conducive to the general good of those they have to instruct, than greater learning would prove with less humility.

Much emulation in reading and speaking has, of late, prevailed amongst the younger candidates; and the improvement in these particulars has been very striking, even within the term of my own observation. Great part of this evident change in oratory may be ascribed to the influence of the present bishop, whose discourses, which he delivers with calm, but energetic solemnity, are particularly impressive. Indeed, it may be truly said, that his lordship's example, as well as his vigilant superintendence, are highly conducive to the preservation of religion in his diocese, as well as to the general amelioration of manners both in his clergy and people, his own character being embellished with all the graces derivable from the high polish of elevated society, combined and corrected by the gentleness and moderation of genuine Christianity.

The service is performed in most country churches alternately in English and Manx; in the towns of Douglas and Castletown, the former language is adopted exclusively. The livings are none of them large, but they are pretty equally distributed; the highest does not exceed £350, nor the lowest fall beneath £80 per annum. The service of a curate is almost unknown, and residence very strictly enforced. I have witnessed, with pleasure, the respect universally shown to the clergyman and his family in several parishes, where such observations have come within my reach; and the peaceful and orderly arrangements of these village-pastors in their houses, has forcibly reminded me of Goldsmith's description of a similar character.

To particularize some cannot be done without injustice to others. But there is one minister in the island, in whose eulogy, I believe, all parties will concur with unqualified approbation. I respect the pious and unaffected humility of this gentleman's mind too much to mention his name. But, as "the friend of Man," a title universally accorded him, he is well known in his little circle, where his paternal care is actively employed to benefit and instruct; nor does he confine his pious endeavours to the narrow limits of his own parish—his writings and exhortations take a more extended range, and the good he is enabled to effect must return in blessings on himself.

The service of the church is attended by the laity with an appearance of devotion, very edifying to witness; nor is the rest of the Sabbath profaned by riots and drunkenness, as is too often the case in larger communities. A quiet walk, or a little chat from house to house amongst the decent villagers, seems to bound the Sunday diversions.

The Methodists are, in this island, an increasing sect. It appears, that from their first institution they have been favourably received here, as has ever been the case, when they have assailed an ignorant or superstitious people. Wesley, who visited them in 1777, says of this place, "We have no such circuit either in England or Ireland; it is shut up from the world; there are no disputes of any kind. Governor, bishop,* clergy, oppose not—they did for a season, but they grew better acquainted with us."

I confess I do not wholly subscribe to the prejudice entertained against this people. I firmly believe, as the candid and ingenuous Dr. Paley observes, "that there is to be found amongst them much sincere and availing, though not always well-informed Christianity." That their devotion is too enthusiastic must be admitted; and where it goes the length of substituting faith for works, the doctrine is undoubtedly more than erroneous, it becomes highly dangerous. But these abstract points are not those which operate on the minds of the multitude, nor are they those which are generally objected to, or even considered by their opponents; and though some far-sighted persons may discern a danger to the church and state, from the prevalence of puritanism, I confess I cannot bring myself as yet to partake of their fears, for I am inclined to think, that the cry of the great mass, if duly analized, would be found to be as much excited by a high strain of devotion in general, as against the Methodists in particular. A very little extra attention to duty, or opposition to prevailing vices, has the effect to raise the hue-and-cry of hypocrisy. According to the present system, drunkenness, debauchery, and profane swearing, are all vices incident to human nature, and for which charity commands us to make every allowance, and continually to bear in mind the precepts of our Saviour against partial judgments. But one seldom sees the same forbearance exhibited in decrying a praying, psalm-singing rogue; his sanctity, even though

---

* Dr. Hildesley was then diocesan.—I cannot help thinking Bishop Wilson would have resisted these innovators with more zeal.

no outward evidence impeaches it, is yet a subject of continual suspicion: in short, hypocrisy, whether real or imaginary, seems to include all the deadly sins; and to evade this charge, no hazard, not even that of our eternal happiness, is thought too much.

The evil consequences to the rising generation of this affected candour in estimating real vices, and this fearful avoidance of assuming virtue, must be obvious. Children, who continually hear all professions of piety ridiculed, and suspected, must naturally look on devotion as useless or affected; and whilst every mention of a future state, and every quotation from Scripture is avoided as Methodistical cant, I would fain know by what intuition they are to obtain the knowledge, which, I trust, we are not yet arrived at the pitch of denying, is necessary to salvation.

My object in this digression is by no means to advocate the cause of enthusiasm, I only seek to decry absolute irreligion. All that is done by the Methodists, and much more than they can effect, would be far better performed by the enlightened and rational clergy of the established church, if they would only exert themselves heartily and conscientiously in the cause; for I fully agree with the author I have before quoted, (Dr. Paley,) who says, "I have never yet attended a meeting of the Methodists, but I came away with the reflection, how different what I heard was from the sobriety, the good sense, and I may add, the strength and authority of our Lord's discourses:" and, therefore, though I would rather have the lower orders instructed in matters of religion, even by the Methodists, than remain completely in ignorance, yet in the Isle of Man, where no such neglect subsists, and where the clergy, from the head of the church to the youngest member of the class, are both adequate to their office, and zealous in performing the duties enjoined on them, I think interlopers are worse than useless.

Further Observations on the Society—An Example presented to the Ladies for their Imitation, deduced wholly from Native *Excellence—The Peasantry—Review of the State of Society at different Periods—Contrast between the Natives and Strangers—Anecdote of the Latter.*

THE situation of the Isle of Man, slowly emerging from a state of depression, has been, for the last three centuries, peculiarly unfavourable to literature. The supply of bodily wants will always supersede the improvement of the mind. Hitherto the people have learnt only to live, they may now "live to learn." But though little has been done at home, the island has nevertheless afforded some excellent specimens of the effects of foreign culture on native talent; and when recalling the names of those who, owing their birth to this confined sphere, have contributed to adorn, instruct, or defend, the parent state, every Manxman will record with pride the distinguished names of Colonel Mark Wilkes, the historian of India; the learned lexicographer, Dr. Kelly; Captains Heywood and Kelly, of the royal navy, gentlemen not more distinguished for courage and enterprise, than for science in their profession: these are all luminaries of the present day, and doubtless there may be many more equally worthy of notice. I have heard of only one native poet, and his talents, though certainly above mediocrity, were suffered to evaporate in local satire, of which the humour is now lost; and in course the momentary corruscations attendant on his essays, have expired with the subjects whence they sprung.

On the whole, I believe it must be admitted, that Mona is not poetic ground; and it seems to me, that the character of the Manx, when it shall be completely developed, will be found better adapted to solid attainments, than to those flights of fancy, which carry the enthusiast into the regions of fiction.

But even to the due cultivation of those talents derived from nature much is still wanting, and the foundation of scholastic learning is yet to be laid. The very heavy expence, as well as the inconvenience attendant on sending boys to England, restrains most families from adopting this plan, whilst those who do it are apt to shorten their course so much that few have the advantage of a regular education; and thus each young man, in comparing the attainments of his contemporaries with his own, finds them so nearly on a scale, that he has no incitement from emulation to advance nearer the goal.

Whenever the present class of pedagogues shall give place to only one or two schoolmasters of real learning, this great disadvantage will be overcome; and as I know no place that offers a fairer opening to persons in this line, I trust the attempt will yet be made: but to the success of such an undertaking moderation of terms are essential at the outset, the value of education not being sufficiently appreciated to command profuse returns, especially before the inhabitants have ascertained the real existence of those abilities, which they have been taught to doubt, from the extravagant and unfounded pretensions by which they have too often been duped.

The Manx ladies would have just cause of complaint if I should pass them over in silent neglect, yet I confess I enter their coterie with some fear, lest those who do not know them should accuse me of flattery, and those who do should charge me with severity.

In speaking of the female part of the community, I shall pass lightly over the occasional visitors, and confine my remarks almost wholly to the natives. Those who have come hither from other countries have seldom presented good specimens. Either extravagance or necessity are badly calculated to form the character of woman in the best mould, and to one or other of these causes may be ascribed most of the emigrations which have hitherto taken place. Future writers will probably have better subjects to describe, but till now the most striking traits exhibited by these fair wanderers have been a sovereign contempt for those they came to live amongst, a prodigious flippancy, vast affectation of high breeding, and pretensions to a rank in their own country not always borne out by facts. With these ladies it was usual to pass their time in querulous regret at the fate which had condemned them to irradiate so low a sphere, and eager anticipations of their return to a more extended circle. The ill policy of showing this aversion to the retreat they had chosen must be plain to any comprehension! no one returns esteem for contempt, and nothing could be more natural than to join in the regret thus loudly expressed, that fortune had compelled them to take a station in society where they were neither welcome nor *invited* guests.

The generality of native ladies belong to that rank most favourable to feminine virtues, neither elevated by superior rank, talents, or attainments, nor sunk in vulgar and degrading ignorance. They are admirably calculated to perform their relative duties, and instances of dereliction are, in consequence, extremely rare. That they have not received the last polish, or acquired those arts which embellish the charms of virtue where she is, and outwardly supply her place where she is not, is most true; but neither do they exhibit those glaring vices, or that offensive disregard to propriety, which we *sometimes* see accompany extraordinary intellectual advantages.

The term *dashing* is not to be found in the Manx vocabulary, nor do the young ladies, or their mothers for them, lay violent hands on admiration, but rather wait with perfect quietness till it is spontaneously offered. I do not, indeed, consider the Isle of Man as the abode of Cupid or the Graces; in general, the marriages contracted by the natives (though they take place at rather an early age) are founded on prudential calculations. No man, however youthful, marries merely for love; yet, as soon as any one is established in business or housekeeping, he naturally looks out for a wife as a necessary appendage to his domestic economy, and in his choice is influenced by parity of circumstances, by early associations, or some such motives, independent of the tender passion. In general, the same quietude of sentiments actuates both sides, yet are these marriages, in most instances, fortunate in their results; a couple thus united live together on the best terms, they co-operate in their pursuits, habit soon gives them an undeviating conformity, and permits their lives to pass

"A clear united stream."

The ladies are, in general, admirable economists, and good mothers: they are rather fond of dress, but even this taste is so circumscribed, that it never leads them beyond the bounds of decency, whilst the vigilant superintendence of a narrow society restrains them from extravagance.

In the course of education pursued by the young ladies, all that is commonly called accomplishment is attained with such difficulty and expence, that the attempt is generally relinquished; for, although in Douglas there are two female schools of tolerable celebrity, yet their plans are too superficial for essential good, and their efforts entirely crippled by the want of masters to assist in those branches of knowledge usually conducted by the other sex.

The style of visiting is like that which prevails in most country towns in England; they meet to play cards, to practise a little extra-judicial inquiry into the proceedings of their neighbours, to relate their own domestic afflictions, to show their new clothes, and to kill time; but for any intellectual attainments, for any "burst of sentiment, or flow of soul," it is as little to be found or expected here, as in any other circle of the same confined dimensions. And I own I have often observed, with smiling wonder, the avidity with which they individually run from house to house all the morning, to repeat the same news, practise the same courtesies, and make the same inquiries separately, which the identical set must hear, see, and answer over again, collectively, in the evening. The only scenes of active and public amusement hitherto established, to bring the young people together, are monthly balls, which are well attended. I wonder nothing like a book society has been attempted amongst the ladies; I am persuaded they have capacities for higher attainments than they have yet pursued, and I should rejoice to see their associations take a superior tone.

I would fain persuade my contemporaries to assume the graces and charms of virtue in her best dress and character; to employ their time in acts of benevolence; to guide the ignorant, stimulate the idle, and substitute active goodness for the negative praise of harmlessness. In no place that I am acquainted with, are there better opportunities for this advance in real worth; the female character here presents almost a spotless surface! there are no prevalent vices to combat! no fashionable crimes to eradicate! all that is required is to improve, embellish, and call forth latent good qualities, and give efficacy to dormant virtues, a purpose which I have little doubt a very few examples would suffice to effect; and I think I cannot better conclude this short essay than with the character of a Manx lady not long since deceased, who, with only the narrow means of cultivation this island affords, presented in her life, and left behind at her death, a complete exemplification of *all* that is valuable in woman. I borrow the words from the sermon preached at her funeral, and I might call on the whole circle of her acquaintance, to say if the picture exhibits one exaggerated feature.

"Her piety, though silent in its exercises, and secret in its springs, powerfully influenced her life and conversation, sweetened her temper, softened her manners, and elevated her views. From the exercises of public worship, from the retirement of her closet, and the perusal of the sacred volume, she returned to the active duties of her family with renewed energy:—'Looking well to the ways of her household, and training up her children in the way they should go, the heart of her husband safely trusted in her, and she did him good all the days of her life.' All her duties were performed with singleness and sincerity; she walked in her family and neighbourhood as the angel of consolation, offering a balm for every wound, and a remedy for every distress. Often have the sick and dying experienced relief from her charitable aid, and often has her well-timed assistance suspended pain, and arrested the progress of misery.

"In discharge of her relative duties she was peculiarly exemplary. Her conduct as a daughter was marked by the most cheerful obedience, and the most watchful attention. No language can convey an idea of the tenderness of her affection for her partner in life;—she was his companion in health, his physician in sickness, ever anticipating his desires and preventing his wishes. Her attachment to her children was tender, rational, and constant: she taught them by her precepts, but still more by her example, to observe and adorn the doctrine of their Saviour in all things.

"The close of such a life might well be expected to be peace; and such it was, solid, substantial, well-grounded peace and hope: for although it was the will of heaven to remove her in the prime of life, and though her sufferings in the last week of her existence were calculated to try her faith and patience to the uttermost, yet she regarded them as the appointment of unerring wisdom, and endured them in silent tranquillity and resignation, exerting herself only to console those whom she was about to leave, and to point their hopes to a future meeting in bliss."*

I believe no Manx woman can peruse this eulogium without some degree of exultation, and I trust also, not without an earnest wish to follow such an admirable example.

The general description given of the Manx peasantry is, that they are sullen, unmoved by benefits, and to a degree beyond all bounds fond of litigation. I am not prepared wholly to deny these charges; but I think I may, without deviating from the strictest truth, offer something in the way of defence and explanation. Assuredly they are not a gracious people; they are slow in their apprehensions, and somewhat cold-hearted in manner, if not in reality, particularly towards strangers, of whom circumstances have engendered a degree of suspicion, which is now almost engrafted in their nature, and which only time, and an improved course of education, can eradicate. The charge of ingratitude also admits of considerable palliation. This sentiment, in uncultivated minds, must ever be in an exact ratio with *their sense* of the benefit conferred. Now it is most certain, that what an English peasant would consider as a state of actual starvation, is scarcely regarded by a Manxman as including any particular deprivation; from their birth they are habituated, without effort or design, to live very hardly. Herrings, potatoes, oatmeal, and these in very moderate quantities, are the general fare equally of the small native farmer and the labourer.

The latter resides contentedly in a cottage of mud, under a roof of straw, so low that a man of middling stature can hardly stand erect in any part of it. If to the common necessaries above stated the good people add a

---

* Extract from a funeral sermon preached on the death of Mrs. Stawell, by the Rev. Thomas Howard, vicar of Braddon.

stock of turf for the fire, and a cow fed in the lanes and hedges, they enjoy the utmost abundance of which they have any idea. A chaff bed for the whole family, a stool and a wooden table, constitute the furniture of the mansion; and here they vegetate in heaps, waiting the recurrence of the herring fishery for the renewal of plenty. When their stores fall somewhat short of their consumption, they take such calamities with patience as matters of course, which *must* happen, but for which the remedy will come of itself in due season; or may be sought in a case of extremity, by spending a day or two in labour at a neighbouring farm.

When therefore a stranger, viewing this scene with compassion, (because to him it would be a state of extreme misery,) satisfies his own feelings by gifts, which the objects of his pity never desired, and scarcely know how to use, ought he to wonder that he excites none of those sentiments of gratitude which the same benefits would naturally produce in other places? should he be angry that the Manxman understands as little of this refined feeling as he did of his own wants?

On the other hand, there are traits of hospitality inherent in the character of these peasants which bespeak a natural generosity, and which it is remarkable are preserved in the greatest purity, where their exercise must be attended with the most considerable self-denial. No cotter, however poor, will refuse to his neighbour or acquaintance a share of his herrings and potatoes, small as the portion may be that is provided for his own consumption; and though their miserable bed be crowded by a whole family, they still find a corner for a native traveller, who seeks the shelter of a lowly roof; and these good offices are extended with the most unaffected simplicity, and accepted more as a right than a favour.

The love of litigation is a charge which it is more difficult to meet with a due apology; yet even on this subject something may be said. In the first place it is almost wholly confined to the lower orders. In the higher circles of the Manx, whether gentry or traders, there is as little disposition to vexatious or petty suits, as in the same classes in other countries, where the access to law is guarded by expence and difficulty; on the other hand, the peasant has been accustomed from infancy to consider the deemster as the guardian of his rights, and an infallible decider of all disagreements, to whom he might apply whenever he felt himself injured or aggrieved, and that, not entirely in the character of a judge greatly elevated above himself, who must be approached with awe, and who from want of experience could enter into none of the petty grievances brought to his cognizance; but, on the contrary, the Manxman feels that this officer has a close and local knowledge of the character, circumstances, and family history of every client in his little district: and he remembers too, that a very short time perhaps has elapsed since the deemster moved in the same sphere with himself. Each man also, partial to his own cause, and knowing the decisions are to be governed by circumstances as they can be made to appear, has a hope, by telling his own story, of prevailing against his adversary. At all events the expence incurred is trifling, and the disgrace of failure none at all.

This habit of referring the merest trifles to judicial authority, diffuses a knowledge of the laws, or rather of the practice, neither beneficial nor improving. Every native man, woman, and *child*, understands the legal terms, and can dilate upon the history of actions, tokens, charges, and appeals, with technical precision; and the pertinacity with which a common peasant will pursue a cause through all the different courts, is both ridiculous and tormenting. I heard an instance in point from very high authority, which I shall repeat as it was related to me.

A man had made a charge of five shillings for digging a

grave, the customary price being only two shillings and sixpence. The affair was contended in the lowest ecclesiastical court, and in course given against the plaintiff, who thence carried it to the bishop, and being still foiled, has had the obstinacy to appeal to the metropolitan court at York, where this ridiculous cause is still pending. But these contentions are generally amongst themselves, and form but a trifling subject of annoyance to strangers, who, with very little temper and caution, may keep clear of these petty inconveniences, which will never wholly subside until the legislature shall impose a tax upon law proceedings, and thereby render them less accessible to the peasantry; or till the deemsters, being remunerated by government at a fixed and competent salary, in lieu of the fees now granted, shall find it for their own ease to discountenance litigation.

The only military force at present in the island are the volunteers, or local militia; there were formerly two fencible regiments of native troops in the pay of government, but these being reduced at different times, a regiment of veterans took their place, who were, however, recalled when the war broke out again. It is probable the present system will not continue long, but that either a permanent force will be raised within the island, or some regiment from Great Britain be stationed here, it being absolutely necessary to have some troops for the protection of the prisons, and also to guard the stores, and enforce the authority of the custom-house officers against smugglers. It is a curious fact, that during the long period of war, when it was universally allowed that a single privateer might have ravaged the island, or laid either of the towns in ashes before assistance or protection could be afforded from England, yet no care was taken to organize those means of defence which were easily within the reach of the inhabitants. It is true that at every commanding point, all round the coast, there were cannon; but these lay dismounted and useless, though, at the same time, government was paying a salary to an ordnance-keeper for his *neglect*. But immediately on the conclusion of peace, an engineer being sent over, has ever since been actively employed in building batteries, arranging stores of ammunition, and mounting the cannon, as if it had been apprehended that, when all the rest of Europe was restored to tranquillity, the arms of the united potentates would be turned against the Isle of Man alone; at any rate, if this idea is considered as futile, I must leave it to clearer politicians than myself to say, why these measures of precaution were not taken before? or why they have been taken now?

If what I have said has failed to convey a general idea of the society and manners of the people, I know not how I shall make my account more accurate. In fact, except a few national traits, which remain permanently fixed, the features of the whole people have ever been liable to great variation, and are constantly influenced by the different classes who come amongst them: of some of the most striking of these changes, it may be amusing, before we conclude, to take a slight review.

In the earliest times we imagine the court of the kings to have been adorned by knights and damsels, whom fancy is allowed to paint in all the spendour of chivalry and romance. Next we find a race of peasants in mud-walled cottages, decked out on holidays, and at fairs, in their *best blankets*, and leaving us in some doubt what kind of drapery was substituted on less important occasions; sunk in extreme ignorance, dozing amidst foggy mountains, and dreaming of an intercourse with fairies and mermaids, or trembling at the power of witches and demons.

The next great revolution converted these half stupified beings into a community having a mixed character between traders and robbers, who united the meanest traits of both professions, living by the exercise of fraud, and a sort of bastard courage called forth only by the prospect of gain, and wholly inapplicable to any better purpose. Hitherto they had formed little connexion with foreigners, or had been little visited by them; all their varieties had sprung from internal circumstances; but at length a new scene opened, since which the changes have been more rapid, and of shorter continuance.

Luxury, as it advanced in Great Britain, continually drove out those sons and daughters of dissipation, who had sacrificed too largely at her altars, to expiate their vices or their follies in other climes; and when the revolutionary war broke out, the continent being closed against such incursions, the Isle of Man became the sole retreat left open to them. At first, the animation and spirit which accompanied persons of this cast threw a charm over their derelictions, and the natives, dazzled by the polished manners and superior acquirements of their visitors, opened their hearts and their houses to them; but this cordiality was short lived. Gold had, at this time, become one of the household gods of the Manx, and it was not possible to preserve this deity inviolate from the attacks of the strangers: hence arose suspicion on one side, and contempt on the other; so that, at last, both parties drew off into separate associations, and all chance of conciliation was at an end. It is now about twelve years since this feud was at its height, and as that was the period of my arrival in the island, I was both astonished and alarmed at the enmity then existing between them. The weekly paper was the instrument of war, and the anger of both sides was vented in repartee and inuendo, in which attacks, it must be owned, the advantage lay with the strangers.

The Manx continually threatened to withdraw the protection afforded to these interlopers, who in their turn warned them, that the island would be ruined by such a measure: they insisted that all the prosperity of the country originated with them! that it was supported by their money, and might be civilized by their example. In fact, to listen only to one side, any one would have supposed these were a class of missionaries, who had made a pilgrimage with the disinterested view of diffusing light and wealth, whilst the Manx as sturdily denied the benefit, and expressed their wish to be left in mediocrity and ignorance, rather than be annoyed by the airs of superiority assumed over them. It was in the height of this contest that a new clan arrived to divert and occupy the public attention. These were a tribe of duellists, or what Addison would have called "*Mohawks*," chiefly drawn from the green shores of Erin; and no sooner had they landed than peace spread her wings, and for many months was heard of no more. I am not exaggerating when I assert, that every evening closed upon a quarrel, and every morning dawned upon a challenge! explanations! apologies! points of honour! and effusions of valour formed the sole subjects of discourse! No meeting, however peaceably arranged between the most intimate friends, could ever break up without a deadly feud, which nothing but lead and gunpowder could allay. For a length of time the whole island (but Douglas in particular,) was in a state of ferment, till the meetings grew so frequent that even terror was worn out, and it began to be observed, that by some lucky chance the heroes still gathered bloodless laurels; so that at last the heroines left off to faint or to fear, and it became necessary to make somebody weep, that every body might not laugh. At length two gentlemen did meet in *real earnest*, and one fell a victim to Moloch; yet such was the apathy with which the scene was regarded, that although at the moment of this melancholy event there were, as usual, a group of the "*Mohawk*" tribe assembled to witness the rencontre, yet did they all take to flight in different directions, and left the unhappy man to breathe his last unassisted and unsupported.

This is the first and last fatal duel upon record in the Isle of Man; since that time the "*Mohawks*" have "*worn their arms with a difference,"* and to a certain degree the peace of the community has been restored; the principals fled the island, and the rest of the parties, dividing the reflected glories of this exploit between them, sat down pretty quietly under the shade of their honours; only now and then taking advantage of the renewed fears of the ladies to mutter an execration, look fierce, and exhibit their skill at snuffing candles with pistol balls.

But as it is out of nature wholly to repress the effervescence of original fire, the "*Mohawks*" next assumed a new fancy; they clothed themselves in long dark cloaks, encouraged the growth of their whiskers and mustaches, girt their loins with leathern belts, in which they stuck pistols and a stiletto, and in this terrific array did a band of these worthies parade the streets of the town; yet I must do them the justice to say, I never heard of any essential mischief achieved by them, though one of them planted the lawn before his house with cannon, and certainly killed all the ducks and geese of a neighbouring farmer with grape-shot; but as he liberally paid the damage, it was, perhaps, as well as any other market to which the good dame could have sent her poultry.

Since this epoch there have been few striking alterations in the state of society, till the passing of the new act. At the present time all is peace and good order; the dissipated are nearly extirpated, the riotous effectually restrained, and, if I am not greatly mistaken in my calculations, the period is arrived when all distinctions being done away, the most easy and social intercourse will henceforth be established between natives and strangers, or rather, considering themselves as subjects of one government, the invidious distinction will be lost altogether in the common and enviable name of Britons.

Some characteristic Superstitions of the Manx.

THE lower and middle orders of the Manx are, in common with all uncultivated people, greatly addicted to superstition; they have the fullest belief in fairies and witchcraft, and to the supernatural influence of one of these imaginary powers nearly all the good or ill that befalls them is ascribed. As these popular prejudices sometimes throw a considerable light on the character of a nation or people, I shall relate a few of the most prevailing legends, as specimens of the general faith.

Each of the two castles of Rushen and Peel has its appropriate apparition. In Rushen are said to be subterraneous apartments, inhabited by genii and giants, their existence having been ascertained by more than one adventurous hero, whose intrepidity has carried them through the mists and obscurity in which the paths leading to these abodes are enveloped. Besides the secluded inhabitants, there are two spirits of different degrees of importance, the one being the apparition of a woman executed for infanticide; the other, no less a personage than the magnanimous Countess of Derby; who, it is constantly affirmed, takes her nightly round on the walls of the castle, where she has been encountered by a multitude of persons, and at great distances of time: but no one has yet had so much compassion on either of these perturbed spirits, as to ask the cause of their wanderings, without which formulæ, according to the established etiquette of ghostly courtesy, it is impossible they should either reveal their uneasiness, or rest in their graves.

At Peel Castle is a spectre of still greater notoriety, called the Manthé Doog, who, so long as the garrison was maintained, made his nightly visits to the guard-room, in the shape of a large black hound. This alarming visitor had continued the practice for so great a length of time, that the soldiers grew familiar with his presence, and one at length, inspired by liquor, took the resolution to follow the animal to his retreat, which none had yet ventured to explore. It was in vain his comrades sought to restrain the hardihood of this champion; he actually set out in pursuit of the mysterious intruder; but on his return, which was somewhat speedier than they had expected, he was deprived of all power to relate his adventures, being both speechless and convulsed, in which condition he remained three days, and then died. This tale is alluded to by Walter Scott, in his poem of Marmion.

"But none of all the astonish'd train
Were so dismay'd as Deloraine;
His blood did freeze, his brain did burn,
'Twas fear'd his mind would ne'er return;
For he was speechless, ghastly, wan!
Like him, of whom the story ran,
Who spake the spectre Hound in Man."

A long story is very gravely related in Sacheverel's account of the island, which I shall repeat in his own words. "In the year 1690, upon the late king's going to Ireland, a little boy, then scarce eight years old, frequently told the family in which he lived, of two fine gentlemen who daily conversed with him, gave him victuals, and something out of a bottle of a greenish colour, and sweet taste, to drink. This making a noise, the present deemster, a man of *good sense* and probity, went into the mountains to see if he could make any discovery what they were. He found the boy, who told him they were then sitting under a hedge about a hundred yards from him. The deemster bade the boy ask why he could not see them;

the boy accordingly went to the place, put off his cap, and made his reverence, and returning, said it was the will of God they should not be seen, but the gentlemen were sorry for his incredulity. The deemster then pulled out a crown-piece, and asked the boy what it was? He answered—he could not tell. He then bade him ask the gentlemen: from whom the child, returning again, told him they said it was silver, and had shown him a great deal of such silver, and some yellow silver besides.

"Another day, a neighbouring minister going into the mountains, the boy told him they were then in a barn hard by, exercising the pike. He went to the place pointed out, and saw a pitch-fork moving about in all the proper postures of exercise; upon which, rushing into the barn, the fork was struck to the roof, but no person to be seen. Another day, the boy came and told Captain Stevenson, that one of them came with his hand bloody, and said he had been in a battle in Ireland. The captain marked the day, and though they had no news for nearly a month after, yet, when it did come, it agreed exactly with the time Colonel Wolseley had given the Irish a considerable defeat.

"I could give you," adds this author, "a hundred other instances during their stay, which was above a month; but, at last, the king came with his fleet into Ramsay Bay, which, one of them telling the other before the boy, he answered, it was well the king was there in person, for if he had sent never so many generals his affairs would not prosper—and, speaking to the boy, told him they must go with the king into Ireland; that he might tell the people of the island that there would be a battle fought between Midsummer and St. Columbus' day, upon which the future fortune of Ireland would depend, which exactly agreed with the battle of the Boyne; that the war would last ten or twelve years, but that, in the end, King William would be victorious over all his enemies."

Nor is the belief in these supernatural appearances become obsolete; to this moment, every damsel who rambles beyond the precincts of the farm-yard at night, incurs the danger of meeting fairies, and it is seldom they return without a circumstantial history of miraculous adventures. Collins, the poet, calls Man the "fairy-land." And as to the influence of witchcraft, it is an article of faith standing on much higher ground than the creed.

If a fisherman makes one or two unsuccessful trips, he instantly proceeds to exorcise his boat by burning gorze or straw in the centre, and carrying the flaming material to every crevice where it is supposed the evil spirit may continue to lurk. If a cow is diseased, or any difficulty occurs in churning, the operation of the *evil eye* is immediately suspected, and a strict inquiry is made as to who may have been lately upon the spot; for the power of doing mischief is by no means confined to a few malignant individuals, but seems to be generally ascribed by every one to an adversary, or a rival.

Conversing on this subject with a farmer of good information on general affairs, he expressed the utmost astonishment, not unmixed with terror, at the scepticism with which I listened to some of these supernatural histories, in confirmation of which he related one story, to the truth of which he offered to bring unquestionable evidence, if my unbelief should yet maintain its ground. He asserted, that two years before that time, he and a neighbour were in treaty for the sale and purchase of a pony, but differing about the price, his neighbour, vexed at his disappointment, *put an evil eye* upon the beast, which *instantly*, and without other visible cause, became so lame as to be wholly useless, and so continued for twelve months; when, by extraordinary good luck, another person called on him, who had on his part the power to discern these unrighteous influences where they had been exercised, and to do them away by a counter charm. No sooner had this man cast his eyes on the animal, than he pronounced his lameness to have originated with the malignant purchaser, and after performing certain ceremonies, he assured my informer that the spell was broken, and that within a few hours the pony would be restored to perfect soundness and strength, all which, in course, happened as foretold.

The witches and fairies of Man are neither supposed to combine, nor to produce exactly the same effects by their power, the former being wholly employed in acts of aggression, whilst the latter have a mixed jurisdiction, and can produce both good and evil by their operations. They are accustomed to perform certain frolics, which show some degree of humour and whim in their propensities: they are also easily assailable by bribes: thus the dairy-maid, who would spare herself unusual exertion, regularly makes the offering of a small pat of butter, or a piece of cheese curd, which is affixed to the wall of the dairy, and is believed to propitiate these invisible agents. The livers of fowls and fish are uniformly sacrificed to the fairies. At Midsummer-eve, when their power is of unlimited extent, flowers and herbs are the only barriers to their incursions, and these are regularly spread on the door and window-sill to protect the inhabitants.

But one of the most curious ceremonies, and which, I believe, is peculiar to the Isle of Man, is, that of *hunting the wren*, founded on a tradition, that in former times a fairy of uncommon beauty exerted such undue influence over the male population, that she at various times seduced numbers to follow her footsteps, till, by degrees, she led them into the sea, where they perished. This barbarous exercise of power had continued for a great length of time, till it was apprehended the island would be exhausted of its defenders, when a knight-errant sprung up, who discovered some means of countervailing the charms used by this syren, and even laid a plot for her destruction, which she only escaped at the moment of extreme hazard, by taking the form of a *wren*; but though she evaded instant annihilation, a spell was cast upon her, by which she was condemned on every succeeding New Year's Day, to re-animate the same form, with the definitive sentence, that she must ultimately perish by a human hand. In consequence of this *well authenticated* legend, on the specified anniversary, every man and boy in the island (except those who have thrown off the trammels of superstition,) devote the hours between sun-rise and sun-set to the hope of extirpating the fairy, and woe be to the individual birds of this species, who show themselves on this fatal day to the active enemies of the race: they are pursued, pelted, fired at, and destroyed, without mercy, and their feathers preserved with religious care, it being an article of belief, that every one of the relics gathered in this laudable pursuit is an effectual preservative from shipwreck for one year; and that fisherman would be considered as extremely foolhardy, who should enter upon his occupation without such a safeguard.

Another tradition, preserved by Waldron in his Account of the Isle of Man, relates, that about fifty years before his residence there, an adventure had been achieved, of which there were living witnesses in his time. It originated in a project, which was conceived by some philosophers, to fish up treasures from the deep, by means of a diving-bell. A venturous hero being enclosed in one of these machines was let down, and, in his descent, continued to pull for more rope, till all they had on board was completely expended, though such had been their precaution, that they had gone out provided with a length of line which, according to their calculation, was sufficient to descend at least double the number of leagues that the moon is computed to be distant from the earth! At such an extreme depth as this adventurer had explored, great wonders might reasonably be expected, and such he encountered, for when, after awaiting his further signal till their patience was exhausted, his companions wound up the rope, and brought the submarine traveller to the upper regions again; he gave a most splendid account of the scenes he had left —"After," said he, "I had passed the region of fishes, I descended into a pure element, clear as air, through which, as I floated, I saw the bottom of the watery world, paved with coral and a shining kind of pebble, which glittered like sun-beams reflected on glass. On looking through the little windows of my prison, I saw streets and squares on every side, ornamented with huge pyramids of crystal, and one building in particular attracted my attention, composed of mother-of-pearl, embossed with shells of various descriptions, and all colours. Having with infinite difficulty forced my enclosure towards this palace, I got entrance into a very spacious room ; the furniture was amber, and the floor inlaid with diamonds, topazes, rubies, and emeralds: I saw also several rings, chains, and carkanets, of all manner of precious stones, set after our fashions, which, I suppose, had been the prey of the winds and waves. These were hanging loosely on the jasper walls, and I could easily have made a booty of immense value, if, at the moment when I had edged my machine near enough to reach them, you had not interposed between me and my good fortune, by the precipitancy with which I was drawn back at the moment of success."*

This story, which, at least, proves the poetical talent of the adventurer, may serve the metrical tale-mongers of the present day, and give a little variety and relief from the tiresome sameness of silver moon-beams and verdant meadows, especially if duly interspersed with the loves of the mermen and maids, who, according to the narrator, inhabit these splendid abodes.

* See Waldron's Works, page 176.

Prices of Provisions—Rent—Servants' Wages, &c.

ALL that remains of my task is to give that promised scale of prices, which may enable persons interested in the inquiry, to form an estimate of the expences incident to a residence in the Isle of Man.

Rent will be found to be the heaviest article of family expenditure. A respectable house of from ten to twelve rooms can scarcely be met with in a good situation, either in Douglas or Castletown, under £30 or £40 per annum. The towns of Ramsay and Peel offer accommodations at a much lower price. Lodgings furnished are let in proportion; unfurnished, few can be met with.

The best mode of providing moveables is from Liverpool, where they can be purchased cheaper, freight included, than in the island; except at sales, whence many persons collect their furniture on very moderate terms: but these transfers of property are much less frequent than they were, when the resort of strangers was greater.

Wages of female domestics are in proportion to their abilities, from £4 to £7 per annum. Those who neglect to hire at May and November are often greatly inconvenienced, as in the intervals few good servants can be met with. The natives will always be preferred on experience, notwithstanding they are somewhat less intelligent, yet are they much more trustworthy than those from the neighbouring counties, for this obvious reason, that persons of good character in that class will hardly find it necessary to leave their native place in pursuit of *lower wages*. Men servants, to occupy the posts of butler, groom, or even footman, are hardly to be procured: their salaries are in consequence quite undetermined.

Butchers' meat is somewhat above the proportionate rate of other articles, except pork, which is often as low as 3d. a pound; for the rest, beef, mutton, and veal, average 7d. Wheat is at this time only 3s. the bushel; fine flower 20s. coarse 17s. the cwt. Oatmeal is an article of general consumption, being made into flat cakes as a substitute for wheaten bread, and always used at the servant's table.

Of well fed and full grown fowls, or ducks the price is 2s 6d. the couple; a goose from 2s. 6d. to 3s. a turkey from 3s to 5s. Fish is abundant and cheap; a good dish may almost always be had for one shilling, sometimes for half the sum. The sorts most abundant, besides herrings, are rock cod, whiting, mackerel, gurnet, haddock, with most kinds of flat fish. None of the shell fish are very plentiful, except crabs. Scollops and lobsters are to be met with in the season; the latter, large and small together, are sold for 9s. the dozen. The oysters on the coast are not good, but a supply sometimes come in from Ireland.

Wines and liquors are articles of luxury, to be had on very moderate terms. Port about 28s. the dozen, which is of an excellent quality; the white wines are neither so good nor so cheap; and with regard to the former, it is much the best plan to import a pipe. This is usually done by economists; and where the quantity is too much for one family, two or more join together, and by this means procure a better article considerably under the retailer's price. Rum is 9s. the gallon, brandy 12s. geneva 10s. As a custom prevails of rewarding all small services with a glass, it is the practice with most people to be provided with an inferior sort of rum for this purpose. Ale is sold in barrels at one shilling the gallon; but this price is far beyond the average of malt and hops; and if families were to adopt the practice of brewing for their own consumption, they would find an essential saving.

Coals are from 26s. to 34s. according to quantity, or scarcity, per ton. Grocery is regulated by the English price, except tea, which is much lower. A new settler is at first much puzzled by the difference between Manx and English money. In general the prices charged in the shops are calculated on British currency, but the dealings in the market, and with the country people, are carried on usually upon the old terms of 14d. to the shilling. Butter is from 10d. to 1s. the pound; eggs twenty for a shilling on an average of the year.

All that I have now stated refers to a residence in the towns; but persons to whom a strict economy is either desirable or necessary, would in all probability find it combined with more ease and comfort at a short distance in the country, where very good family houses are easily attainable, with ten or twenty acres of land, on moderate terms. The wages of a labourer are from £12 to £14 per annum with his board; or if he maintains himself, and is a superior workman, 12s. per week in summer, and 10s. in winter. The price of a good cow in full milk is from £10 to £14 according to the size. The quantity of milk averages about four gallons per diem; two of these will supply a moderate family with seven or eight pounds of butter per week, besides the ordinary consumption of milk and cream. If, in addition, they can raise their own grain, potatoes, and poultry, the articles to be purchased with money come within a very moderate compass. I know several families of eight or ten persons who have adopted this system, and live in the utmost ease and abundance on £300 per annum, many of them *keeping a carriage*, by which, however, I mean simply a convenience for moving from place to place, combining neither show nor state, driven by the labourer in his Sunday clothes, sitting behind the same horses he at other times follows in the plough or the cart: for as there are no taxes on these sort of vehicles, nor even a turnpike to add to the charges, the first cost is the whole consideration, and this may be large or small according to the taste or the ability of the purchaser.

The foregoing estimate, I think, cannot fail to prove the assertion, that in point of expence the Isle of Man offers a favourable retreat for persons of middling fortune: for if the advantage and recommendations thus set forth, are not considered as more than a counterbalance to the few defects and inconveniences which I have stated with equal impartiality, it must be that *I* have failed in my intended description of both; or that an undue weight is given to points which, in fact, though material blemishes in the constitution, are yet far from being generally felt. In writing the history of the island, and particularly of its present state, I should have been justly chargeable with disingenuity if I had disguised or omitted palpable facts; but nothing can be more true, than that numbers have resided for years without feeling the operation of these evils, which are like a latent or an hereditary distemper, neither felt nor seen till concurring circumstances awaken or call forth the lurking evil.

A short space of time, a little correction of defects in the laws, and a hearty co-operation with future settlers, is, I am persuaded, all that is wanted to restore the island to a higher degree of prosperity than it has ever yet known. The Isle of Man has within itself the seeds both of ease and plenty; and surely the wisdom to give them due cultivation, will not be wanting in a people who have in the last few years made such rapid advances in intellectual improvement.

To Europe; upon, I think, as useful a time exercise, that is point of extent, the U. S. of [A]... of a reasonable return for pains and trouble taken, the objects and recompense etc. thus set forth, in not considered as more than a counterbalance to the laws, debts and circumstances which I have stated with equal impartiality; it must be that I have told in my candid description of both; or that to undue weight is given to points which, in fact, though material blemishes in the constitution, are yet for form's sake generally felt. In writing the history of this Land, and particulars of it, pass it over, I will have been pretty obliged to with delicacy, if I had dispensed as connected to public interests; but nothing can be worse than that any has been, which is a satire and feeling the opposition to those evils which enable a just cause, in a thirsty distempter, well. Men are in the case, acting a contusion or where no evil finds it, but in its self.

A short episode of time, a little correction or defects in the land, and be in co-operation with future settlers, etc. I am persuaded, will it is wanted to restore the island to its former complete quality to this that we know it is, of Man has within itself the sole basis of existing up, instead of the wisdom to equal than its culture to a stand. How it could be in a people who live to the adverse in they to seek fresh advances in intellectual attainment.

APPENDIX.

No. 1.

Rev. Mr. Wilson's Letter to the Earl of Derby.

MY LORD,

NOTHING but a sense of duty and gratitude would have put me upon this liberty; but because I have reason to believe it concerns your lordship, I can willingly hazard all future favours your lordship designs me, rather than be silent in a matter of this moment; though I have no reason to fear any such consequences. I do, therefore, with all imaginable submission, offer these following particulars to your consideration.

First, Though several of the debts be, as your lordship urges, unjust, and, perhaps, most of the bills in part unreasonable, yet is it very probable that a great many are really just; and if these are not paid, those who suffer have just complaint to God and man, which must certainly have an ill influence on your lordship's affairs.

Secondly, That several in this neighbourhood are undone, if they are not speedily considered; they are forced to the last necessity, some to sell their estates, others to leave their country, or lie in jail for debts which are owing to them from your lordship. They come day after day with tears and petitions, which nobody takes any notice of; and so your lordship never comes to know what they suffer. Your lordship sees what methods the rest, who are more able, are taking; and you best know what may be the consequence: but however it ends, if their demands are just, they will still have reason to complain of the wrong that is done them.

Your lordship is never suffered to know the influence these things have on your temporal affairs; but I am ready to make it out, whenever your lordship shall think it your interest to inquire into this matter, that you constantly pay one-third more for what you want than other people do. I know very few care or are concerned at this; but I cannot but see and lament this hardship, which cannot possibly be remedied till your lordship has taken some order with your creditors, and reformed those who have the disposal of your monies.

I am not able to foresee how these things will end, and one cannot tell what they may be forced to attempt. It is too likely that if any disturbance happen in the government, their wants may make them desperate, and their numbers insolent. I have been lately told, some of them have threatened some such thing. And now, my lord, if I have said any thing unbecoming me, I hope your lordship will pardon me, and think it a fault of indiscretion rather than design. I mean honestly, and that your lordship may think so, I do protest in the presence of God, that I had rather beg all my life than be so far wanting to my duty, as not to have given you these short hints, which your lordship could not possibly have, but from some faithful servant, as I presume to subscribe myself, &c. &c. &c.

THOMAS WILSON.

No. 2.

Bishop Wilson's Character of his Wife, extracted from the Prayer composed by him on her Death.

The memory of the just is blessed.—*Prov. x. 7.*

ALMIGHTY God, the author of life and death, who dost not afflict willingly, nor grieve the children of men; I do, in all humility, submit my will entirely to thine, most humbly beseeching thee to accept of my thanks and praise for all the graces and favours vouchsafed to my wife, now in peace; for her great modesty and meekness of spirit; for her remarkable duty to her parents, and love to her relations; for her great love to me and my friends, and for her fidelity to her marriage-vows; for her tender affection for her children, in performing all the offices of a kind and pious mother; for her peculiar care of her family, and the prudence and mildness by which she governed it; for her unaffected modesty in her own and her children's apparel, and the great humility of her conversation with all sorts of persons; for her great compassion for the poor and miserable, and her cheerful compliance with me in relieving them.

I bless thy holy name for these, and all other fruits of thy holy Spirit; but above all, I most heartily thank the Lord for her piety to him during her health, and for his mercies to her in the time of sickness; for her hearty repentance, stedfast faith in the promises of the Gospel's unfeigned charity; her humble submission to God's good pleasure, and patient suffering what his hand had laid upon her; for all the spiritual comforts the gracious God did vouchsafe her, the opportunities of receiving the blessed sacrament, the prayers of the faithful, the ministry of absolution, and the assistance of her pious friends at the hour of death.

With these reflections I comfort my soul, stedfastly believing, that none of these graces and favours were lost upon her; but that she departed in the true faith and fear of God; and therefore I do humbly pray to thee, Oh blessed Jesus, in whose hands are the souls of the faithful, after they are delivered from the burthen of the flesh, that we may in thy good time meet in joy, and have our perfect consummation in bliss, both in body and soul, in thine eternal kingdom, &c.

See Life of Thomas Wilson, 4to. vol. I. p. 32.

No. 3.

Bishop Wilson's Address to his Children.

MY DEAR CHILDREN,

IF I do not live to tell you why I have saved no more for you out of my bishopric, let this satisfy you: that the less you have of goods gathered from the church, the better the rest that I leave you will prosper. Church livings were never designed to make families, or to raise portions out of them, but to maintain our families, to keep up our hospitality, to feed the poor, &c. And one day you will be glad that this was my settled opinion; and God grant that I may act accordingly!

Remember, that the daughter of a priest, if taken in a fault, was to be put to death under Moses's law. Lev. xxi. 9.

I never expect, and I thank God I never desire, that you or your children should ever be great; but if ever the providence of God should raise any that proceed from my loins to any degree of worldly wealth or honour, I desire they will look back to the place and person from whence they came. This will keep them humble and sober minded. But above all, I desire they will never think themselves too good to be servants.

APPENDIX.

No. 4.

Bishop Wilson's Letter to the Keys.

To the Twenty-four Keys, Representatives of the Commons of this Isle.

GENTLEMEN,

AMONG the many indignities put upon us, the bishop and vicars general, of late years, by the temporal court, that of being fined at the last Tynwald is not the least afflicting. In regard that whatsoever is said to be done at that solemn assembly, (as is the order for fining us,) will by posterity be understood to have been done with the knowledge and approbation of the whole, which consisting of the governor, council, deemsters, and twenty-four keys, we desire to know whether you, the said keys, were made acquainted with, or gave your consent to, the said order, or to our present imprisonment?

And forasmuch as we were that day openly charged with exercising a spiritual tyranny, you who dwell in several parts of this isle, may do us the justice of testifying whether you know or believe there be any just cause for so heavy, and (as we persuade ourselves) so groundless an imputation.

THOMAS SODOR AND MAN.
WILLIAM WALKER, } Vicars General.
JOHN CURGHEY.

Dated Castle Rushen, July 10, 1722.

APPENDIX.

The Answer of the Keys.

MY LORD AND REV. GENTLEMEN,

WE the Keys of Man, as well to satisfy your lordship, and you the ecclesiastical judges, as to justify ourselves to posterity, do hereby certify and declare, that though we were present at the Tynwald during the whole time of the sitting of the court, and until the same was dismissed as usual, we were neither made acquainted with nor gave our consent to the order you mention; neither was any such order there made or concerted; and therefore we could not but be much surprised to hear of your being then fined, and afterwards imprisoned.

As to the charge of exercising a spiritual tyranny, we do solemnly testify (as we are in duty bound) that there is no cause to us known for so strange an imputation, being verily persuaded, that you have been so far from assuming to yourselves an undue authority, that the church was never better governed than in your time, nor justice more impartially administered in the ecclesiastical courts of this isle.

J. STEVENSON,	PHIL. MOORE,
ROBT. CURPHEY,	J. WATTLEWORTH, JUN.
WM. CHRISTIAN,	JAS. CHRISTIAN,
SIL. RATCLIFFE,	JOHN CURGHEY,
THOS. CORLET,	JOHN MURRAY,
JAMES BANCKES,	EDMUND CORLET,
THOS. CHRISTIAN,	JOHN CHRISTIAN.

I, Thomas Stevenson, not being present at the Tynwald, agree with my brethren only in respect of the latter clause.

THOS. STEVENSON.

Mem. Five of our members were absent at the signing hereof.

JOHN STEPHENSON.

Castletown, July 11, 1722.

See Appendix to the Life of Thomas Wilson, 4to. vol. 1, p. 112.

No. 5.

TO THE KING'S MOST EXCELLENT MAJESTY.

THE humble petition of Thomas Wilson, D. D. in behalf of his father, the Bishop of Man, and the inhabitants of the island, humbly sheweth,

By the late embargo, and an act of Parliament just now passed, the corn and provisions are prohibited from being exported to the Isle of Man, from any port of the three kingdoms; by which means your petitioner's father, and the inhabitants of that place, labour under the inexpressible want of provisions, especially bread corn; so that, if not speedily relieved, many thousands are in imminent danger of being starved. And what adds to their melancholy circumstances is, that it hath pleased God to afflict them with a pestilential flux, owing, in a great measure, to the want of wholesome food.

In this deplorable case they have no other way left, but to apply to his sacred majesty, the father of his people, that he will be graciously pleased to order a certain quantity of bread corn from the ports of Liverpool or Whitehaven; they giving security that it shall be landed and expended only for the use of the inhabitants of the Isle of Man. The granting of which will for ever lay the said bishop and the inhabitants under the most lasting sense of gratitude, and the sincerest acknowledgments for a favour to which they are to owe their health and lives.

No. 6.

Letter to the King.

MAY IT PLEASE THE KING'S MOST SACRED MAJESTY

To receive the most grateful acknowledgments of the ancient Bishop of Man, for his majesty's great condescension and late royal favour to the son of the bishop, whose obscure diocese, and remote situation, might justly have forbid him all expectations of so high a nature from a royal hand. May both the father and the son ever act worthy of so distinguishing a favour! and may the King of kings bless his majesty with all the graces and virtues which are necessary for his high station and for his eternal happiness, and enable his majesty to overcome all the difficulties he shall meet with abroad,* and bring him back to his kingdoms here in peace and safety; and finally to an everlasting kingdom hereafter; which has been and shall be the sincere and constant prayer of his majesty's most grateful, dutiful, and faithful subject and servant,

THOMAS SODOR AND MAN.

Isle of Man, May 3, 1743.

* The king was in Hanover.

Letter to his Son at the same time.

I AM both surprised and pleased with the unexpected favours conferred upon you, both by the king and the Bishop of Salisbury. I hope in God you will answer the great ends of his providence, in raising you such friends, and in putting into your hands such unlooked-for talents, in order to improve them to his glory, and to your own salvation. For my own part, I have ever received such favours with fear, lest I should be tempted to dishonour God by his own gifts; and it shall be my daily prayers for you that you may never do so. This was the case with the wisest and greatest of men, whose history and fall were part of this day's service of the church.

Enclosed you have a letter to his majesty. Perhaps, you may not approve of the style *(his* instead of *your* majesty,) but I know it to be more becoming, and will be better accepted by a foreigner, and therefore it shall pass.

I have also written to the Bishop of Salisbury, to whom my most grateful service and thanks. According to my notion of writing to his majesty, I ought not to have subscribed my name; but I have done it, lest you should have thought otherwise.

No. 7.

Heads of a Bill, proposed in Tynwald, for Amendment of the Criminal Law.

ISLE *of Man to wit.*—WHEREAS, by an act of Tynwald, promulgated in the year of our Lord 1737, it is enacted, that "No court, judge, or magistrate, within this isle whatsoever, shall have power or authority for the future to impose or inflict any fines or punishment upon any person or persons within the said isle, for or on account of any criminal cause whatsoever, until he, she, or they be first convicted by the verdict or presentment of four, six, or more men, as the case shall require, upon some statute law in force in the said isle." And whereas doubts have been entertained whether such act of Tynwald extends to treasons and felonies at and by the common law of the island, or only to other smaller crimes, offences, and misdemeanors.—We therefore, &c. And be it enacted, &c. &c. That the said act of Tynwald shall not be construed to extend to any treason or felony which subsists at, by, and under the common law of the island.—And whereas it is expedient that certain treasons, felonies, misdemeanors, crimes, and offences should be described with greater certainty than has hitherto been done by the laws of the island; and that certain other crimes and offences should be enacted and declared to be treasons, felonies, and misdemeanors.—Be it therefore further enacted,

TREASONS.

1. That the felonious and traitorous compassing or imagining the death of our sovereign lord the king, of our

lady the queen, or of their eldest son and heir, is and shall be held to be *high treason*, and punishable by death.

2. That the felonious and traitorous violation of the king's companion, or king's eldest daughter, unmarried, or the wife of the king's eldest son and heir, is and shall be held to be *high treason*, and punishable by death.

3. That the felonious and traitorous levying war against our sovereign lord the king in his realm, is and shall be held to be *high treason*, and punishable by death.

4. That the felonious and traitorous adhering to the king's enemies in his realm, the giving them aid and comfort in the realm, or elsewhere, is and shall be held to be *high treason*, and punishable by death.

5. That the felonious and traitorous counterfeiting the king's great seal, or privy seal, or his sign manual, or privy signet, is and shall be held to be *high treason*, and punishable by death.

6. That the felonious and traitorous counterfeiting the king's money, or the bringing false money into the said isle, counterfeit to the king's coin, knowing such money to be false, to merchandize, and making payment withal, is and shall be held to be *high treason*, and punishable by death.

7. That the felonious and traitorous slaying the king's governor, the king's lieutenant governor, the members of the council, or any of them, the deemsters, or either of them, the keys, or any of them, being in their places, doing their offices, is and shall be held to be *high treason*, and punishable by death. And be it further enacted, &c. That nothing shall be adjudged to be high treason in the said isle, but what is in and by this act enacted, declared, and described to be high treason, and that no person or persons shall be attainted of any of the treasons enacted, declared, and described by this act, except on some open and overt act and deed, charged against him, her, or them.

FELONIES.

8. That the unlawful and felonious killing of another, with malice aforethought, either express or implied, is and shall be held to be felony and *murder*, and punishable by death.

9. That the felonious ravishment and carnal knowledge of a woman, against her will, is and shall be held to be felony and *rape*, and punishable by death.

10. That the felonious ravishment and carnal knowledge of a female child, under the age of ten years, either with or without her consent, is and shall be held to be felony and *rape*, and punishable by death.

11. That the felonious and carnal knowledge, against the order of nature, by mankind with mankind, or with brute beast, is and shall be held to be felony and *buggery*, and punishable by death.

12. That the felonious breaking and entering into the dwelling-house of another by night, with an intention to commit a felony, any person or persons being then inhabiting in such house, is and shall be held to be felony and *burglary*, and punishable by death.

13. That the felonious, wilful, and malicious burning of the house, mill, out-house, office, barn, stable, ship, boat, or vessel, of another, any person or persons being then in any such building, ship, boat, or vessel, other than the perpetrator or perpetrators of such burning, or aiding and assisting therein, is and shall be held to be felony and *arson*, and punishable by death.—And that the felonious, wilful, and malicious burning of any stack of corn, stack of hay, stack of straw, stack of furze, stack of turf, stack of ling, stack of fern, stack of wood, or stack of potatoe haulm, of another, any such stacks being adjoining to any house, out-house, office, barn, or stable, in any of which buildings any person or persons shall then be, other than the perpetrator or perpetrators of such burning, or the

aiding and assisting therein, is and shall be held to be felony and *arson*, and punishable by death.

14. That the felonious and forcible stealing, taking, and carrying away from the person of another, of goods or money, of any value, by violence, or putting such person in fear, is and shall be held to be felony and *robbery*, and punishable by death.

15. That the felonious *returning from transportation*, or the being seen at large within the said isle, without lawful cause, before the expiration of the term for which the offender was ordered to be transported, or had agreed to transport himself, or herself, is and shall be held to be felony, and punishable by death.

16. That the felonious and false making, *forging*, counterfeiting, or altering, or causing, or procuring to be falsely made, forged, counterfeited, or altered, or the willingly acting or assisting in the false making, forging, counterfeiting, or altering any act of Tynwald, or any decree, judgment, or execution, or any record or process of any of the courts of the said isle, or any verdict of any jury, or deposition of any witness, duly taken and signed by or before any court, magistrate, or jury, within the said isle, or any deed, charter, writing sealed, court roll, will, writing testamentary, bond, writing obligatory, memorial of the inrolment or registration of any deed or will, bill of exchange, promissory note for the payment of money, acquittance, receipt, either for money or goods, release or discharge of any debt, account, action, suit, or demand, the number of any principal sum of any accountable receipt for any note, bill, or other security, for the payment of money, or any warrant or order for payment of money, or delivery of goods, with the intention to defraud any person or corporation whatsoever, is and shall be held to be *forgery* and felony, and punishable by death, or transportation for life, at the discretion of the court of general gaol delivery, according to the malignity of the offence.

17. That the felonious *uttering, or publishing as true, any false*, forged, counterfeited, or altered act of Tynwald, or any decree, judgment, or execution, or any record or process of any of the courts, or any verdict of any jury, or deposition of any witness, duly taken and signed by or before any court, magistrate, or jury, within the said isle, or any deed, charter, writing sealed, court roll, will, writing testamentary, bond, writing obligatory, memorial of the inrolment or registration of any deed or will, bill of exchange, promissory note for the payment of money, indorsement, assignment, or acceptance of any bill of exchange, or promissory note for the payment of money, acquittance or receipt, either for money or goods, release or discharge for any debt, account, action, suit or other demand, the number of any principal sum of any accountable receipt for any note, bill, or other security for the payment of money, or any warrant or order for the payment of money or delivery of goods, with the intention to defraud any person or corporation whatsoever, knowing the same to be false, forged, counterfeited, or altered, is and shall be held to be felony, and punishable by death or transportation for life.—And be it enacted, that an act of Tynwald, passed in the year of our Lord 1797, *intituled*, "An Act for the punishment of Forgery, &c." shall, as to all offences which shall be committed after the promulgation of this act, be and stand repealed.

18. That the felonious and unlawful stealing, taking, and carrying away of the personal goods of another, of the value of ten shillings or more, is and shall be held to be *grand larceny*, and punishable by death, or transportation for life, at the discretion of the court.—Provided, nevertheless, that the felonious and unlawful *stealing, taking, and carrying away of one or more sheep*, or of any lamb, goat, or kid, of whatsoever value the same respectively may be, is and shall be held to be grand larceny, and punishable by transportation for life.

19. That the felonious *receiving of stolen goods, of the value of ten shillings* or more, knowing them to be stolen, is and shall be held to be felony, and punishable by death, or transportation for life, at the court's discretion.

20. That the felonious, wilful, and *malicious burning* of the house, mill, out-house, office, barn, stable, ship, boat, or vessel of another, or others, no person or persons being then therein, other than the perpetrator or perpetrators of such burning, or aiding and assisting therein; and that the felonious, wilful, and malicious burning of the stack of corn, stack of hay, stack of straw, stack of furze, stack of turf, stack of fern, stack of potatoe haulm, or stack of wood, of another, none of such stacks being adjoining to any house, out-house, office, barn, or stable, in any of which buildings any person or persons shall then be, other than the perpetrator or perpetrators of such burning, or aiding and assisting therein, are and shall be respectively held to be felony and *arson*, and punishable by transportation for life.

21. That the felonious, wilful, and *malicious shooting* at any person, with intent to slay or wound such person, where death does not ensue, &c. is and shall be held to be felony, and punishable by transportation for life.

22. That the felonious, violent, and *malicious wounding*, disabling, mutilating, and disfiguring of another, is and shall be held to be felony and *mayhem*, and punishable by transportation for seven or fourteen years, at the discretion of the court.

MISDEMEANORS.

23. And be it further enacted, by the authority aforesaid, that the making a *wilful, corrupt, and false oath*, in any matter or cause, legally depending in any suit or variance, by any warrant, citation, process, writ, action, bill, libel, complaint, petition, information, or indictment,

in any of the courts within the said isle, or before any magistrate, jury, person or persons, duly authorized by the laws of the said isle, to administer such oath, is and shall be held to be wilful and corrupt *perjury*, and a high misdemeanor, and punishable by fine, and imprisonment, and the loss of an ear, to be taken off at the public market-place.

24. That the unlawful and corruptly *causing or procuring* any person to commit wilful and corrupt perjury as aforesaid, is and shall be held to be *subornation of perjury*, and punishable by fine, and imprisonment, and the loss of an ear.

25. That the falsely and designedly obtaining any monies, goods, wares, or merchandises, from any person or persons, by means of any false token, counterfeit letter, or by any other false pretence or pretences whatsoever, with the intention to cheat or defraud any person or persons, is and shall be held to be *cheating and swindling*, and a misdemeanor, punishable by fine and imprisonment, and corporal punishment.

26. That the knowingly *sending or delivering any letter or letters*, with or without a name or names subscribed thereto, or signed by a fictitious name or names, letter or letters, threatening to accuse any person or persons of any crime, punishable by the laws of the said isle, with intent to extort or gain money, goods, wares, or merchandises, is and shall be held to be a misdemeanor, and punishable by fine and imprisonment, and corporal punishment.

27. That the unlawful stealing, taking, and carrying away of the personal goods of another, under the value of ten shillings, is and shall be held to be *petty larceny*, and a misdemeanor, punishable by fine and imprisonment, and corporal punishment.

28. That the doing of *wilful and malicious mischief* and damage to any of the buildings, lands, trees, shrubs, mounds, dikes, fences, ships, boats, horses, sheep, cattle,

or to any other goods and chattels of another, shall be proceeded against in the manner prescribed in and by an act of Tynwald, passed in the year 1753, intituled, "An Act for the better preventing Petty Larceny and Trespass," and shall be punishable as a misdemeanor by fine and imprisonment, besides compensation to the party aggrieved, in the manner prescribed by the said act.

29. That the unlawful killing of another, without malice either express or implied, is and shall be held to be *manslaughter*, and a misdemeanor, punishable by fine and imprisonment, and corporal punishment. Provided that, in all trials for murder, if the jury shall be of opinion, and find that the party accused has been guilty of man-slaughter only, the said jury shall, by their verdict, find him or her guilty of manslaughter; and that, in all trials for manslaughter, if the jury shall be of opinion, and find that the party accused has been guilty of murder, the said jury shall, by their verdict, indict him or her as for murder.

30. That if any woman shall *conceal her being with child*, during the whole period of her pregnancy, and shall not call for aid, and make use of help and assistance in the birth, and the said child shall be found dead or missing, such mother shall be held to be guilty of a misdemeanor, punishable by fine and imprisonment; provided, nevertheless, that nothing herein contained shall extend, or be construed to extend, to discharge the mother of any such child from trial and punishment for murder, in case it shall appear that such child shall have been murdered by such mother, or by her procurement.

31. That the malicious striking and making *affray in any of the Courts of Justice of the island*, or the using threatening and reproachful words to the judge or court, the judge or court being then sitting, is and shall be held to be a misdemeanor, and punishable by fine and imprisonment.

32. That the wilfully *obstructing the execution of law-*

ful process; that the *breaking prison* by a person lawfully imprisoned; that the *forcible rescuing*, or attempting to rescue a person who shall be lawfully imprisoned; that *the escaping*, or attempting to escape, by a person lawfully arrested; that the voluntarily permitting, or negligently *suffering, a person to escape,* who shall be lawfully arrested or confined, are and shall be severally held to be misdemeanors, punishable by fine and imprisonment.—Provided always, and be it further enacted and declared, that nothing herein contained shall extend, or be construed to extend, to affect, abridge, or alter, the power of courts of justice and magistrates to punish contempts as formerly accustomed; and that the house of keys, the clerk of the rolls, and the registers of the ecclesiastical courts, when in the execution of their respective offices, have, and shall have, the power of punishing contempts in like manner as any court or magistrate within the said isle.

33. That the *receiving of stolen goods,* under the value of ten shillings, is and shall be held to be a misdemeanor, and punishable by fine and imprisonment, and corporal punishment.

34. That the *compounding any treason, felony,* or misdemeanor, or the taking money or goods from a person accused of any crime, to forbear to prosecute, is and shall be held to be a misdemeanor, and punishable by fine and imprisonment, and corporal punishment.—And that so much, or such part of an act of Tynwald, promulgated in the year of our Lord 1737, as regards the compounding or agreeing not to proceed in any criminal prosecution, shall, as to all offences to be committed after the promulgation of this act, be and stand repealed.

35. That the *bribing*, or attempting to bribe, any magistrate or person connected in the administration of justice, to do any thing contrary to the duties of his office; or for any magistrate or person concerned in the administration of justice, to accept, or offer to accept a bribe, to do any

thing contrary to the duties of his office, is and shall be held to be a high misdemeanor, punishable by fine and imprisonment, and disqualification to serve his majesty in any place of public trust.

36. That the *attempting to influence a jury*, or any of the jurors, corruptly by promises, persuasions, entreaties, money, entertainment, or the like; or for the jury or any of the jurors to be so corruptly influenced, is and shall be held to be a misdemeanor, and punishable by fine and imprisonment.

37. That the *stirring up suits* and quarrels between his majesty's subjects, either by law or otherwise, is and shall be held to be a misdemeanor and barratry, and punishable by fine and imprisonment.

38. That the *assembling of three persons or more* together, with an intent mutually to assist one another against any who shall oppose them in the execution of some enterprise of a private nature, with force and violence against the peace, or to the manifest terror of the people, whether the act intended were of itself lawful or not, such assembling is and shall be held to be an *unlawful assembly*, and the persons concerned shall be punishable as for a misdemeanor, by fine and imprisonment.—And if, three persons or more shall violently, riotously, and in a tumultuous manner, against the public peace, and to the manifest terror of the people, do any act, whether lawful or unlawful, such persons are and shall be held to be guilty of a riot, and shall be punishable as for a misdemeanor, by fine and imprisonment.

39. That the *violently entering* into the possession of lands or tenements in the occupation of another, with menaces and force, without authority of law, is and shall be held to be a *forcible entry* and misdemeanor, punishable by fine and imprisonment.

40. That the unlawful keeping possession of lands or tenements, by menaces and force, is and shall be held to

be a *forcible detainer*, and a misdemeanor, and punishable by fine and imprisonment.

41. That the *spreading false news*, knowing the same to be false, with intention to produce discord, and tumults, and strife, between his majesty's subjects, shall be held to be a misdemeanor, and punishable by fine and imprisonment.

42. That the *challenging another*, by word or letter, to fight with deadly weapons, either expressed or implied, or knowingly to be the bearer of such challenge, shall be held to be a misdemeanor, and punishable by fine and imprisonment.

43. That the *assaulting another, with an intent to commit murder*, rape, or robbery, or any other capital crime, is and shall be held to be felony, and punishable by transportation for life, or for any term of years, not less than fourteen, at the discretion of the court.—Provided, that nothing herein contained shall be construed to extend to do away or alter the mode of proceeding in a summary way, without a jury in cases of common battery or passionate and provoking words, as heretofore accustomed.—Provided also, and be it enacted, that the fines imposed by an ordinance made in the year of our Lord 1661, for batteries and passionate words, provoking the same, and recognised by an act of Tynwald, promulgated in the year of our Lord 1737, be respectively altered and increased in manner following; that is to say, that the fine upon each offender in cases of common battery, shall be any sum not exceeding forty shillings, nor less than ten shillings; and that the fine upon each offender in cases of provoking language, shall be any sum not exceeding fifty shillings, nor less than thirteen shillings and fourpence, according to the degree and nature of the offence, as the court or magistrate shall think proper to affix, order, and award the same.—And that the committing a common assault, without a blow being struck, or battery actually committed,

shall be tried and punished in like manner as a common battery, as before mentioned.

44. That the having two wives or two husbands at the same time, shall be held to be *bigamy* and a misdemeanor, and punishable by fine and imprisonment, unless one of the parties has been continually abroad for seven years, or unless one of the parties has been absent within the island for seven years, and the remaining party has no knowledge of the other's being alive within that time, or unless there has been a legal divorce between the parties.

45. That the *malicious defaming* or injuring another, by publishing any libellous printing, writing, sign, or picture, concerning him or her, in order to provoke him or her to wrath, or to expose him or her to public hatred, contempt, or ridicule; or the scandalous publishing of any obscene, indecent, or immoral picture, printing, or writing, are and shall be severally held to be misdemeanors, punishable by fine and imprisonment.

46. That *all unlawful, indecent, and scandalous actings and doings*, not herein before specified, to the disturbance of the public peace, and against good order and good morals, of notorious evil example, are and shall be held to be misdemeanors, and punishable by fine and imprisonment.

PUNISHMENT.

And be it further enacted, &c. That all and every person or persons who shall be lawfully convicted of any of the treasons, felonies, misdemeanors, and offences herein before particularly described, enacted, and declared, shall be liable to, and shall suffer such capital punishment, transportation, corporal punishment, imprisonment, and fine, as to each respective treason, felony, misdemeanor, and offence, is herein before severally appointed, specified, declared, and annexed.—Provided always, that in cases of felony, no imprisonment shall be for a longer period than   nor less than save and except in such cases as are herein and hereby otherwise declared and enacted; and that in cases of misdemeanor, no imprisonment shall be for a longer period than two years, nor less than three months, and no fine to a greater amount than five hundred pounds.

TRIAL FOR TREASON AND FELONY.

And be it further enacted, by the authority aforesaid, that all the said treasons and felonies shall be tried in the Court of General Gaol Delivery, upon the prosecution of his Majesty's attorney-general of the said isle, for the time being, for, and in the name and behalf of the King, and upon indictments previously found in the accustomed manner of finding indictments in cases of treason and felony, by the law of the said isle.

TRIAL FOR MISDEMEANORS.

And that the said misdemeanors shall be tried either upon information preferred by the attorney-general, in the name and on the behalf of our Sovereign Lord the King, or by petition, at the instance of a private prosecutor or prosecutors, in the presence of the deemsters, or one of them, by and before a jury of six good and lawful men of the sheading, wherein the party or parties accused, or some, or one of them, do or shall reside, or of such other sheading as may be ordered, on good cause shown, which jury shall be impannelled, by order or warrant of a deemster, and shall consist of an equal number of men from and out of each and every parish within such sheading; and that it shall be lawful for a deemster, on complaint lodged, by information or petition as aforesaid, and affidavit made to the truth thereof, to issue his order or warrant for apprehending and imprisoning any person or persons, charged with having committed any of the said misdemeanors, until he, she, or they, give in good and sufficient security, at the discretion of such deemster, to appear and stand trial for such misdemeanor, when thereunto lawfully required.

And be it further enacted, that prosecutions for such misdemeanors shall be commenced, and effectually prosecuted within two months from the time of the apprehending and imprisoning of any person or persons charged with having committed any of the said misdemeanors, and not afterwards, unless good cause be shown to the said deemster why the same should be postponed.—And that, whenever, and as often as any person or persons so charged as aforesaid, shall have been so apprehended and imprisoned, such person or persons shall have it in his, her, or their power to apply for, and bring on his, her, or their trial, and shall also be entitled to, and obtain, such time for making his, her, or their defence as the deemster, on application made, shall think reasonable.—Provided always, that in all prosecutions for grand larceny, if the jury by whom the same shall be tried, shall be of opinion, and find that the goods stolen are under the value of ten shillings, such jury shall proceed and find a verdict as for petty larceny.

And that, in all prosecutions for petty larceny, if the jury by whom the same shall be tried, shall be of opinion, and find that the goods stolen are of the value of ten shillings, or more, such jury shall proceed, and, by their verdict, indict the offender or offenders of grand larceny.—And be it enacted, by the authority aforesaid, that the several provisions and enactments, respecting grand larceny and petty larceny, contained and enacted in and by an act of Tynwald passed in the year of our Lord 1629, and also in and by an act of Tynwald passed in the year of our Lord 1753, shall, as to all offences which shall be committed after the promulgation of this act, be, and the same are hereby severally repealed.

Manx Coin.

ITS ancient bearing was a ship; but the arms are now, and have been for centuries, *Gules*, three armed legs proper, or rather argent, conjoined in fess at the upper part of the thigh, fleshed in triangle, garnished and spurred topaz. So long as the King of Man wrote "*Rex Manniæ et Insularum*," they bore the ship; but when the Scots had possession, with the Western Islands, the legs were substituted. It has been said of the three legs, that with the *toe* of the one they spurn at Ireland, with the *spur* of the other they kick at Scotland, and with the third they bend to England.

In 1733, the impression on the copper circulation was the arms of Man, three legs, with J. D. between the bend and the motto (as now) "*Quocunque Jeceris Stabit;*" on the reverse, the eagle and the child on a chapeau, motto "*San Changer;*" beneath the chapeau, the date. In 1758, the Ducal coronet, with a cipher A. D. with the date under: the reverse, as before, without the initials J. D. In 1786, the King's head, with the date under, motto "*Georgius III. Dei Gratia;*" the reverse as before.

The three legs refer to the relative situation of the Island with respect to the neighbouring nations of England, Scotland, and Ireland, previous to the union between any two of these; since which the symbol entirely loses its propriety, and has become obsolete and unmeaning. While England, Scotland, and Ireland, were belligerent nations, the existence of Monabia as an independent state, must depend on an armed neutrality, and the alternate protection which it might be able to challenge from any one, against the hostile aggressions of the other two.

The legs are *armed*,—which denotes *self-defence*. The spurs denote *speed;* and while in whatever position they are placed, two of them fall into the attitude of supplication; the third, which will be upward and behind, appears to be kicking at the assailant, against whom the other two are imploring protection. The *vis* of the symbol is, that if England should seek to oppress it, it would soon engage Ireland or Scotland; if either of these should assail it, it would hasten to call England to its defence. The motto, which is an Iambic Dimeter—Quocunque jeceris stabit—*Which ever way you throw it, it will stand*, is very ingeniously contrived to agree, both in sense and style, with the intention and attitude of the legs, whether taken in English or Latin. You cannot change the position of the legs in the plain, so as to alter their attitude, and no transposition of the words will change their sense. The occult moral of this emblem presents the instructive parable of—"A brave man struggling with the storms of fate."

The character is constituted by the conjunction of humility, energy, and fortitude. His attitude is that of supplication; but it is at the same time that of activity. He is only on one knee: with one limb he implores assistance, with two he serves himself. With the sense of dependence on strength superior to his own, he combines the most strenuous exertion of his own energies: to the modesty of supplication, he conjoins the discretion of armour and the activity of the spur. Whatever lot Providence may apportion to such a man,—wherever it shall cast him, he will stand.

Reader, thou'st seen a falling cat
Light always on its legs so pat;
A shuttlecock will still descend,
Meeting the ground with nether end:—
The persevering Manxman thus
A shuttlecock or pauvre puss,
However thro' the world he's tost—
However disappointed, crost,

Reverses, losses, Fortune's frown ;
No chance or change can keep him down :
Upset him any way you will,
Upon his legs you find him still ;
For ever active, brisk, and spunky,
"*Stabit, jeceris, quocunque.*"

Traditions and Superstitions.

THERE are but few records of the Island. The greatest part of them, in troublesome times, were carried away by the Norwegians, and deposited among the archives of Drunton, in Norway, where it is alleged they still remain : though it is reported, a Mr. Stevenson, a worthy merchant of Dublin, a few years since offered the then Bishop of Drunton a considerable sum of money for the purchase of them, designing to restore and present them to the Island ; but the Bishop would not part with them on any terms. The loss of these ancient records renders it impossible to ascertain how long the Island has been discovered, or by whom ; and to make up this deficiency, they relate the following marvellous history :

Some hundred years (say they) before the coming of our Saviour, the Isle of Man was inhabited by a certain species called *Fairies*, and that every thing was carried on in a kind of supernatural manner ; that a blue mist, continually hanging over the land, prevented the ships that passed by from having any suspicion there was an Island. This mist, contrary to the laws of nature, was preserved by keeping a perpetual fire, which happening once to be extinguished, discovered itself to some fishermen who were then in a boat on their vocation, and by them notice was given to the people of some country, (but what they do not pretend to determine) who sent ships in order to make a further discovery: that, on their landing, they had a fierce encounter with the little people (the fairies), and having got the better of them, possessed themselves of Castle Russin or Rushen, and by degrees (as they received reinforcements) of the whole Island. These new conquerors maintained their ground some time, but were at length vanquished by a race of giants, who were not extirpated until the reign of Prince Arthur, by Merlin, the famous British enchanter, who, by the force of magic, dislodged the greatest part of them, and bound the rest in spells which they believe will be indissoluble to the end of the world. They pretend also, that this Island afterwards became an asylum to all the distressed Princes and great men in Europe, and that those uncommon fortifications made about Peel Castle were added for their better security; but of this we shall treat hereafter.

The tradition of what happened on suffering the domestic fire to be extinct, remained in such credit with them, that hardly a family in the Island, but kept a small fire continually burning: every one, at that time, confidently believing that if no fire were to be found, most terrible revolutions and mischiefs would have immediately ensued.

It is ignorance which is the cause of these excessive superstitions; but these few hints are not sufficient to show the world what a MANXMAN formerly was, and what power the prejudice of education had over weak minds. If books at one time had been of any use among them, one would have imagined that the Count of Gabalis had been not only translated into the Manx tongue, but that it was a sort of rule of faith to them; since there is hardly a fictitious being mentioned by him in his book of absurdities, to which they would not readily have given credit. It is doubtful, idolizers of the clergy as they once were, whether they would not have been refractory even to them, had they preached against the existence of fairies, or even against their being commonly seen; for though the priesthood were a kind of gods among them, yet still tradition was a greater god than they; and as they confidently asserted that the first inhabitants of their island were fairies, so they maintained, that these airy beings had still their residence among them. They called them the *good people*, and said they lived in wilds or forests and on mountains, and shunned great cities, because of the wickedness committed therein. All the houses were blest where the fairies visited, because they fled from vice. A person would once have been thought impudently profane, who should have suffered his family to go to bed, without having first set a tub or pail full of clean water for these guests to bathe themselves in, which the natives averred they constantly did, as soon as ever the eyes of the family closed, wherever they vouchsafed to come. If any thing happened to be mislaid, and found again in some place where it was not expected, they told you a fairy took it and returned it: if you chanced to fall and hurt yourself, a fairy laid something in your way, to throw you down, as a punishment for some sin you had committed.

The Scenery of the Island; Longevity of the Islanders, &c.

THE inhabitants, like the Swiss and Highlanders, are warmly attached to their native mountains, and not without reason; for the whole country is, in a high degree, beautiful, there scarcely being any of the same extent that can equal it in scenes of romantic grandeur. It has been considered by many judges of the picturesque, as inferior in these qualities to the Isle of Wight, only from its being destitute of the same luxuriant growth of wood. Let the lovers of the romantic travel no farther than to the distance of about two furlongs, from the southern extremity of the Isle, where is a small rocky Island, called the Calf of Man. This is fenced round by gloomy caverns and stupendous precipices; is tenanted by a great variety of sea fowl, which form a most striking and picturesque scene on the water, sitting in innumerable tiers one above another, and adorning with their white breasts the dark and towering rocks which encircle the Island,—their shrill discordant tones increasing the effect of the sensations that arise from the wildness of the scenery. The surface is rather barren; but there is every thing bearing the character of the sublime, tending to raise the bolder emotions of the mind, rather than amuse it with gentle sensations. The eye is regaled from its heights with the azure vault of heaven, and beneath, the briny surface is covered with swelling sails, either impelled with the cheerful breeze, or agitated by bleak winds or driving storms, while the surrounding earth presents a verdure—wild and innocent. On the edge of an awful precipice is the remains of an hermitage, said to have been the retreat of a person, in Queen Elizabeth's reign, who imposed on himself a residence in this dreary solitude, as a penance for having murdered a beautiful woman, in a fit of jealousy.

The longevity of the inhabitants is proverbial; but it is chiefly confined to the natives, and to those only who pass their lives in rural occupations, breathing the mountain air, habituated to early hours, living on simple diet, remote from the more populous towns, and unsophisticated by the refinements and luxuries of high life; for where these creep in and diffuse their baneful influence, it would be as absurd to look for the venerable head, silvered o'er with age, the ruddy countenance, and the vigorous strength of patriarchal times, as to hope to extract ice from a sunbeam, or fire from the mountain snow. Candidates for longevity, cannot expect to attain this distinction by merely migrating to a country celebrated for it, unless they conform to the simplicity of nature, and study her salutary rules, who teaches her votaries to banish all superficial wants. And although it cannot be doubted, but that the free use of ardent spirits tends to shorten the scanty pittance of human existence, it is yet matter of surprise, that, in a country like the Isle of Man, where the *dram*, from its inferior price, is universally accessible, there are not to be found more instances of fatal devotedness to intoxication. The generality of the Manx may be distinguished for sobriety: slaves to riot and debauchery are to be found every where.

The following epitaph on a tombstone, in the churchyard of Kk. St. Ann, (generally called Kk. Santon) in this Island, proves the truth of these observations, showing also, that the "miserable conceit" of punning on the dead, survived longer in the Isle of Man than in any other country:—

TO THE MEMORY OF DANIEL TEAR,
Who died Dec. 9, 1787—aged 110.

Here, friend, is little Daniel's tomb:
    To Joseph's years he did arrive;
    Sloth killing thousands in their bloom,
    While labour kept poor Dan alive.
How strange, yet true, full seventy years
    Was his wife happy in her *Tears*.

N. B. This person was a native. Sir Wadsworth Busk, Attorney-General of the Island, erected the stone, and wrote the verses; but it was generally thought he was really older than 110.

EXTRACT

FROM THE

JOURNAL OF A MODERN TRAVELLER;

OR,

A Trip with the Manx Herring-Fleet

IN 1821.

IN the month of September I arrived at Peel. It was the height of the season for the herring-fishing; and just at this time the shoals were lying along that part of the coast which extends from Peel Castle to the Calf of Man. A great proportion of the male population of the island were consequently drawn to this place. It is from the herring-fishery that a great part of their subsistence is derived. There are few families of the interior, even those who reside in the most sequestered glens, or on its highest mountains, who do not delegate some of their members to share the scaly produce of the sea. The traveller who, at this season, passes round the island, can form but a very inadequate idea of its inhabitants. He may see, on every hand, the laborious females plying the sickle, and in long ranks of twenty or more sweeping away the golden produce of the fields. But of men, he will see few; except such as by age and infirmity are disqualified, or by sufficiency disinclined, to try their fortune on the propitious ocean, which for centuries has brought its treasures to the shores of Man. It is computed that not less than 3500 are annually employed in the herring-fishery. If the stranger should chance to be pursuing his journey on the Saturday, he will notice groups of these marine adventurers returning to their rustic dwellings to pass the sabbath in rest and devotion. Indeed, in this respect, they are a laudable example to fishermen of other countries. If their sentiments be even charged with somewhat of superstition, they are such as are truly delightful to a Christian observer. Such deeply-rooted prejudices, in favour of religious observances, can only be the result of a system of pastoral care and holy instructions with which this island was favoured many generations ago. At this day, their religious prejudices are so strong against the practice of employing the Sabbath in fishing, or even going out late on a Sabbath evening, though they must necessarily wait till the same hour on the Monday evening, that it would not be in the power of any logic or rhetoric, any gain or necessity, to induce them to desecrate any part of God's day of rest by their sea-faring occupations.* It is devoutly to be wished that this sacred feeling (call it superstition if you please) may long continue. If these hardy islanders would have Zebulon's blessing, "to suck of the abundance of seas, and of treasures hid in the sand," they will ever do well to pay the homage of awful reverence to that supreme Being whose "way is in the sea, and whose path in the great waters;" and who, in a just "controversy with the inhabitants of the land," might say, "The fishes of the sea shall be taken away." (Hosea iv. 1, 3.)

The return of these countrymen on Monday to the place of rendezvous, where the fleet has remained at anchor during the day of holy rest, is not a little interesting. Every Manxman musters his pony, accoutred with a rustic

---

* The herrings being fish of *passage*, it has been pronounced lawful by the Church of *Rome* to employ the Sabbath in fishing for them; and a whole chapter in the *Decretals* is assigned to the discussion: but, on this subject, we may rejoice that the Manxman's religion is proof against the pope's infallibility.

saddle, composed of old stockings, sheep-skins, and pack-thread, shouldering his white bag filled with his homely food for a week's consumption; and plods away with his home-made sandals to his appointed harbour. It is not unusual for his wife, and one or two of his children, to accompany the cavalcade, riding the meagre nag; and with fervent wishes for their good fortune, cheering the road with domestic hilarity, and desiring to see the last of the parent-fisherman.

You may, from these circumstances, in some degree imagine the busy scene of preparation which was taking place on my arrival at Peel. The weather was fine, the wind favourable, and on every hand this plodding community were as full of transactions as can be conceived. The fishermen were converging from every quarter, bending beneath the load of nets which they were conveying to their respective boats; and a strange hollaing and bustling in a crowded harbour, while taking advantage of the returning tide, prevailed in every quarter. An anxiety to ascertain every information relative to the fishery carried me round among the busy throng; but not being satisfied with the usual currency of the answers given to strangers, I resolved to take *a night's excursion with the fleet*, when, away from the intrusion of the objects on shore, I might contemplate, from the actual scene of operations, what was justly anticipated to be a highly interesting spectacle.

Before we enter upon the detail of our nocturnal occupations, it may be necessary to give a general idea of those *migrations* which bring to this quarter a portion of the countless myriads of herrings which traverse the ocean.

Herring is a word derived from the German *heor*, an army, which expresses their number when they migrate into our seas.

"Herrings are chiefly found in the North sea. In those inaccessible seas, that are covered with ice during a great part of the year, the herrings find a quiet and safe retreat from all their numerous enemies: there neither man, nor their still more destructive enemy, the sun-fish, or the cachalot, the most voracious of the whale kind, dares to pursue them. It is true, there are fisheries elsewhere, but none so copious. It hath been observed, that the arrival of the herrings on the coast of Shetland is certain, and almost to a day, on or before the 22d of June.

"It is commonly said, that nobody ever saw a herring alive, and that they die the minute they are taken out of the water; but there are instances to the contrary.

"The herring is a fish of passage; so that it is allowed to catch them on holidays and Sundays: in the Decretal there is an express chapter to this effect.

"The winter rendezvous of the herrings is probably the icy sea, within the arctic circle; as this sea swarms with insect food in greater abundance than in our warmer latitudes. From this sea the great colony of these fishes sets out about the middle of winter; and this colony is composed of such numbers as to exceed the power of imagination. But they have no sooner left their retreats than they have to encounter with a multitude of enemies. The sun-fish and cachalot devour them in great abundance; and besides, the porpus, the grampus, the shark, cod-fish, haddocks, pollocks, and the numerous tribe of dog-fish, find them an easy prey, and desist from making war upon one another. To these enemies we may add innumerable flocks of sea-fowl that chiefly inhabit the northern regions towards the pole, which watch the outset of their perilous migration, and spread among them extensive ruin. In this state of danger, the defenceless emigrants crowd closer together, as if they could thus secure themselves against the attacks of their enemies. The main body begins to separate, at a certain latitude, into two great divisions; one of which moves to the west, and pours down along the coasts of America, as far south as Carolina, and becomes so numerous in the Chesapeak bay as to be a nuisance to the shores. The other division takes a more eastern direction towards Europe, and falls in with the great island of Iceland about the beginning of March. Upon their arrival on that coast, their phalanx, which hath already suffered considerable diminution, is nevertheless found to be of such extent, depth, and closeness, as to occupy a surface equal to the dimensions of Great Britain and Ireland; but subdivided into columns of 5 or 6 miles in length, and 3 or 4 in breadth; each line, or column, being led, according to the ideas of fishermen, by herrings of more than ordinary size. The herrings swim near the surface, sinking occasionally for 10 or fifteen minutes. The forerunners of those who visit the British kingdoms appear off Shetland in April or May, and the grand body begins to be perceived in June. Their approach is known to the fishers by a small rippling of the water, the reflection of their brilliancy, and the number of soland geese, or gannets, and other aerial persecutors, who are eager to devour them, and who, with the marine attendants, may serve to drive shoals of them into bays and creeks, where many thousands of them are taken every night from June till September. Although the Shetland islands break and separate the grand body of the herrings into two divisions, they still continue their course towards the south. One division proceeds along the east side of Britain, and pays its tribute to the Orkneys, the Murray firth, the coasts of Aberdeen, Angus, and Fife, the great river Forth, the coast of Scarborough, and particularly the projecting land at Yarmouth, the ancient and only mart of herrings in England, where they appear in October, and are found in considerable quantities till Christmas. The other division pursues its course from the Shetland islands, along the west side of Britain; and these are observed to be larger and fatter than those on the east side. After passing the Shetland and the Orkney isles, they crowd in amazing quantities into the lakes, bays, and narrow channels of the shires of Sutherland, Ross, and Inverness; which, with the Hebride isles, especially the Long island, form the greatest stationary herring fishery in Britain; that upon the coast of Shetland excepted. Sometimes this shoal, in its southern progress, edges close upon the extensive coast of Argyleshire; fills every bay and creek; and visits, in small detachments, the firth of Clyde, Lochfine, and other lakes within the entrance of that river; the coast of Ayrshire, and of Galloway, to the head of the Solway firth. This shoal proceeds from the western shores of Scotland towards the north of Ireland; where, meeting with a second interruption, they are again divided into two brigades. One shoal passes down the Irish channel, visits the Isle of Man, and affords an occasional supply to the east coast of Ireland, and the west coast of England, as far as the Bristol channel. The other shoal skirts along the west coast of Ireland, where, after visiting the lakes of Donegal, it gradually disappears, and is finally lost in the immensity of the Atlantic. Herrings, it is observed, are not seen in quantities in any of the southern kingdoms, as Spain, Portugal, or the south parts of France, on the side of the ocean, or in the Mediterranean, or on the coast of Africa.

"Were we inclined," says a well-known writer, "to consider this partial migration of the herring in a moral light, we might reflect with veneration and awe on the mighty power which originally impressed, on this most useful body of his creatures, the instinct that directs and points out their course, that blesses and enriches these islands, which causes them at certain and invariable times to quit the vast polar deeps, and offer themselves to our expecting fleets."—" This impression was given them, that they might remove for the sake of depositing their spawn in warmer seas, that would mature and vivify it more assuredly than those of the frigid zone. It is not from defect of food that they set themselves in motion, for they come to us full of fat, and on their return are almost universally observed to be lean and miserable. What their food is near the pole, we are not yet informed, but in our seas they feed much on the oniscus marinus, a crustaceous insect, and sometimes on their own fry. They are in full roe to the end of June, and continue in perfection till the beginning of winter, when they begin to deposit their spawn. Though we have no particular authority for it, yet, as very few young herrings are found in our seas during the winter, it seems most certain that they return to their parental haunts beneath the ice, to repair the vast destruction of their race during summer, by men, fowl, and fish."

Having selected a vessel with a decent crew, and a steady, intelligent, and communicative captain, (as you may style him,) and clad myself in a garb adapted for the purpose, I went on board. At 3 o'clock in the afternoon the May-flower cleared off from the pier, and o'er the swellings of a majestic tide bore away to the expanding deep.

Having understood that it was the custom of the Manx fishermen to use a *short prayer* on going out to their occupation, I felt some disappointment in observing no religious ceremony: but my suspense was soon dissipated. Turning off from the rocks, on which the venerable castle reared its pile of mouldering fragments, the captain exclaimed, " Hats off, boys," when every man, with his face in his hat, and upon his knees, implored, for a minute, the protection and blessing of the Almighty, in the way he thought best. It was a gratifying spectacle. I cannot certify that the same expression of devotion was manifested in *every* vessel; but I presume it is, to this day, a general practice.

Having been previously informed by a respectable islander, that some years ago he had seen a great number of the fishermen upon their knees in the market-place, imploring the divine goodness, and receiving the admonitions of a Christian minister, I was jealous of this glory having departed; and at the sound of "Hats off, boys," a sensation of gratitude, tenderness, and sympathy, thrilled through my soul, which may be better conceived than described, and which can never be banished from my recollection. Solemn and affecting scene! How different from the loud oaths and vociferated curses of the ruthless seamen! How admirably adapted is such a ceremony, to remind the poor fisherman of an all-pervading Providence, by whose decree his uncertain subsistence might be swept away in a moment! And let us not start back with a suspicious coldness from these indications of devotional feeling, and, classing them with unmeaning superstitions, afford them a jealous toleration, as being only adapted to the vulgar. There may be, there must be, among such a motley assemblage, both hypocrisy and superstition; but there is, in many, a holy sense of dependence, gratitude, and veneration, which systems of national education may long labour to produce, and which would be, if lost, a great and awful calamity.

> Oft as the fleet from Mona's shore
> Bears to the deep its changeful sail,
> Let each his pray'r devoutly pour,
> And consecrate the welcome gale!

We sailed out seven miles, and then returned three. During this, the men were busily employed in preparing the nets, which occupied nearly two hours. The nets are brought on board in separate pieces, generally about 25 fathoms long and 7 deep. The usual number of pieces is nine or ten. These are then joined together to make one complete length, which, when extending behind the boat, will reach from 400 to 500 yards. Stones are fastened to the bottom of the net to cause it to sink, and buoys are tied to the top by cords, regulated by the number of fathoms it may be thought necessary to allow the net to sink. The net is then carefully rolled up, so as to facilitate its being passed, in its whole length, over the side of the boat.

The nets being prepared, the weary fisherman, stretching himself on the fore-castle, soon falls into a slumber, tired with the sleepless labours of the preceding night; while some of his companions, more wakeful because more interested, are keeping a watchful eye in every direction, to hail the appearance of those *signs* which may direct them in the choice of their situation for fishing.

The *fleet*, being now engaged in the same anxious circumspection, presented a lively scene. With foresails down, to steady and slacken their sailing, they were all intent upon selecting the most favourable spot. A space of about ten miles in length, and from two to three in breadth, was now traversed to and fro, in rapid alternations, by about 350 vessels. The fishermen are very scrupulous about counting the vessels, superstitiously saying, as I heard myself, "If they count the ships, they shall catch no fish."

The fleet did not consist exclusively of Manx vessels. Many come, during the season, from Ireland, Scotland, and St. Ives in Cornwall. A little jealousy will necessarily be excited by the intrusion of these foreign fishermen; but that suspicious feeling seems to be wearing off, and giving way to the more liberal principle, that all have an equal title to the blessings of the sea. It is very certain that their interference cannot cause the Manxmen to catch fewer herrings. The mode of fishing adopted by the men of St. Ives is by many thought superior to that of the Manxmen; which is very probable, as they are, generally, more successful. The rapid interchanges of the vessels crossing and recrossing each other in their frequent tackings—the majestic rolling of the sea, whose cerulean waves were emblazoned by reflecting the golden clouds of an autumnal evening sky—the high spirits of the fishermen, who hailed an unusual promise in the "signs," which were making their appearance—the novelty and the peculiarity of the scene—caused an indescribable interest, which was intensely kept up at this hour of the evening by an anxiety to witness the approaching labours.

It was now six o'clock. The signs were hailed on every hand. At the frequent animated cry of the sailors of "Down again, Down again," my attention was directed to the striking of the *gannet*, a bird which chiefly stays on the southern cliffs of the Calf of Man.*

I observed these birds often flying and hovering in certain directions, when suddenly raising themselves to the height of from 200 to 300 feet, and fixing their wings to cleave the air with peculiar facility, they descend with amazing force and velocity in a line quite perpendicular, and plunge into the wave like the falling of an anchor. It has been proved that they can descend from 10 to 20 fathoms into the water. They remain under the surface about 15 seconds, and having succeeded in their errand fly off to their rocky retreats.†

Half an hour afforded the birds of prey their sufficient supply, when the horizon was soon cleared of these feathered invaders. This entertainment was, however, quickly succeeded by the appearance of the porpoises. This animal, the "phocena delphinus" of Linnæus, is the smallest of the cetaceous tribe: those we saw were about six feet

* *Gannet* is the name used for the "Pelecanus Bassanus" of Linnæus, or the *soland goose*. Mr. Ray supposed the gannet to be a species of large gull; and he was led into the mistake by never having an opportunity of seeing this bird except flying, and in the air it has the appearance of a gull. On this supposition he gave it the title of *cataracta*, a name borrowed from Aristotle, and which admirably expresses the rapid descent of this bird on its prey.

† The Cornish mode of taking these birds, which cannot easily be shot, is, by fastening a pilchard to a board, and immersing it a little below the surface of the water; which when the gannet perceives, he precipitates himself with such violence from his aerial elevation, that his beak passes through the board, and he dashes his brains out.

long. At first, they rolled and spouted, at a distance, in different directions; afterwards, wheeling their finny backs in gentler volutions, they approached close to our boat. There is something in the idle, heedless whirl of these brawny creatures, taking their pastimes near, that affords peculiar amusement to a stranger in maritime excursions.

Availing themselves of these signs as the groundwork of their reasonings, the spectator was not a little amused to listen to the anxious disputation of the wiser ones. Every one thinks his own opinion best; and to please all, there may be sometimes no alternative but to strike sail where they are, and take their chance. It is, however, generally the case, that every vessel is quite satisfied with its situation, though some miles distant from others, which of course have the same predilection for the place they have chosen. Not far from us I observed a boat carrying a *flag*, which I found to be what is recognized by the honourable distinction of the *Admiral's boat*. The admiral rides near the centre of the fleet, and is appointed for the adjustment of differences between the boats; and the striking of his flag is the signal for the fleet to commence their work of fishing, which never takes place till *sunset*.

It was seven o'clock when the magnified orb of the blazing sun descended below the briny horizon, gleaming over the wide interposing main a broad flame of crimson, and left, in a few moments, behind him the milder reflections of the clouds, illumined by the effulgence of his setting. The admiral's flag was struck—the mainsail of each boat was quickly descending on the deck—the rusty teagles were screaming—the busy sailors shouting—and the vessels, spread far and wide upon the waters, were now stationary, and exhibited only a forest of naked masts as far as the darkening atmosphere would admit the perception of a vessel.

This was the hour of *adventure*. The nets were soaked with a few buckets of water to assist their sinking; each individual fixed himself at his post; one to unrol the net, one on this side to adjust the stone weights, one on that to adjust the buoys, and two immediately before these to lift the net over the side of the vessel. In fifteen minutes the whole length was heaved over-board, and committed, in a trail of 500 yards, to the deep. They had now to trust to the providence of God. And I was unspeakably gratified to find that the conviction of an all-disposing Providence was not absent at a crisis when their hopes and fears were left in full operation. The sound of sacred harmony came on the gale of departing day from a vessel stationed to windward of us. It was a *hymn* sung lustily by the crew, who were reposing after their nets were struck. An unexpected salutation! A glow of sacred sympathy warmed my breast. I acknowledged the identity of that religion which can inspire the song of praise upon the Manxman's fishing-boat, as well as in the prison of Philippi. I conceded feelingly to the truth, that he that loveth God will love his brother also; and though I never saw, and never shall see, those untutored singers of Israel, I must confess, I felt that I must, as a Christian believer, love them. Remarking upon this to my fellow-sailors, I inquired if they never employed themselves in this way; and the captain, noticing the gratification afforded me by the vocal exercises of the adjacent crew, observed that "they were no great singers, but it was customary with them to have a word of prayer." "Boys, come aft," was no sooner spoken, than the willing company were seen upon their knees around me. A young man, not knowing my clerical office, commenced without ceremony, a simple, unaffected, and earnest prayer, to which I listened with peculiar pleasure, from the conviction that it was the evidence of a sincerity and a piety which were invaluable to its possessor; and still more so, because I found myself in a *house of prayer*, though tossed on the rude billows of the ocean. When this supplication ended, the claims of office, and the bias of a devotional frame, constrained me to add my unworthy orison. Never did I realize more solemnly the presence of Jehovah, "who plants his footsteps in the sea, and rides upon the storm;" whose breath causeth "the waves thereof to rage and swell, till deep calleth unto deep at the noise of his waterspouts." I felt it incumbent upon me to implore his blessing upon our companions in the surrounding fleet, that they might "fear God, and worship him who made the sea and the fountains of waters;" and that they might be prepared to surrender their strict and solemn account to Him to whom "the sea must give up her dead;" that whenever they supplicated for mercy, they might be strong in faith, giving glory to God, and not "like the wave of the sea, that is driven of the wind and tossed;" that God would give success to their precarious occupation, and cause the net to be "cast on the right side of the ship;" and that the poor fishermen might not "toil all night, and catch nothing." I could not but supplicate for the island on whose shores we were billowed, that it might ever "wait for God's gracious law;" that the produce of the sea might ever be continued to them; and that the *Gospel-net* might be cast among them by a holy and zealous ministry; and that these blessings might be extended to the Islands of other climes, till "the abundance of the sea shall be converted unto God." Rising from our devotions, I was greeted with a fervent expression of their Christian affection.

The stars now glittered in the milky-way, and the bolder fires of the revolving planets supplied the place of the more powerful radiance of the absent moon. The lighthouses at the extremities of the island were sending abroad at intervals a stream of benignant brightness. The blaze of these flickering beacons, so delectable to the bewildered mariner, brings with it associations of reflection and sympathy, which, if they be less affecting in sublimity than the contemplation of the bright orbs suspended on high by the merciful Creator, are not less allied to those sentiments of tenderness and sensibility, which are elicited by empicturing the melancholy scenes of shipwreck.

Though not unusually dark, it was sufficiently so to give effect to the glistening appearance of the shoals of fish that approached the vessel. If any thing could make one covet darkness, in such a situation, it would be that one might witness the flouncing and struggling of the finny multitudes that are entangled in the meshes of the net.

About 10 o'clock all hands were engaged to haul in the net, which is drawn, not as many suppose after the method adopted to circumvent and enclose the fish, but leisurely, over the side of the boat. The net, being suspended perpendicularly, only catches those fish of the shoals which by traversing to and fro are entangled by the gills. At least, this is the Manx method.

The drawing in of the net is a beautiful sight. Perhaps from ten to twenty herrings in every lineal yard come tumbling over the side of the boat, if they have tolerable success. The net assumes a luminous appearance in the act of drawing, and the captured creatures, flouncing about for a few minutes, exhibit all their phosphorescent beauty, and expire. The idea of herrings being never seen alive is therefore not quite correct.

Our success being only tolerable, the mainsail was hoisted, and we drove a few miles to the southward. The same operations were again performed. Our trail, during the second shooting of the net, got entangled with that of an adjacent vessel, which obliged them to haul it again on board. This created great confusion. It will unavoidably often occur; and is always very unpleasant, by raising a tumultuous shouting and blaming each other. This is the only disagreeable you may encounter, with the exception that if the weather prove rainy or stormy you are obliged to retire to the *den*, a miserable receptacle, and rightly named, truly. With a fire on the floor, you go *in* where the smoke comes *out*; and when entered, can neither stand nor sit, but are necessitated to stretch your longitude where you can, amid all that is sickening and wretched. Whoever ventures on a fishing excursion must prepare and fortify himself to endure the horrors of the miserable den.

During the whole period, the net was cast three times; and the number of fish taken was 8 or 10 maize, or about 7000. This is considered good success. It sometimes occurs, that one boat will take 40 or 50 maize; and in the year 1802, it was known for one boat to bring home 180; at which plentiful season 100 maize was not an unusual product. Such seasons have, however, been unknown of later years. The May-flower, our vessel, has gained 70 guineas in one night's trip; but she is thought fortunate now in clearing from 5 to 10 guineas.

The net having been drawn on board for the last time at 5 o'clock in the morning, sails were hoisted for returning home. The wind being contrary, we did not reach Peel before 8 o'clock. The interim was employed in clearing the nets of the few fish remaining entangled, and talking over events of the neighbourhood, and fishing anecdotes. Wearied with midnight vigils, I hailed with joy the long illuminated line of opening day. I watched the increasing day-break till the sun rose behind the heights of Knockaloe and Slieauny-froghane, and gleamed on the welcome tide that was bearing us homeward.

To watch the returning fleet, whose sails are expanded to the morning sun, is truly pleasing; and the stranger who will, just at the proper time, ascend the summit of Knockaloe, will be able to see this in perfection, and will be abundantly repaid for the toil of climbing the steep ascent.

On entering the harbour we were hailed by small boats, having buyers on board, who go round among the fishing boats to ascertain their success, and offer prices for their herrings.

APPENDIX.

It may be necessary here to explain the manner of dividing the product of the night's fishing. A boat is generally considered to carry 9 men and 9 pieces of net; and the product is divided into twelve shares; one of which goes to every fisherman, two to the owner of the boat, and one for the nets, which is apportioned to the owners of them respectively. Thus the captain, by taking *two* of his own men, and providing the boat and the nets, would just divide the product equally with the six fishermen who go along with him.

It may be calculated, according to *our* night's success, that each fisherman may earn from 10 to 20 shillings a night. This however would be extremely erroneous, if taken as a general example. They are sometimes unable, through stormy weather, to go out above twice or three times in a week; and often, when they go, catch but few herrings—sometimes none. There is no danger of their becoming rich. They deserve all they get. Their long absence from the domestic circle—their chief labour being required during the hours of midnight—their constant exposure to the horrors of the storm and tempest—and the painful uncertainty of their success—will constrain every one to acknowledge that their bread is hardly earned, and that the fisherman is worthy of his hire.

When we reflect that the chief subsistence of upwards of 3000 poor Islanders depends upon this precarious source, it must be a gladdening event when the fleet returns from the labours of the night with two or three thousand pounds worth of herrings. Yet, out of this good, arise two serious evils, which every means should be employed to correct. The one is, that success in fishing induces excess in drinking. Intoxication is the bane of this Island. It is to be regretted that the low price of spirituous liquors affords such a facility for indulgence in this destructive crime. The other evil is a disgusting indolence when on shore, resulting from the nature of sea-faring occupations.

APPENDIX.

Accustomed to their fishing, they become almost useless at home. The females toil in the fields, and cultivate the farm, while the men, having no engagements at sea, lounge away the vacant day in the corner of some neighbouring tap-room, talking over the wonderful exploits and escapes of the preceding season. As agricultural arrangements are now carrying forward with increasing spirit, it is hoped that the male population will derive a political and moral advantage. There is no doubt that if the time that is employed in fishing were employed in farming, it would as well repay the poor man for his labour. He that can convince the Manxmen of this truth will confer a benefit as great as his task will be difficult.

Being once more on terra firma, I found myself in the midst of a busy population. General anxiety to know what had been our success manifested itself. The herrings began soon to be circulated as a trading commodity. Carts from Douglas and different parts of the country were carrying away the shining purchase; lusty females were conveying off their baskets with the milky-looking contents; and the smoky-visaged paupers came buying the day's meal at 5 for a penny, pleased, at so reasonable a rate, to replenish the table of their hardy families.

The fishermen, on landing, brought along with them their nets, which were forthwith shouldered to the adjacent hill, where I observed scores of them laying them abroad to dry, and mending the broken meshes, to be ready for the next excursion.*

A circumstance at this time happened, which created an additional movement, particularly among the younger tribes. One of the fishermen venturously attempting to bring to shore a small skully-boat, which he had overladen with herrings, it was overturned by the heavy surge which

---

* For an account of the manner in which the herrings are *salted* and *dried* for exportation, the reader is referred to page 149.

was driving upon the beach. The children of the town were quickly crowded upon the shore, attempting, with wonderful amusement to themselves, to snatch from the driving waves the floating fry. The merriment was great to the freakish children; but the poor man, who had lost about 10,000 herrings, was not so pleased to see their mirth at his expense.

While the weather continues favourable, the fishing operations, which I have attempted to describe, are kept up during the season without intermission; and I frankly confess, few specimens of industry have afforded me greater entertainment or satisfaction than the herring-fishing of the Isle of Mån.

FINIS.

J. Gleave, Printer.

46-350- 19-25-61

CPSIA information can be obtained at www.ICGtesting.com
Printed in the USA
LVOW05s0102160415

434713LV00015B/260/P